ROMANESQUE & GOTHIC

DECORATIVE METALWORK

AND

IVORY CARVINGS

IN THE

MUSEUM OF SCOTLAND

VIRGINIA GLENN

National Museums of Scotland

Published by NMSE Publishing
a division of NMS Enterprises Limited
National Museums of Scotland
Chambers Street
Edinburgh EH1 1JF

British Library Cataloguing in Publication Data
A catalogue record for this book is available from the
British Library.

ISBN 1 901663 55 8

Design and production management
by Elizabeth Robertson.
Printed and bound by J W Arrowsmith Limited,
United Kingdom.

Front cover: Detail of the Guthrie Bell Shrine, H1, pages 94-9.
Iona, mid-12th to late15th century, iron, copper alloy and silver gilt.

Back cover: Skye Chess Piece, L2, pages 178-81.
Scotland, mid-13th century, walrus ivory.

CONTENTS

IN MEMORY OF MY PARENTS TOM AND DORRIE GLENN

PREFACE

This catalogue covers a wide variety of material from many sources over four centuries. Like any prudent author, I have to admit that it will be punctuated by errors and omissions. My hope is that its publication will make these collections more accessible and encourage readers to correct and expand our knowledge of them.

More omissions will occur in this preface than any other section of the book, because here I would like to thank all the scholars, colleagues and friends who have helped me, for their patience and unfailing assistance. I have tried to acknowledge them in individual entries where they have made specific contributions, but in six years of writing and research so many people have come to my rescue that it is impossible to include them all by name. This does not mean that I am less than sincerely grateful.

For a generous grant which made the necessary travel to London, France, Scandinavia and Ireland possible I have to thank the British Academy.

Within NMS I enjoyed much encouragement from Mark Jones as Director and Dale Idiens and David Caldwell as successive Keepers of History and Applied Art. All the members of my own department have enthusiastically made suggestions of one sort or another. However, Jackie Moran, who probably has most practical knowledge of these objects, cheerfully met the greatest demands on her time during the hectic preparations for the opening of the Museum of Scotland, while NMS Documentation tolerated me scribbling in their busy registry. Without the museum's excellent library I could not have attempted this project and they brought all their resources to bear on obtaining obscure books and references with speed and efficiency. I am particularly beholden to Andrew Martin's knowledge of the manuscripts and papers of the Society of Antiquaries of Scotland.

It is also invidious to single out curators in the many museums in Scotland, England and abroad whose expertise I have enjoyed. John Cherry, Keeper of Medieval and Modern at the British Museum, with whom I had many long and valuable debates, was a constant support with a keen understanding of the Scottish context. Marian Campbell and Paul Williamson, Victoria and Albert Museum; Cormac Bourke, Ulster Museum; Raghnall Ó Floinn, National Museum of Ireland; Elisabeth Taburet-Delahaye and Danielle Gaborit-Chopin, the Louvre; Geneviève François, Centre national de la recherche scientifique; Poul Grinder-Hansen and Michael Andersen, Copenhagen Nationalmuseet; Göran Tegnér, Stockholm Statens Historiska Museum; Henrik von Achen, Bergen Museum, Universitetet i Bergen; Øystein Ekroll and Erik Jondell, Nidaros Domkirkes and Erla Bergendahl Hohler, Universitetets Oldsamling, Oslo, were also notably unstinting with their time and expertise. For help with seals in general I owe much to Marie-Claude Delmas and Alain Dionnet, Archives de France, T Alexander Heslop, University of East Anglia and Alan Piper, Archives and Special Collections, University of Durham. Very precise guidance was given by Alan Borthwick, National Archives of Scotland, who read all the relevant entries and saved me from a number of pitfalls. John Higgitt and Philip Bennett, University of Edinburgh, advised me on aspects of medieval illumination and language.

In Edinburgh the helpful staff and impressive resources of the National Library of Scotland and the University of Edinburgh Library have made my work easier and pleasurable, as have those of the British Library, the Warburg Institute, the Conway Library of the Courtauld Institute and the Bodleian. With the expert assistance of numerous archivists I have also benefited greatly from access to the manuscript collections of those institutions and also to the holdings of the Public Record Office, Kew, Cumbria County Archive, Trinity College Library, Dublin, the Rigsarkivet, Copenhagen, the Riksarkivet, Oslo and the Archives du Nord, Lille. Knut Espelid of Bergen University Library supplied me with essential references to Norwegian historical sources.

My especial gratitude goes to two major contributors to the work. Richard Fawcett of Historic Scotland kindly acted as independent reader and made many pertinent suggestions. Geoffrey Barrow answered a stream of questions on Scottish history with the infallible learning and good humour which he has extended to generations of students and researchers. Membership of The Scottish Medievalists has given me the opportunity to pick the brains of many others at their annual Pitlochry conferences.

The production of this book reflects the skills of many individuals including the designer Elizabeth Robertson, Jim Lewis who drew the maps, the editor Helen Kemp, the indexer Anne McCarthy, and Lesley Taylor and Cara Shanley of the publishing division of NMS Enterprises Limited. Unless otherwise stated, the photographs were taken by the museum's own highly-specialist photographers, whose work has been invaluable to this title. To them I should like to give many thanks.

Last, but not least, I am grateful for the continuing support we have received from the Trustees of the National Museums of Scotland and from Dr Gordon Rintoul who succeeded Mark Jones as Director of NMS in 2002.

Virginia Glenn
Research Associate
Department of History and Applied Art
National Museums of Scotland
September 2003

SCOTTISH COUNTIES AS DESIGNATED BY THE
LOCAL GOVERNMENT (SCOTLAND) ACT 1889

It was deemed simplest to continue to use these geographical designations in the catalogue text for two reasons. Many of the objects were first published when they were current, so pursuing references in the original literature should be more straightforward, particularly as the changes from earlier 19th-century administrative regions were comparatively minor. Recent reorganizations were more radical and some county names disappear altogether, while it seems likely that further local government amendments will result in more confusion.

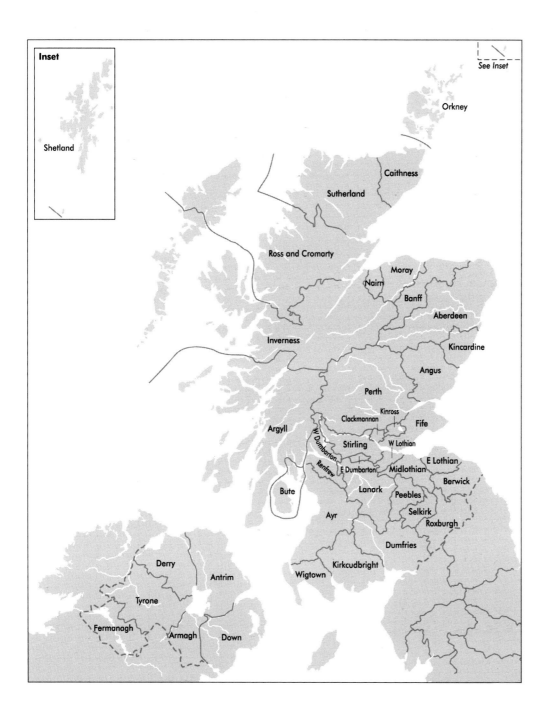

NOTES FOR READERS

Each section is preceded by a map of the find sites where known.

The material has been divided into sections as indicated on the contents page.

Opposite the number of many entries (*eg* Al) is the reference to the catalogue of the temporary exhibition *Angels, Nobles and Unicorns*, Edinburgh 1982 (*eg* B39, followed by the page number 26). It was there that much of this material was last published. Where there is no reference, the object was not included in that exhibition.

Purely for convenience of reference, each object has been given a name, *eg* LEUCHARS DISH FRAGMENT.

The numbers below the object names are the NMS acquisition numbers (*eg* H.NT 142).

Measurements are in millimetres throughout unless quoting from another publication.

The term 'the museum' refers to the National Museums of Scotland (NMS) in its present form or any of its previous manifestations, *ie* the Royal Scottish Museum, the National Museum of Antiquities of Scotland and the original collections of the Society of Antiquaries of Scotland. The Museum of Scotland specifically denotes the building opened in 1998, where most of this material is presently on display.

INTRODUCTION

The artefacts described in this catalogue formed, in succession, the basis of the later medieval section of the Society of Antiquaries of Scotland's own collection and that of the National Museum of Antiquities of Scotland; altogether a sequence of acquisition stretching back to the 1780s. Today they provide core displays in the Museum of Scotland.

Various considerations prompted the creation of a new catalogue of this well-known material. The last summary list was published as long ago as 1892. Ninety years later most of it was included in the catalogue of the temporary exhibition *Angels, Nobles and Unicorns*, which declared its purpose as offering not a definitive work of scholarship but a base which scholars might use in their more specialised work. Despite this modest claim, it has proved a useful tool to many readers in Britain and further afield.

In addition to these two single volumes, many of the objects were covered in the Society's *Proceedings* usually at the time when they were exhibited to the members or acquired for the museum. Many were, indeed, published at considerable length and by major scholars. Some of these papers are, and shall remain, the last word on the subject.

However, an initial benefit of the new catalogue is to bring the findings of all this earlier work together in one book. Also, modern students have advantages over even their most learned predecessors. A huge amount of comparative material has become known and readily accessible, particularly in the last three decades.

This has occurred principally through a series of international exhibitions with their accompanying publications, through the improved quality and comparative simplicity of modern photography and through the labours of several generations of scholars and curators for whom travel and communication have become easier and more affordable. In addition to this, techniques of scientific analysis can now be applied where previously the art historian had to rely on instinct alone.

Although both institutions are integral parts of the National Museums of Scotland (NMS), it was decided not to include the medieval collections of the adjacent Royal Museum in this book. They also include important objects of very high quality which tell an interesting story, but one of nineteenth- and early twentieth-century antiquarian collecting in Scotland and elsewhere. The decorative metalwork and ivory carvings covered here all have a known, or at least a plausible, Scottish provenance traceable to between AD 1100 and the early sixteenth century. As such, they are evidence from which we can make valuable deductions about a period in the nation's history for which documents are frequently sparse or altogether non-existent.

Unfortunately, civil war and religious iconoclasm have left us with an even more fragmentary picture of medieval art in Scotland than in most Protestant countries. To compare our surviving pieces with the great riches of the national museums in Copenhagen, Stockholm, Oslo and Bergen – for example – is almost to despair. Nevertheless, detailed study of what remains provides glimpses of the lifestyle, taste, status, wealth and foreign connections of Scottish institutions and individuals between the twelfth century and the Reformation.

The reasons for the scanty survival of Scotland's medieval material culture have often been debated. The country was certainly smaller, poorer and less populous than mighty neighbours like France or even England. Much of the terrain was too wild and mountainous for cultivation and remains largely uninhabited to

fig 1: THE MACE OF ST SALVATOR'S COLLEGE
Silver gilt, by Johne Maiel, Paris, 1461, reproduced
courtesy of the University of St Andrews.
(detail)

this day. This, however, applies even more strikingly to Norway, where enviable quantities of pre-Reformation religious art survive.

David McRoberts examined the processes behind the sixteenth-century destruction of Scottish churches, religious houses and their contents in a masterly article of 1959. He pointed out that in about 1540 Scotland had thirteen cathedrals (although a few were quite small) and over one thousand parish churches, some of them very wealthy like St Nicholas in Aberdeen or St Giles in Edinburgh. There were also very prominent and rich collegiate churches, for example the chapels of Stirling Castle and King's College, Aberdeen. Numerous abbeys, friaries and nunneries were again in many cases well endowed. Forty years later most of their buildings were in ruins, their furnishings and treasuries despoiled. This increasingly Calvinist iconoclasm was exacerbated by internal political opportunism and repeated attacks by the English already forcibly converted to Protestantism by Henry VIII. Curiously, the destruction wrought by what John Knox himself described as 'the rascal multitude' in their populist forays was more total than the depredations of Henry's methodical commissioners in England. By comparison, the Lutherans of Scandinavia took a much more relaxed approach to religious change, resulting in neglect rather than annihilation of Catholic churches and their contents.

The documentary evidence is, however, that from at least the twelfth century the ecclesiastical metalwork in use in Scotland was on a par with much of Europe. Robert Bartlett's recent exciting discovery of a description of the translation of St Margaret's relics in 1180 at Dunfermline, reveals a *theca* shining with gold leaf and ornamented with figures, features one recognises from the major shrines of similar date still to be seen in the Rhine and Meuse area. By the end of the fifteenth century religious communities in medieval Scotland had acquired the vestments, service books, altarpieces and vessels customary for celebration of the mass in quantities equal to their European neighbours. To cite just one cathedral, Glasgow in 1432 listed a pure gold chalice and paten in its inventory; among its silver were fourteen chalices, some gilt and some with patens; three altar crosses; two croziers, one gilt; ten shrines and reliquaries; a large and a smaller censer; a ship for incense and twenty-three bowls, phials and minor vessels. This was in addition to jewels, brooches and a large collection of vestments. John Dowden, editing the Glasgow documents in 1899, pointed out that Aberdeen Cathedral's inventories show it to have been even more amply supplied. The quality and sophistication of the fifteenth-century maces of the University of St Andrews demonstrates what at least some of the listed plate may have looked like (fig 1).

Secular patrons, notably the royal family and their close adherents, also had opulent tastes. The Renaissance aspirations of the court of James IV (1488-1513) were reflected not only in the presence of distinguished musicians, poets, churchmen and an Italian alchemist, alongside the King's Gaelic harpist, but in the great halls which he built at Stirling and Edinburgh Castles. The wardrobe accounts tell of the lavish accoutrements acquired to furnish this lifestyle, with its international connections (at least six languages were spoken at the court) and cult of jousts and tournaments. The Flemish Book of Hours commissioned to mark the marriage in 1503 of James and Margaret Tudor, sister of Henry VIII, is the most brilliant of their extant illuminated manuscripts and testifies to the magnificence they could command, while their decorated marriage contract and *The King's Quair* show Scottish artists evolving their own related style (fig 2). However, of the treasure and jewels, virtually all that remain are the crown, sceptre and sword of the 'Honours of Scotland' in Edinburgh Castle, all much altered in succeeding reigns.

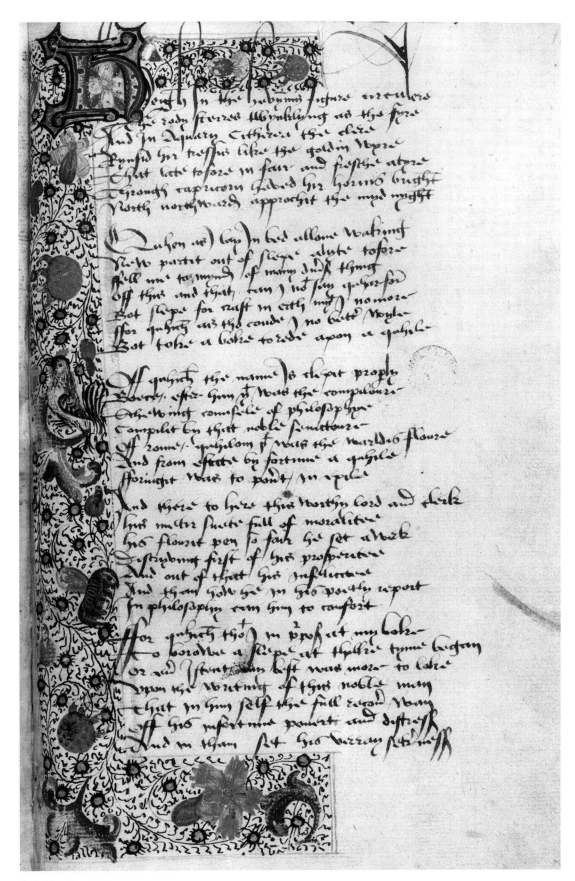

fig 2: **The King's Quair**
MS Arch Selden B 24, fol 192 recto, paper, Edinburgh
or Roslin, after 1489, reproduced by permission of the
Bodleian Library, Oxford.
260 x 175 (pages cropped)

This was not simply a very late flowering of a taste for luxury in Scottish royal circles. An inventory survives of the trousseau received in Bergen in 1293 for Isabella de Brus, daughter of the earl of Carrick and sister of Robert Bruce, when she married King Erik of Norway. In addition to her clothes lavishly trimmed with fur, she had couches, hangings and cushions embellished with cloth of gold and miniver and a coverlet with the arms of France. There were also sixty-eight items of silver weighing altogether over eighty marks (in modern terms over 600 oz) and two crowns, one smaller than the other.

Isabella is not the only very wealthy lady of the thirteenth century about whose possessions we have a little information. In the political faction rivalling the Bruces, Derbforgaill (1209-89), whose name has been Latinised as Devorgilla, Devorguilla, Dervorguilla and Dervorguilla, the last of which most accurately reflects the Gaelic, was the mother of the ill-fated king, John Balliol. She is remembered as benefactress of Glasgow Cathedral, foundress of Sweetheart Abbey in Dumfriesshire and Balliol College, Oxford and was a great heiress in her own right. Three richly illuminated books which she owned have survived in the University of Edinburgh, Princeton and Bodleian libraries, but none of her plate or jewellery, which may well have surpassed Isabella's in both quantity and quality. From the impressions of her seal on the 1282 statutes of Balliol College and four of their other charters it is clear that the matrix was made by a very fashionable and accomplished engraver. The intricate heraldry is carried out with great precision and the figure of Dervorguilla herself is elegant and graceful, with extraordinarily fine detail on the coiled hairstyle, delicate veil and embroidered robe. Even the little trees on each side of the Lady of Galloway are of clearly differentiated types remarkable on such a tiny scale (fig 3).

fig 3: SEAL OF DERVORGUILLA
Red wax, attached to the College Statutes, English or French, 1282, reproduced by permission of the Master and Fellows of Balliol College, Oxford.
H 64, W 38

Although interesting and precious, remnants of medieval luxury such as the Bute Mazer and the early silver spoons in the Museum of Scotland would probably pale into insignificance beside the treasures of these greater families. To form any kind of picture of the lives of major medieval courtiers in Scotland, this has to be borne in mind.

The collection and preservation of what did survive has been a major concern of the Society of Antiquaries of Scotland since its foundation in 1780. In two lengthy essays to mark the Society's bicentenary, R B K Stevenson charted the progress of its museum through various premises in the Old and New Towns of Edinburgh. In 1851 ownership of the collections was conveyed to the nation and gradually government funding was obtained for the housing and staffing of the forerunner of the National Museum of Antiquities of Scotland. However, the Society continued to play a major part in the administration of the museum and in raising finance for it. In 1891 it moved to purpose built galleries in Queen Street, which were shared with the Scottish National Portrait Gallery which today occupies the entire building. The Museum of Scotland, Chambers Street, in which this material is now displayed was opened by Her Majesty the Queen on St Andrew's Day 1998. It was specially designed to show the Scottish collections from prehistory to the present day.

Many of the names which appear in this catalogue are those of luminaries of the Society of Antiquaries of Scotland. Daniel Wilson, perhaps the most internationally celebrated, is the subject of a book by Marinell Ash and collaborators published in 1999. Joseph Anderson's career as 'the foremost figure in all matters relating to Scottish archaeology' was covered by David Clarke in the millennium *Rhind Lectures*, published in 2002. Scholars and collectors in large numbers turned to David Laing, who died in 1878 in his eighty-sixth year, for advice on acquisitions and antiquarian research. His vast archive of papers is lodged with the library of the University of Edinburgh and will certainly yield further insights into the formation of this collection in due course. The Keeper of the National Museum of Antiquities from 1919 to 1938, John Graham Callander, did much to reorganise the medieval collections between the wars. The work of all these figures was extensively published, first in *Archaeologia Scotica* then since 1852 more methodically in *Proceedings of the Society of Antiquaries of Scotland* (*PSAS*). Research actively continues on the Society's manuscript records which will further refine the published accounts.

Wilson and Anderson instigated a scientific approach to archaeology in Scotland. However, most of the material catalogued here did not come from systematic exploration, but was found by chance or preserved more or less accidentally. Consequently, it must be remembered that the evidence it provides is to some extent random. Many important sites await proper archaeological investigation, some as major as the royal palace at Roxburgh, which would provide a much fuller account than at present. Smaller excavations like Finlaggan on Islay, recently carried out by NMS, have already furnished valuable new information, in that case about the lifestyle of the Lords of the Isles.

Despite this haphazard pattern of acquisition the maps of the find sites show that in many cases they have considerable historic significance. It is interesting to compare them with the two earliest known maps of Scotland, both made by the English and published by Hume Brown over a century ago.

The mid-thirteenth-century map of mainland Britain by Matthew Paris shows important towns at Berwick, Roxburgh, Edinburgh (which he indicates as castellated), Glasgow, Dunfermline, Dundee, St Andrews, Arbroath and as far north as

Aberdeen. Both he and the maker of the Gough Map (fig 4), perhaps a century later, believed that the Forth and Clyde estuaries met in the middle creating SCOCIA ULTRA MARINA, a separate northerly island which could only be reached overland by means of Stirling Bridge. Of the far north west Paris says there are vast and trackless seas, impassable marshes (fit however for cattle and shepherds) and mountainous woody regions harbouring an uncivilised race of herdsmen.

In 1295 communications were sufficiently good for Edward I to march from the Borders as far as Banff and Elgin, the latter described in the English chronicle of his journey as 'a goode Castell and a good towne'. The thoroughfares were adequate for him to take with him thirty thousand foot soldiers and five thousand heavily armed horsemen. On only one occasion in the 'Voyage of Kynge Edwarde' does the writer record that the night was spent 'in tentis'. Everywhere else on this expedition of more than three hundred miles from south to north there was a castle or religious house which could accommodate the royal party at least, mostly described as 'faire' or 'good'. The complexity and effectiveness of these land routes was documented by Geoffrey Barrow in 1992.

The Gough cartographers, working with the extra information collected during this English invasion, had a much greater accretion of facts at their disposal.

fig 4: GOUGH MAP
MS Gough Gen. Top. 16, vellum, English, mid-14th century,
reproduced by permission of the Bodleian Library, Oxford.
(detail)

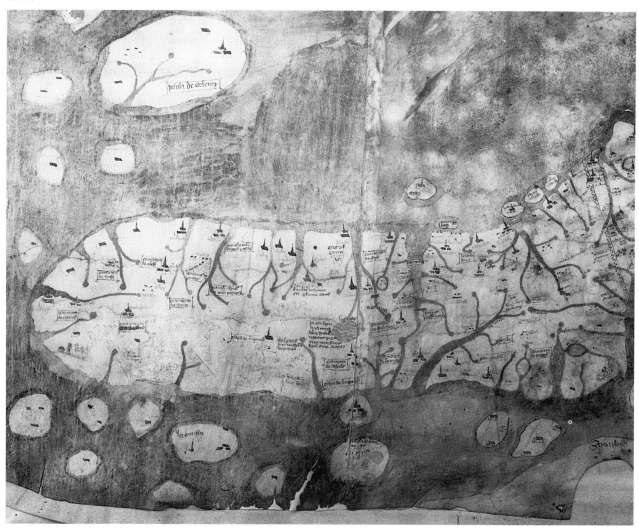

There are many more towns, castles and religious institutions on their map, with added geographical features such as rivers, mountains and lakes. By this time English knowledge extended northwards not just to Elgin, but as far as the town of Wick. Kildrummy Castle had obviously made a lasting impact as it is shown as a major fortification under the *Comitatus de Marr* (the earldom of Mar).

Much more was also known about the islands surrounding Scotland. A large church is drawn on Orkney, representing the twelfth-century cathedral of St Magnus, Kirkwall. A smaller one on the island of May represents the Benedictine foundation linked to Reading Abbey. Rothesay Castle is shown on the *Insula de Bote*, although the actual island of Bute has been removed from the Firth of Clyde into the Irish Sea. Dwellings also appear on *Les Outisles* (the Hebrides), but the view of the west and central Highlands is just as bleak as that of Matthew Paris. The area is shown as largely empty except for a reference to much hunting south of Badenoch and an abundant wolf population in Sutherland.

The distribution of provenances for the items in this catalogue largely conforms to this picture. By far the greatest concentration for every category except ivory and bone occurs on the east coast, with some sites in the central belt and numerous instances stretching across the Borders into Dumfries and Galloway. The plentiful discoveries in the latter area are probably more of a tribute to the activities of local enthusiasts, inspired by Dumfriesshire and Galloway Natural History and Antiquarian Society, than an indication of its wealth and importance in the Middle Ages.

Most of the material described in this volume follows, even if at some remove, contemporary norms of style and taste in England, France and the adjoining areas of Northern Europe. However, the six objects in the *West Highland* section are in a distinct style associated with the area, as are the two whalebone caskets (L9 and L10). The playing pieces and some of the jewellery found on the western islands have similar characteristics, but combined with strong Scandinavian influence, while the Lewis Chessmen seem actually to have been imported from Norway.

This scattering of Nordic features and the comparative proliferation of later medieval finds up and down the east coast point to two of Scotland's most important trade routes. Faster, easier and in times of trouble safer than travel overland, the influence of sea links cannot be overestimated. The sea route from Scandinavia, down the west coast of Scotland to Man and Ireland, was established by the Vikings. The evidence of some of these artefacts is that it was still in use by traders in the twelfth, thirteenth and probably later centuries. It was on the east coast, however, that growing ports and prosperous royal burghs forged commercial links not only with Bergen and Denmark, but with the Low Countries and the Baltic, a process shown in detail by Michael Lynch and others in McNeill and MacQueen's *Atlas of Scottish History*. Scotland's main exports were wool, hides and fish, but most of what was imported in return was luxury goods. Alexander Grant (1984) cites wine, exotic foodstuffs, quality cloth and pottery, armour and military equipment. One Scottish ship captured by the English in 1394 carried brass plates and pots, candelabra, keys and locks amongst its very varied cargo. With these imports would have come foreign merchants and foreign ideas.

The Romanesque and Gothic decorative metalwork and ivory carvings in the Museum of Scotland illustrate the history of Scotland at a seminal period of the country's development. Firmly established as an independent nation with its own monarchy and a thriving network of religious institutions, between 1100 and 1500 it built up through political alliances, royal marriages and expanding trade links a secure and relatively powerful position amongst its European neighbours.

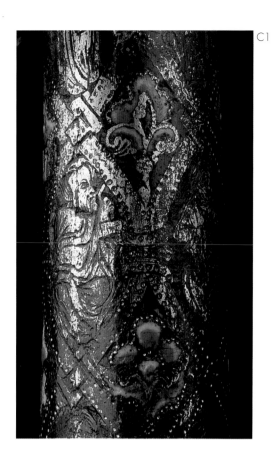

Detail showing Tier III.2 of enamel decoration

C1 THE WHITHORN CROZIER
Copper alloy, gilt and enamelled
English (?), c1175
(pages 29-33)

Detail showing Tier I.4 of enamel decoration

C2 **THE BUTE MAZER** (detail of the print)
Silver, gilt and enamelled
Scottish, after 1314, before 1330
(pages 34-8)

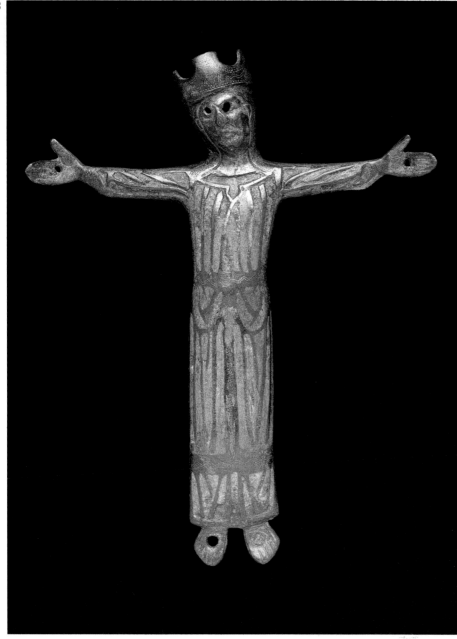

C3 CERES CRUCIFIX FIGURE
Copper alloy, gilt and enamelled
French, Limoges, c1225-50
(pages 38-9)

C6 WAUCHOPE CASKET HASP
Copper alloy, gilt and enamelled,
lapis lazuli
French, Limoges, early 13th century
(pages 41-2)

C4 BORVE PLAQUE
Copper alloy, gilt and enamelled
Scottish or Scandinavian, mid-13th century
(pages 39-40)

C4

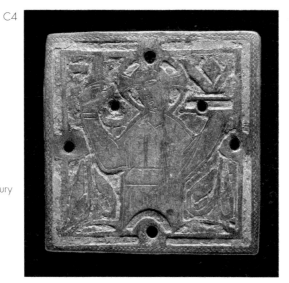

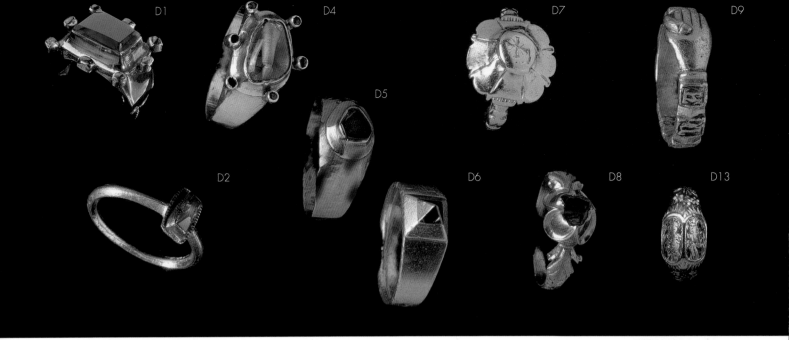

RINGS D1 WHITHORN
Amethyst, sapphire and gold
Scottish (?), 13th century
(page 48)

D2 WHITHORN
Amethyst and silver gilt
Scottish (?), 13th century
(page 48)

D4 CANONBIE
Sapphire, emeralds and gold
Scottish or English, mid-13th
century (page 49)

D5 CANONBIE
Ruby and gold. Scottish or
English, 13th century (page 50)

D6 HOLYROOD
Diamond and gold
Scottish (?), c1300 (page 50)

D7 WEISDALE VOE
Gold. Scottish or
Scandinavian, early 14th
century (page 51)

D8 DUNKELD
Ruby, gold and (lost) enamel
Possibly Italian, late 14th
century (page 51)

D9 FEDE DEVICE
Silver, gilt and originally
enamelled. Scottish or English,
late 15th century
(page 52)

D13 TANTALLON
Enamelled gold
English, 15th century
(page 54)

E21 KAMES BROOCH
Pearls and gold
Scottish, mid-13th century
(pages 67-8)

E15 DOUNE BROOCH
Gold
Probably Scottish, late 14th or early 15th century
(page 64)

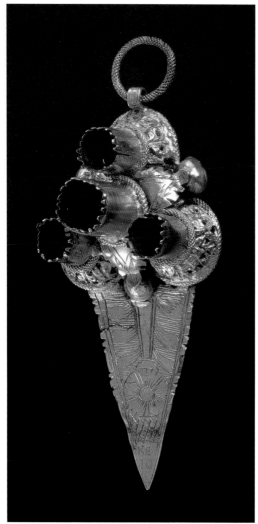

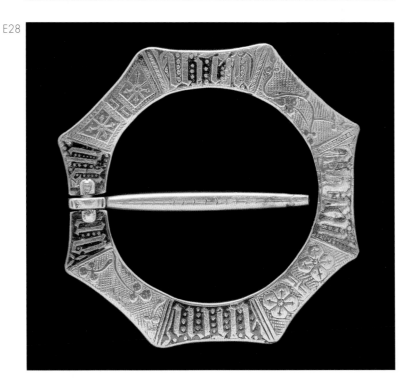

E22 KINDROCHIT BROOCH
Silver, gilt and enamelled
Scottish, late 15th century
(page 68-9)

E28 MULL BROOCH
Silver and niello
Scottish, mid-15th century
(pages 72-3)

F3 KILRENNY RELIQUARY PENDANT
Silver gilt and glass
Scottish, late 15th century
(page 84-5)

G3 IONA FILLET (detail)
Gold
West of Scotland, c1200
(page 91)

H1 **GUTHRIE BELL SHRINE**
Iron, copper alloy, silver gilt
West of Scotland, mid-12th to late 15th century
(pages 94-9)

H3 **TIBBERMUIR CORPUS**
Copper alloy gilded
Scottish, mid-12th century
(pages 104-105)

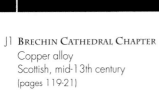

front

back

SEAL MATRICES   J1 **BRECHIN CATHEDRAL CHAPTER**
Copper alloy
Scottish, mid-13th century
(pages 119-21)

J4 **COUPAR ANGUS ABBEY**
Silver
Scottish, before 1449
(pages 125–6)

H6 THE COIGREACH OR 'QUIGRICH'
Rock crystal and silver gilt
Scottish, 13-15th centuries, with re-used 12th-century filigree
(pages 107-15)

L1(g) L1(a) L1(k) L1(e) L1(j)

THE LEWIS CHESSMEN

(from left to right)
BISHOP, KING, WARDER, QUEEN Walrus ivory
WARDER Whale tooth
Scandinavian, late 12th century
(pages 149-77)

L9

L9 EGLINTON CASKET
Whale bone and copper alloy
Scottish, c 1500
(pages 186-9)

COPPER ALLOY

I

This mixed group of material contains both secular and ecclesiastical metalwork. Most of it was probably produced locally, but A1, A4 and, possibly, A2 are interesting imports. The quality of the pieces ranges from the elegance of the jewelled spur, presumably an indication of MacDonald wealth and status, to the awkward proportions of the aquamanile, an object inexpertly based on a popular European form of vessel.

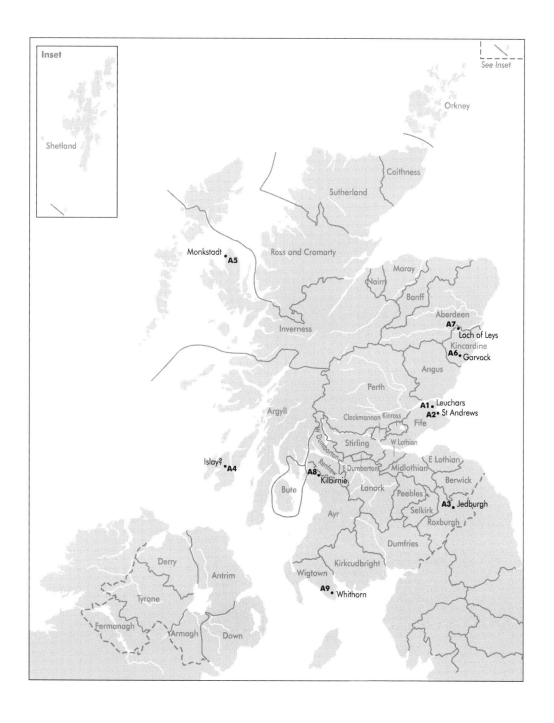

A1
LEUCHARS DISH FRAGMENT
[H.NT 142]

Northern Germany, mid-12th century
Copper alloy; hammered, engraved
DIAM 254 (approx)

CONDITION
Extensive losses all round edge, small holes in central area, cracked, bent and corroded.

INSCRIPTIONS
NI/NI IRA(?)/VI: NI/I: [gap] : AI: V: V: AI: (round the rim) IRA/A/A (in the centre) IR / A (at the monster's mouth) (Roman)
[for INVIDIA IRA 'envy anger']

PROVENANCE
Found by Dr J B Mears at the Castle Mound, Leuchars, Fife, who presented it to the museum in 1931.[1]

+ + + + + + + + + + + + + + + +

In the centre a striding figure, wearing a round helmet with a knob on the top, a hauberk and hose, brandishes a broad sword at shoulder height and clasps a pointed shield to his chest. The visor of his helmet is raised to show one eye. The shield is decorated with four groups of three lines radiating from a round central boss, and the scabbard, which protrudes behind the figure, with paired lines and a saltire cross. In front of the figure a monstrous humanoid head with jagged tufts of hair and closed eyes opens its mouth to show four jutting fangs.

On the fragmentary rim the feet of five figures are visible, four of them grouped in confronting pairs. Five wide radiating motifs separate the figures, marked by a single vertical line on one side and a double on the other and engraved with alternating horizontal bands of short vertical dashes and shallow curved V-shapes.

The whole is crudely and rather sketchily engraved, although the drawing is lively and animated.

+ + + + + + + + + + + + + + + +

These bowls have survived in considerable numbers in northern Europe, although their places of manufacture have never been securely identified. More carefully engraved examples with elaborate iconography based on the lives of saints, particularly Thomas the Apostle[2] and Ursula, are known, but more cursory products like A1, with somewhat misunderstood inscriptions and abbreviated scenes based on moralistic texts, are much more common.[3]

Comparison with other complete bowls, in the British Museum, Rome and Cologne, makes it possible to identify the wide radiating bands as tree-trunks, with figures similar to the central knight engaged in conflict against a woodland background.[4] On the same grounds, it is suggested that the monster's head is emerging from a tree stump.

In the later 12th century, Leuchars Castle was a stronghold of the de Quincis. Robert de Quinci came of a family from near Béthune on the French Flemish borders which had settled in Northamptonshire after the Conquest.[5] By the end of Malcolm IV's reign he had become an important figure in Scottish affairs and had married the daughter and heiress of Ness, Lord of Leuchars, a major native landowner in central Scotland.[6] Close contacts with England continued, his son Saer became earl of Winchester in 1207, but family ties with northern France were not forgotten and documents of Robert's were witnessed in 1170 and later by four associates from communities within about 20 kilometres of his native Cuinchy.[7]

The bowl could have been brought to Scotland by a family member, have been a gift from one of their

A1

Flemish contacts or simply part of the normal equipment of a rich and powerful household with active international communications.

NOTES: [1] *PSAS*, vol LXVI, 1931, 15-16, fig 2. [2] London 1984, 253-4, cat no 259. [3] Weitzmann-Fiedler 1981, *passim*. [4] Ibid 118, cat no 137, pl 125, fig 137. [5] Barrow 1992, 80. [6] Barrow 1971, 6, 43. [7] Barrow 1973, 318-19.

A2   B28, 22

St Andrews Bowl and Cover

[L.1946.1]

Northern Germany or Scotland, 12th century
Copper alloy; raised, engraved
DIAM 101, H 41 (bowl); DIAM 103, H 1 (cover)

CONDITION
Brittle and corroded, sections missing from the base, sides and rim of the bowl and from the centre and edge of the cover.

PROVENANCE
Found before 1898 about five feet below the surface during grave-digging between St Rule's Tower and the south corner of the east end of St Andrews Cathedral.[1] It entered the museum collection in 1946.

✦ ✦ ✦ ✦ ✦ ✦ ✦ ✦ ✦ ✦ ✦ ✦ ✦ ✦ ✦ ✦

The hemispherical bowl with a flattened base has a raised circle in the bottom on which is engraved a geometric ornament consisting of a double outlined concentric six-petalled flower within a circle; the petals joined by double concave arcs, the central compass point clearly marked. Three outer circles define the depression surrounding the raised centre. The flower and circle motif is repeated on the underside of the bowl. There is a border of roughly engraved lines just below the flattened rim.

The cover is round and slightly dished. In the centre double engraved outlines define a Celtic cross with a circle in the middle, framed by one inner and four outer concentric rings. The edge is bent downwards to fit the rim of the bowl.

✦ ✦ ✦ ✦ ✦ ✦ ✦ ✦ ✦ ✦ ✦ ✦ ✦ ✦ ✦ ✦

Copper-alloy bowls classed as 'Romanesque', with concentric geometric decoration loosely comparable to this have survived in Prussia, Berne, Cologne and Wroclaw in Poland.[2] Although it was found less than ten kilometres from A1, which could suggest a common source of supply, the engraving on A2 is so simple and the design so basic that it may well be a native Scottish example of the genre.

The engraving on the cover is shallower than that inside the bowl, the double outlines further apart, and there are four surrounding circles instead of three. It may be an unrelated paten which has been bent at the edges to form a close fitting lid for the bowl.

NOTES: [1] Fleming 1899, 76-8. [2] Weitzmann-Fiedler 1981, 129-30, pl 144, figs 175-8; A2 is fig 176 bis, incorrectly identified on page 129 as from the Helmsdale hoard, which is actually late Roman.

A2

A3
JEDBURGH MOUNT
[H.XB 10]

Scotland, mid-12th century
Copper alloy, gilt, glass; cast, gilded
H 145, W 101, D 7 (approx)

CONDITION
Very brittle and corroded, part of the ring and a fastening (?) device missing.

PROVENANCE
Found during an excavation sponsored by the Scottish Development Department (Ancient Monuments) in 1984 in the chapter house, Jedburgh Abbey, since then in the care of the museum.[1]

✦ ✦ ✦ ✦ ✦ ✦ ✦ ✦ ✦ ✦ ✦ ✦ ✦ ✦ ✦ ✦

The cast mount consists of a ring with three projecting arms, the whole half-round in section. The two longer arms placed diametrically on the ring have a green glass 'gem' in a high plain setting. Half-way between them is a shorter arm with a blue glass 'gem' in a matching setting. A fourth arm opposite the latter consists of half a fastening (?) device, flat and circular in shape with a round hole in the square terminal. The other three arms each have a hole pierced for a fixing pin.

The metal has all been gilded and has cast decoration. There are fans of formalised leaves on the ring at the intersections with the two longer arms. Three widely angled V-shaped notches ornament the ring below the arm with the blue gem. Double lines mark the two longer

arms above the green gems and at the ends, frame the ornament on the ring and punctuate it midway between. The reverse is completely plain.

✦ ✦ ✦ ✦ ✦ ✦ ✦ ✦ ✦ ✦ ✦ ✦ ✦ ✦ ✦ ✦

The mount is clearly designed to be applied to a flat surface and a book cover has been plausibly suggested,[2] but this makes the circular lug difficult to explain.

The foundation by David I of the Augustinian house at Jedburgh is recorded in a document of between 1147 and 1151.[3] The building of the abbey church, architecturally one of the most splendid in Scotland, probably began almost immediately afterwards.[4] The few stylistic features of the mount suggest that is also mid-12th century in date, but the circumstances of its discovery neither confirm nor deny this as it was excavated in the chapter house, which was largely remodelled in the early 14th century and yielded finds which were obviously residual, including a coin of Aethelred II (978-1016).[5]

NOTES: [1] Lewis and Ewart 1995, 55-9. [2] Caldwell 1995, 86-8. [3] Barrow 1999, 139-40, no 174. [4] Fawcett 1995, 159-66. [5] Lewis and Ewart, loc cit.

A4   B36, 25-26
ISLAY CRUCIFIX FIGURE
[H.KE 12]

Northern Europe (?), mid-12th century
Copper alloy; cast, engraved
H 146, W 136, D 22

CONDITION
Complete, but very corroded and worn to the point where some of the modelling, for example the face, is indecipherable.

PROVENANCE
Bought for the museum in 1894 from the collection of the late Gourlay Steell.[1]

✦ ✦ ✦ ✦ ✦ ✦ ✦ ✦ ✦ ✦ ✦ ✦ ✦ ✦ ✦ ✦

The figure of Christ Crucified from a processional or altar cross is bareheaded with long straight hair falling from a centre parting to the shoulders. The straight slightly raised outstretched arms have large hands with round holes in the palms. A sunken chest shows little indication of musculature or ribs and the stomach is thrust forward. Tapering legs part widely from the knees and the feet are long and sloping with no nail holes.

The head is tilted to the figure's right, but otherwise the pose is very frontal, emphasised by the symmetrical drapery pattern of the knee-length perizoma. It has a horizontal girdle in three ridges joined at the front by a tasselled knot from which two streamers fall to just above

A3

the knees. There is a vertically ridged pad on each hip and a pattern of vertical lines and beading down each side, with two panels of inverted V folds at the front.

✛ ✛ ✛ ✛ ✛ ✛ ✛ ✛ ✛ ✛ ✛ ✛ ✛ ✛ ✛ ✛

Gourlay Steell was elected to the Royal Scottish Academy in 1859 and became Animal Painter to Her Majesty in Scotland in 1873 at the same period as his brother was Queen Victoria's Sculptor-in-Ordinary. From 1882 until his death in 1894 he was curator of the Scottish National Gallery.[2] His collection, like that of Noel Paton and other 19th-century Scottish artists, was probably formed to provide historical 'props' in his compositions. A portrait by Gourlay Steell of his young son shows the boy standing next to a carved 17th-century chair, with a powder horn hung from the back and an elaborate 18th-century basket-hilt sword propped against the seat.[3] He might have acquired A4 on one of his trips to Colonsay or Jura,[4] but it is equally likely that he bought it from a dealer in Edinburgh or London who ascribed the Islay provenance to it.

The condition of the object is such that stylistic considerations can be only tenuous. However, a comprehensive corpus of these figures places it with Romanesque examples surviving from northern Germany and the French-Belgian borders.[5]

NOTES: [1] *PSAS*, vol xxviii, 1894, 237. The museum also purchased a 17th-century Highland belt with heavily decorated brass mounts. A late 17th-century mirror with an earlier provenance at Holyrood Palace from Steell's collection was sold at Christie's South Kensington, 2 May 2002, Lot 254. [2] Cursiter 1949, 96, 112-13, 116. [3] I am indebted to Susanna Kerr of the Scottish National Portrait Gallery for this information. [4] Laperriere 1991, 233, 235. [5] Bloch 1992, 84, 90, cat no I E 13, pl 20.

A4

MONKSTADT SPUR

[H.ML 94]

Text by Blanche Ellis

Western Europe, possibly Scotland, 12th century
Copper alloy, gilt, quartz, glass; cast, engraved, gems cut
and polished
w 70 (span between terminals), L 134 (overall); L 53 (neck
including goad 23)

CONDITION
Missing loop, five missing stones, surface affected by
lengthy immersion.

PROVENANCE
Recorded in 1862 in the collection of Lord MacDonald at
Armadale Castle, then said to have been found in the bed
of Loch Monkstadt, Skye, when it was drained about 30 years
previously.[1] Purchased by the museum at auction in 1976.[2]

+ + + + + + + + + + + + + + + +

The straight neck is of rounded lozenge section, with a
broad based quadrangular goad. The spur sides are of D
section and, despite some distortion, sweep elegantly
forward into deep curves under the wearer's ankle before
rising to their terminals. The terminals are of figure-8
form, one has lost most of one ring while the complete
one is slightly bent. They are extremely small and the
rivets which would have held the spur leathers are
missing. The front edge of the surviving ring of the
broken terminal shows signs of wear. Although they are
of the usual form for rivet terminals of their period, they
are strangely designed to rise diagonally backwards
above the top edges of the spur sides.

The decoration of the spur originally included
cabochon 'gems' in high oval collets, each retained by
four claws: one jewel on each top surface of the goad,

another on top of the neck and three along each side. The
upper surfaces of the sides, neck and goad are incised
with a pattern of flowers and leaves, plain and cross-
hatched within interlaced narrow bands. The lower parts
of the neck and sides and the inner surfaces of the sides
are undecorated. There are slight traces of gilding around
the stone settings on the sides.[3]

+ + + + + + + + + + + + + + + +

Except for the arrangement of its terminals, the form of
the spur is similar to that of an undecorated iron spur
excavated from a sealed context dated 1080-1150 at
Goltho, Lincolnshire.[4] The Monkstadt spur may also be
compared with the copper-alloy prick spur with geometric
decoration from the site of Linlithgow Palace, which is
the latest form of medieval prick spur common from the
mid-12th and the 13th centuries.[5] Another 12th-century
spur of different form with shorter almost straight sides,
has a similar neck and goad to A5 and is incised with a
pattern of stylised fleurs-de-lis within narrow flowing
bands. It is mercury gilded, but not jewelled.[6]

Throughout history spurs have very occasionally
been decorated with jewels. In 1399 Jean Froissart commented that the spurs used at English coronation
ceremonies were 'with one point without rowels'. This
was worthy of note because prick spurs were already unusual by that date and suggests that those in ceremonial use
were already quite old. They continued to be used until
they were melted down after the execution of Charles I.
The 1649 inventory of his goods described them as 'One
paire of silver gilt Spurres with buckles sett with 12 slight
stones and crimson silke strapps'.[7]

Other late-medieval jewelled examples include the
pair of French gilded copper-alloy rowel spurs, now in
New York, which belonged to Bertrand de Goth who died
in 1324, each of which has a rock crystal stone set on

A5

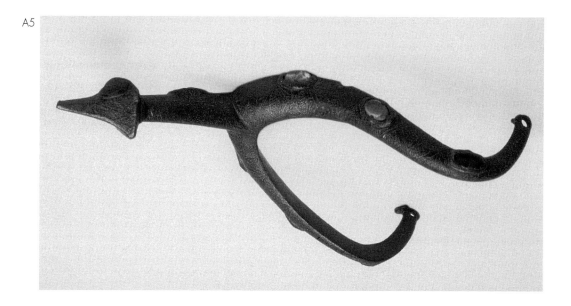

either side of its rowel box.[8] A large, late copper-alloy prick spur in Bologna has claw settings for missing jewels and a buckle so similar to those on the de Goth examples that it is clearly contemporary with them.[9]

Although A5 appears in general to be a functional spur for riding, the strangely awkward, diagonally upward angle of the terminals would have caused problems, with the undersole leather chafing on the side of the spur. A possible alternative is that it was made as payment for land tenure. Payment of rent in the form of a pair of spurs is known from a number of places in Britain, usually for estates, but also for Shottesbrook Church, Buckinghamshire.[10] In 12th- and 13th-century Scotland this custom was also practised. A Kelso charter records a gift of Malcolm IV to Serlo his clerk, between 1153 and 1165, of about 52 acres of land for 'certain gilt spurs annually.[11] For a pair of gilt spurs in each case, Robert de Brus granted land and a mill in Annandale in 1218.[12] Iron spurs were sufficient for land in Glen Esk, Angus about the same period,[13] but gilded metal was again the material of a pair (*calcaria subaurata*) exchanged between Maud and her brother John of Wilton for a similar transaction concerning a property in Tarvit, Fife before 1238.[14] The tradition continued there, the rent for the same land still being *unam par calcarium deauratorum* between 1283 and 1285.[15]

The possibility has been considered that A5 might have been made in the style of the 12th century to coincide with the drainage of the loch in the early 19th century, but despite the impractical terminals, its general form, detail and condition tend to support its authenticity.

NOTES: [1] Smith 1862, 103-4. For a summary of the MacDonald lands at Monkstadt, see page 147. [2] Christie's, London, 14 April 1976. [3] Smith 1862, 104, also noted this. [4] Beresford 1987, no 166, 180, fig 160, 185. [5] Caldwell and Lewis 1996, no 121, 854, illus 23, 857, where the spur is dated 'early 14th century'. Now NMS H.ML 1, as a purely utilitarian object it has not been included in this catalogue of 'decorative' metalwork. [6] Private collection, said to have come from a field near Norwich. [7] Blair 1998, vol II, 275-82, where he discusses the Froissart reference (taken from Buchon 1840); Millar 1972, 50. [8] Dean 1926, 129-30; Grancsay 1955, no 78. [9] Boccia 1991, no 189, 102. [10] Verbal communication from E Rigold. [11] Kelso Liber 1846, no 216, 178. [12] Macquarrie 1983, 73, 75-6. [13] National Archives of Scotland ms GD 45/16/1737. [14] Barrow 1974, 29-30. [15] Ibid, 36; information on rent spurs in Scotland assembled by Virginia Glenn.

GARVOCK CENSER
[H.KJ 26]

Scotland, 13th century
Copper alloy; raised, cast, saw pierced, punched
DIAM 101, H 151, W 124 (with loops)

CONDITION
Generally good, finial slightly misshapen, one hanging loop missing from cover.

PROVENANCE
Found in 1846 under the floor of the old church at Garvock, Kincardineshire; exhibited to the Society of Antiquaries of Scotland in 1887,[1] and deposited in the museum that year by the Rev. William Stephen.[2]

✛ ✛ ✛ ✛ ✛ ✛ ✛ ✛ ✛ ✛ ✛ ✛ ✛ ✛ ✛ ✛

The censer is in two parts, a bowl and a cover, each with four horizontal loops for suspension chains. The bowl is hemispherical with a plain high foot. A border of double circles is stamped around the rim. The underside of the base has been repaired at an early date with a circle of copper alloy held in place with four pins, which is engraved with a trial (?) pattern of a flower formed by compass arcs.

The cover is stepped up to a tapering hexagon, crowned with a cast hexagonal finial. The lower part mirrors the bowl shape and has the same double circle border at the rim and below the first step. It has four quadrilobe apertures, surrounded by three double circles, spaced midway between the hanging loops. Above this curved section are two tiers of keyhole-shaped perforations (fourteen below, ten above) separated by a sloping ledge.

The inside of the censer is entirely plain.

✛ ✛ ✛ ✛ ✛ ✛ ✛ ✛ ✛ ✛ ✛ ✛ ✛ ✛ ✛ ✛

A6

Medieval European copper-alloy censers from the 12th century onwards have survived in large numbers. This example with rudimentary architectural articulation and simple punched decoration is probably a local product of the 13th century.

NOTES: [1] Gammack 1887, 180. [2] NMAS 1892, no KJ 26, 294.

A7   C46, 44
LOCH OF LEYS CANDLEHOLDER
[H.MGI 111]

Scotland, 14th century
Copper alloy, gilt; cast, chased, engraved, gilded
H 155, W 73, D 123

CONDITION
Toes of the left foot missing, top of the head dented, surface slightly corroded and pitted, most of the gilt worn or missing.

INSCRIPTIONS
A (?) (Lombardic)

PROVENANCE
Bought by the museum in 1982 from a local man whose grandfather was said to have found it on the site of a crannog, Loch of Leys, Kincardineshire.[1]

+ + + + + + + + + + + + + + + +

A schematised figure of a young man kneels on his right knee, his left arm resting on his outstretched left knee

A7

and his right arm curving forward to form a faceted loop with a round hole.

His short bobbed hair with fringe, long bulging eyes slanting downwards from a flat triangular nose and the three horizontal ridges indicating mouth and chin are cast and chased. His knee-length tunic with a standing collar has double cast folds at each knee and in his lap, with six horizontal ridges cross his back. There is a pattern of small punched circles on his shoulders and an 'A' (?) roughly engraved and punched on his chest.

The casting appears to be mostly solid, with a bronze plug on the top of the head. The whole was originally gilt.

+ + + + + + + + + + + + + + + +

This type of candleholder occurs quite widely in Northern Europe, an example in Oslo is described as Anglo-Norwegian and dated to the second quarter of the 12th century.[2] The hair and costume details of A7 place it much later, alongside figures in Paris and Schwerin.[3] The closest comparison is with a candleholder found in 1980, during building works on a site in Newcastle upon Tyne with no known medieval history. It was acquired by the British Museum in 1983.[4]

NOTES: [1] Caldwell, D H notes in NMS, Department of History and Applied Art files; of five 14th- to 16th-century utilitarian bronze vessels, also found in the loch when it was drained in 1850, two were presented to the museum and three are at Crathes Castle. Caldwell suggests in his notes that the crannog may have been an early predecessor of the latter 16th-century building.
[2] Swarzenski 1954, 64, pl 148, fig 329. [3] Von Falke and Meyer 1935, figs 212-13. [4] Information kindly supplied by John Cherry.

A8   E86, 95
KILBIRNIE AQUAMANILE
[H.MC 41]

Scotland, 14th century
Copper alloy; cast, engraved
H 179, W 73, L 224

CONDITION
Generally good, the surface worn by polishing, a hole has been broken in the left flank and a patch applied to the left haunch.

PROVENANCE
Found in 1868 or 1869 in mud displaced by the dumping of refuse by the Glengarnock Iron Company in Kilbirnie Loch, Ayrshire. The aquamanile was discovered in the bottom of a wooden dug-out canoe along with a three-legged brass pot. The site was about 20 feet away from a crannog.[1] It entered the collection of W J Armstrong of Fairlie,[2] and was purchased for the museum in 1885.[3]

+ + + + + + + + + + + + + + + +

The vessel cast in the shape of a lion with a large head stands squarely on four short thin legs with small schematised paws. A round hole in the top of the head retains part of the hinge for a lid, now missing. There is a further round hole, possibly for a decorative gemstone, in the chest.

The animal has small round ears, downturned teardrop-shaped eyes with roughly engraved lashes, a flat nose and a broad muzzle with a spout protruding from its jaws. Its tail curls down between its legs and ends in a tuft against its right flank. A strap handle joins the back of the head and the lion's rump; with a bevelled lump at the top, a wide domed horizontal upper section and an irregular flat sloping band below.

+ + + + + + + + + + + + + + + +

The established European norm for these vessels is here so debased that the serpent normally depicted as arching over the animal's back and serving as a handle is virtually unrecognisable, the characteristics of mane and paws have been omitted and the proportions are grotesque. Presumably it was produced by a craftsman unfamiliar with either the appearance of real lions or current fashions in aquamanile design.

NOTES: [1] Cochran Patrick 1886, 385. [2] Anderson 1878, 54-6. [3] *PSAS*, vol VIII, 1885, 10.

A9
WHITHORN PINNACLE
[K.2001.3]

Scotland, mid-14th century
Copper alloy, gilt; cast.
H 30, W 7, L 7

CONDITION
Broken, bent and corroded.

PROVENANCE
Found in an unidentified grave at the cathedral church at Whithorn in 1960 with a late 12th-century enamelled crozier [C1] and a 14th-century silver chalice and paten [B6].[1]

+ + + + + + + + + + + + + + + +

A miniature decorative architectural pinnacle consisting of a finial with a ball top, rising from a square collar with four diagonally placed leaves above and a curved moulding underneath. The slender square section spire below has a single moulded collar, then three notched collars. At the bottom there is a gabled niche with a single lancet on each of the four faces. The base is broken off, although some heavily corroded fragments remain.

+ + + + + + + + + + + + + + + +

This is part of an elaborately decorated object such as a pax or a morse.

NOTE: [1] See C1 page 32 for details of the excavation.

A8

A9

II SILVER

To have only eight items in this section is a sad reflection of the destruction wreaked on church treasuries and personal belongings dating from the later medieval period in Scotland. The sophisticated shapes and the refined engraving of the Iona spoons hint at what these lost riches might have included.

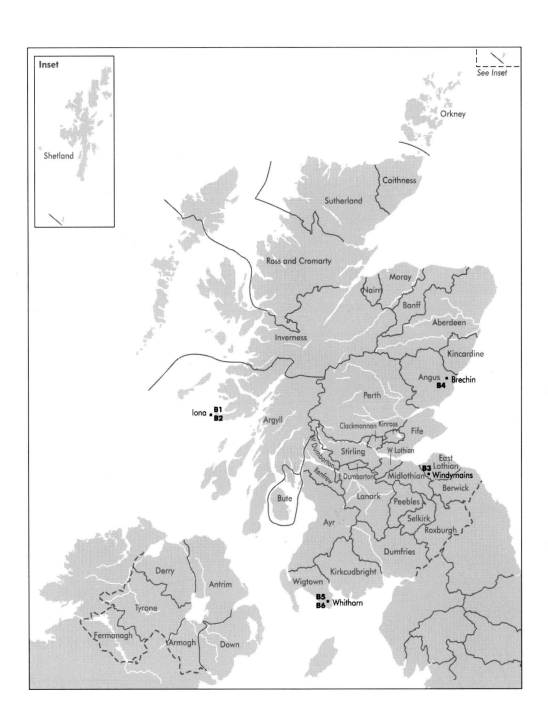

Three Iona Spoons
[H.HX 32, 33, 34]

Scotland or England, *c*1200
Silver, partly gilt; cast, engraved, raised
W 48, D 20, L 204 (HX 32, complete specimen)

CONDITION
H.HX 32 is in excellent condition, see below for H.HX 33 and H.HX 34.

PROVENANCE
Discovered in 1922 during routine maintenance work, by HM Office of Works underneath a stone at the west corner of the base of the south respond of the chancel arch of the nunnery, Iona. The spoons were wrapped in coarse linen with another spoon [B2] and a gold fillet [G3].[1]

✛ ✛ ✛ ✛ ✛ ✛ ✛ ✛ ✛ ✛ ✛ ✛ ✛ ✛ ✛

The three spoons are of approximately the same pattern. H.HX 32 is the best preserved and slightly more elaborate than the others. It has a berry knop with seeds in a calyx of four notched petals above a plain round collar. The stem is in four sections, cylindrical with two vertical engraved lines flanked by pairs of dots representing buds; cast and gilt to represent a twig with buds sprouting through the bark; a flat gilt bar with a square motif containing a four-petalled flower within a lozenge, above a panel of repeating crescent-shaped leafy scrolls inside a plain narrow border.

The stem is joined to the bowl by a flattened grotesque animal head with vertically projecting ears and long oval eyes, its jaws clamping the top of the bowl. The bowl is a deeply curved pointed oval, its engraved decoration consisting of plain lines marking a border all round and a leafy motif at the centre top. This is asymmetrical with a V-shaped frond spreading upwards from a central dot and fleshy curving leaves, with edges curling back, sprouting below. The border and this motif are gilded. Except for the knop and the cast 'bark' section of the stem, the back of the spoon is entirely plain.

H.HX 33 is heavily corroded and part of the bowl is missing and cracked. The knop is smaller and the decoration generally less sharply defined than on H.HX 32.

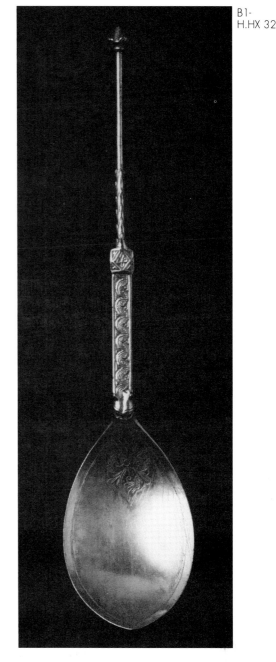

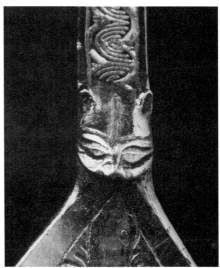

H.HX 34 is in even poorer condition, the stem broken, part of the bowl missing and it has been coated with silver paint, which further obscures the already corroded surface. It appears to be closer in design to H.HX 33 than to H.HX 32.

The latter two spoons are rather poorer copies of H.HX 32, which may have been an imported prototype imitated by less skilled local craftsmen.

+ + + + + + + + + + + + + + +

The nunnery on Iona was founded by Ranald, son of Somerled, who died about 1210, for Bethag his sister who was prioress.[2] The architectural style of its handsome church places it in the first quarter of the 13th century and strongly suggests that it was influenced by Irish models.[3] Clearly the house was well endowed; around 1210 it commissioned from a scribe in Oxford the richly illuminated Iona Psalter,[4] described by one writer as 'a product of the highest quality' (fig 5).[5]

Conflicting views have been published on the dating, purpose and place of manufacture of the four Iona spoons. Although we know from documentary sources that silver spoons existed in some numbers, in England at least, from the 11th century onwards,[6] very few examples survive for comparison before 1300 and none can be firmly dated on the basis of their provenance.

The Taunton spoon, found during excavations at the castle in 1928,[7] has a stylised blossom at the top of the bowl which is held in the jaws of an animal head at the bottom of the stem, features very similar to those on the Iona spoons. Its flat stem has a zigzag panel, below a slightly wider square of strapwork. Only fourteen

fig 5: **IONA PSALTER**
MS 10,000, fol 37 recto, vellum, English c1200, The Trustees of the National Library of Scotland.
H 420 W 300

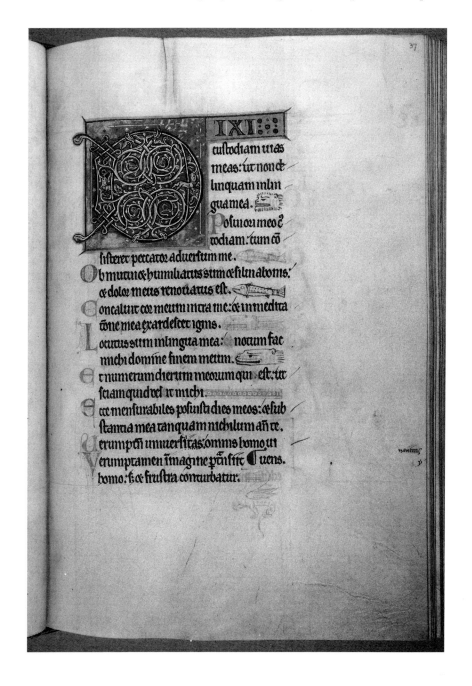

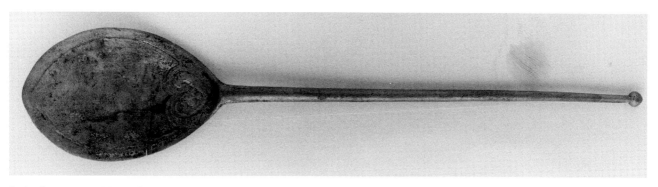

fig 6: SPOON FROM WOOD QUAY, DUBLIN
Copper alloy, Irish, before 1210, National
Museum of Ireland – Ard Mhúsaem na hÉireann.
L138, w41

millimetres longer than H.HX 32, it strongly resembles it except for the plain upper stem and the inclusion of a second smaller animal head below the finial.

The Pevensey spoon, discovered in a pit under the stairs at the entrance to the castle keep, is rather longer,[8] but the very damaged bowl shares the pointed shape curving down at the sides and the biting animal head with the Taunton and Iona examples. Like B2, below, it retains traces of niello. The stem, however, is quite different with a flat elongated oval bar containing a scroll with spiral ends, below a square four-petalled flower and a beaded twisted terminal. A further spoon in the Nationalmuseet in Copenhagen also has the biting animal head and oval stem, engraved with a shaggy lion. It was part of a hoard along with coins, mainly English, dating to 1257 and earlier.[9] Now wrongly reconstructed as a double spoon, its original form was probably close to Pevensey.

Finally, a copper-alloy version with a plain stem and berry knop has the B1 bowl shape, outlined with a single engraved line and simplified blossom in an inverted heart at the top (fig 6). Now in the National Museum of Ireland, it comes from a site at Wood Quay in Dublin datable to 1210 and represents a less costly version of this type.[10] Apart from this last and the Danish spoon, archaeological evidence gives few clues to the dating in any of these cases, including Taunton and Pevensey Castles.

The context of the Iona find is obscure. Clearly the spoons and fillet had been carefully hidden, possibly, but by no means certainly, at the time of the Reformation. The items may all come from the nunnery's treasury and in the absence of any concrete evidence to the contrary there seems no reason why all five objects should not date from about the time of its consecration in 1203.[11] Attempts have been made to relate the stem decoration on B2 to English manuscript illumination of the mid-12th century, but similar borders of simple geometric four-petalled flowers in lozenges or rectangles persisted into the 13th century as line filling ornaments, for example in the Iona Psalter itself (fig 8).[12] The

Augustinian Psalter (fig 7) probably from Holyrood Abbey features elongated serpents' heads in profile comparable to B1 in particular and dates from about 1200.[13] Both books also use leafy petal decorations with turned back wavy edges and curving stems, a form which may first have appeared about 1130, but was still in use at St Albans at the turn of the century.[14] In any

fig 7: AUGUSTINIAN PSALTER
MS Bamburgh Select 6, fol 47 verso, vellum,
Scottish c1200, reproduced by permission of
Durham University Library.
(detail)

case, goldsmiths were generally conservative about adopting motifs from the more easily handled medium of the painter and there is usually a marked time lag before the most recent fashions make their mark on even sophisticated metalwork. The animal head and the bowl shape are still visible on an unprovenanced pewter spoon assumed to be English and tentatively dated to about 1300.[15]

In favour of the Iona spoons being for purely domestic use is the total absence of religious imagery in the decoration and their discovery in association with an entirely secular personal ornament. Against this is their delicate structure, considerable fragility and very shallow capacity. The down-curved sides of the shallow bowls mean that they would have held only a few drops of liquid, compatible with their use for adding water to the communion wine in the chalice,[16] but not with the convenient consumption or serving of any form of foodstuff. It is certainly known that ecclesiastical dignitaries and churches owned ceremonial spoons and often in sets.[17]

All these spoons have features in common with 12th- and 13th-century northern European metalwork,[18] but are generally regarded as English. However, it is interesting to note that only the Pevensey spoon was found at a distance from the sea routes linking south-west England, Ireland, Scotland and ultimately Scandinavia. Unless further specimens come to light with more specific origins, their place or places of manufacture will remain largely speculative.

NOTES: [1] Curle, 1924, 102. [2] McDonald 1997, 222. [3] RCAHMS 1982, 23-4. [4] National Library of Scotland MS 10000. [5] Morgan 1988, 76. [6] How 1952, 23, n 1; Abbot Wulketul restored twelve silver spoons to Croyland Abbey in 1085; Roger, Archbishop of York, left 40 silver spoons among his plate in 1181. [7] Gray 1930, 156-8; How 1952, 30, pl 4 II; London 1984, 280, cat no 297. [8] Simms 1932, 73-4; How 1952, 28, pl 3 II; London 1984, 281, cat no 299. [9] Grinder-Hansen and Posselt 1992, vol I, 74, fig 64, 143, vol II, 15-18, cat no 81. [10] Ó Floinn, information kindly communicated by letter. [11] Oman 1959, 36, pl IV 11; London 1984, 280, cat nos 298a and 298b, where Stratford argues for a mid-12th-century date on stylistic grounds and maintains that the Taunton, Iona and

Pevensey spoons were all probably for secular use. [12] For example, folio 19v. [13] MS Bamburgh Select 6, on deposit with the University of Durham Library; Doyle 1957. [14] Rickert 1965, pl 92(A); London 1984, 132, cat no 83. [15] London 1987, 281, cat no 210. [16] How 1952, 23, n 1. [17] Watkins 1947, part I, 5, 37, 82, part II, lxxxi, xci, 128-9, 143; Oman 1959, 35. [18] London 1984, convincing comparisons are drawn with engraved borders on the Dune drinking bowls 285, 287, cat nos 306, 308, called here Angevin or German and dated to the last quarter of the 12th century.

B2   C42, 41-2
IONA SPOON
[H.HX 35]

Scotland or England, *c* 1200
Silver; cast, engraved, raised, niello
W 42, D 15, L 165

CONDITION
Extensive corrosion, particularly to the bowl, niello now completely lost from decoration.

PROVENANCE
The nunnery church, Iona.[1]

✣ ✣ ✣ ✣ ✣ ✣ ✣ ✣ ✣ ✣ ✣ ✣ ✣ ✣ ✣

The spoon has a conical knop above a plain round collar. The stem is in two sections, the upper part a flattened cylinder widening slightly towards the bottom; the lower

fig 8: IONA PSALTER
MS 10,000, fol 33 recto, vellum, English *c*1200,
The Trustees of the National Library of Scotland.
(detail).

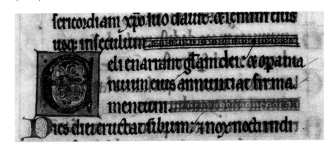

B2

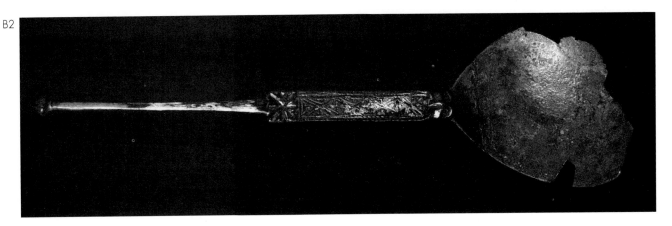

a flat bar with a square motif containing a six-petalled flower, above a panel of elongated lozenges each containing a quadrilobe flower head.

The stem is joined to the bowl by a flattened grotesque animal head with backswept ears and large oval eyes, its jaws clamping the top of the bowl. The condition of the bowl is such that it is impossible to say if it was originally decorated. It is curved and was probably a pointed oval similar to H.HX 32. The back of the spoon is entirely plain.

✛ ✛ ✛ ✛ ✛ ✛ ✛ ✛ ✛ ✛ ✛ ✛ ✛ ✛

The design is related to that of the B1 spoons, but B2 was shorter, has a simpler knop, lacks the twig-like decoration on the upper stem and has more integrated and geometrical decoration on the lower stem, which takes the flower in lozenge motif and runs it into a continuous frieze[2] even more comparable to the Iona Psalter (fig 8).

NOTES: [1] For exact provenance see B1, above. [2] For comments on purpose and dating see B1, above.

B3
WINDY MAINS SPOON
[H.MEQ 16]

C41, 41

Scotland or England, first half of the 14th century
Silver; cast, punched, raised
W 46, D 16, L 138

CONDITION
A wide split at each side of the bowl.

PROVENANCE
Found in 1813, while removing gravel, by Mr Archibald Park in 'Windymains Water', East Lothian, four feet below the bed of the river. Presented to the museum by Mr Park of Morningside in 1864.[1]

✛ ✛ ✛ ✛ ✛ ✛ ✛ ✛ ✛ ✛ ✛ ✛ ✛ ✛

The spoon has a knop in the form of an acorn, the cup decorated with punched circles, on a slightly flattened cylindrical stem bevelled at the bottom where it joins a plain round bowl, slightly pointed at the top.

✛ ✛ ✛ ✛ ✛ ✛ ✛ ✛ ✛ ✛ ✛ ✛ ✛ ✛

A number of plain silver spoons with acorn knops similar to this example have been found in England and Northern France.[2] A pair of Rouen spoons in the Victoria and Albert Museum come from a hoard buried about 1330,[3] while another bears the earliest English hallmark – the 'Grecian' leopard's head mark thought to have been used in London between 1300 and 1350.[4]

The two farms of Windy Mains and Old Windy Mains lie immediately adjacent to Keith Marischal. Keith Water (presumably the same stream as 'Windymains Water') borders both Keith Marischal and Old Windy Mains. The earliest parts of the present Keith Marischal House date from 1589, but the ruins of a church begun about 1200 stand in the grounds.[5] The Keith family had been prominent since the 12th century when they first held the hereditary office of marischal of Scotland and they formed a major part of the 'Bruce establishment'.[6]

Sir Robert Keith became marischal during the reign of John Balliol, was captured by the English and sent to Bristol for safety in 1300, returned to Scotland and eventually joined Robert Bruce in 1308. He played a heroic part leading the only Scots cavalry at Bannockburn and became an indispensable administrator to the king, for all of which he was rewarded with substantial grants of land in the north-east of Scotland resulting in the removal of the main family interests from East Lothian.[7]

Silver spoons of this type would not be unexpected in a household such as Sir Robert's. His departure from Keith Marischal in the 1320s could indicate an early 14th-century date for the spoon, consistent with current fashion in England and France.

NOTES: [1] *PSAS*, vol V, 1864, 303; How 1935, 147-8, fig 10; Oman 1959, 38. [2] How 1952, 42-3, fig 4 III; London 1987, 280-1, cat no 209. [3] Lightbown 1978, 20, 33, 97. [4] How 1952, 64-5, pl 15 III. [5] McWilliam 1978, 37, 269. [6] Grant 1984, 126, 129. [7] Barrow 1988, 113, 208, 217, 227, 284.

B3

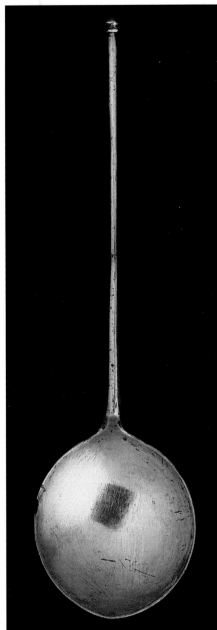

BRECHIN SPOON
[H.MEQ 14]

Scotland or England, early 14th century
Silver; cast, raised
w 46, D 18, L 165

CONDITION
Small pieces missing from the back of the stem and the edge of the bowl, some corrosion.

PROVENANCE
Found while digging a grave near the principal entrance to the churchyard of Brechin in 1785 with fragments of other spoons and pennies of Alexander III of Scotland and Edward I and II of England.[1] Presented to the Society of Antiquaries of Scotland by Lord Gardenstone in the same year.[2]

✝ ✝ ✝ ✝ ✝ ✝ ✝ ✝ ✝ ✝ ✝ ✝ ✝ ✝ ✝

The spoon has a conical knop above a round collar, a long cylindrical stem and a plain circular bowl.

✝ ✝ ✝ ✝ ✝ ✝ ✝ ✝ ✝ ✝ ✝ ✝ ✝ ✝ ✝

The close resemblance between this spoon and another Rouen spoon from the *c*1330 hoard has been pointed out.[3] The finials are almost identical, as are the bowl shapes and the profiles, although the form of the stem is perhaps nearer to that of the Windy Mains spoon, B3, above.

NOTES: [1] *Archaeologia Scotica*, vol III, 1831, 41-2, 44, 45. [2] Wilson 1849, no 40, 41 or 42, 94. [3] Curle 1924, 107-109; How 1935, 147-8, fig 10; How 1952, 38-41, pls 2 III, 3 III; Oman 1959, 36-8, pl IV 12.

WHITHORN CHALICE AND PATEN
[H.1992.1837, 1838]

Scotland or England, early 13th century
Silver, gilt; raised, chased, engraved, gilded
DIAM 121, H 111 (chalice, to bottom of tang)
DIAM 135, D 2 (paten)

CONDITION
Chalice: Some holes in the bottom of the bowl and the original stem and foot removed.
Paten: Rather bent and misshapen, about a quarter of the rim missing.
Some wear to the gilding on both pieces.

PROVENANCE
Found in 1957 in the grave of a bishop, at the cathedral church at Whithorn, with a gold and amethyst ring [D1], two bronze buckles, a fragment of gold braid and the remains of a wooden crozier.[1]

✝ ✝ ✝ ✝ ✝ ✝ ✝ ✝ ✝ ✝ ✝ ✝ ✝ ✝ ✝

The chalice has a completely plain hemispherical bowl, with a later square section tang crudely attached.

The circular paten has a round and then a stepped moulding at the outer edge of the wide sloping rim, which is bevelled into the dished

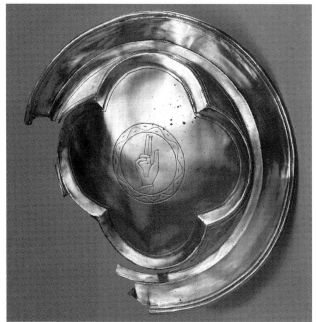

centre. The centre is filled by a quatrefoil framed by a further bevel. Chased and engraved outlines emphasise the changes of plane. Engraved in the middle is a double circle with a wavy line and dashes between, around the *Manus Dei*. The central compass point from which the design was laid out is clearly visible. On the reverse the outlines of the quatrefoil and the inner circle are marked with an engraved line.

✛ ✛ ✛ ✛ ✛ ✛ ✛ ✛ ✛ ✛ ✛ ✛ ✛ ✛

B5 closely resembles the chalice and paten found in the grave of Richard de Gravesend, bishop of Lincoln from 1258 until his death in 1279 (fig 9). The shallow round chalice bowls with everted lips have the same profile, the engraved central motifs of the hand of God raised in blessing on the patens are treated in almost identical manner, and both are framed by double circles with wavy lines between.[2] Only the depressed quatrefoils differ slightly, being cusped on the Lincoln paten. Presumably the Whithorn chalice also had a more or less elaborate knop and a foot in similar style to that of Gravesend's chalice, possibly removed because it had been damaged. There was evidence in the grave of a wooden substitute to which it was attached by the present tang.[3]

This does not give us a precise date for B5. It was common practice in the Middle Ages for out-of-date plate or substitutes in base metal to be used as grave goods. The Lincoln chalice and paten may considerably pre-date Gravesend's death.[4] Stylistically, it seems rather less developed than the Dolgelly chalice and paten of about 1230-50 and the Scandinavian examples derived from similar English prototypes.[5] The Whithorn chalice and paten could be almost half a century earlier than the ring found in the same burial [D1].

NOTES: [1] See the commentary to C1, page 32.   [2] Ottawa 1972, 92, pl 68, cat no 49A.   [3] National Archives of Scotland, DD/27/1582, Historic Scotland file.   [4] London 1987, 237, cat no 111.   [5] Reykjavík 1997, 102-104, 117, cat nos 27a, 27b.

fig 9: CHALICE AND PATEN OF BISHOP GRAVESEND
Silver, English, before 1279 probably first half of the 13th century, copyright Dean and Chapter, Lincoln.
H124 (chalice), DIAM 114 (paten)

Excavated fragments of Whithorn chalice and paten.

B6 Reconstruction drawing of Whithorn chalice by Marion O'Neil

B6
WHITHORN CHALICE AND PATEN
[K.2001.1 & K.2001.2]

Scotland, mid-14th century
Silver; raised, incised, punched
Chalice DIAM 130, H 180 approx (based on the reconstruction drawing)

CONDITION
Broken and corroded all over.
Chalice: Stem intact and attached to part of the foot; rest of foot broken into seventeen fragments; bowl, one large portion with rim reconstructed, eight other large fragments and numerous small ones.
Paten: Central portion intact but cracked; rim in thirteen fragments.

PROVENANCE
Found in a grave at the cathedral church at Whithorn in 1960 with a late 12th-century enamelled crozier [C1] and a mid-14th-century pinnacle [A9].[1]

+ + + + + + + + + + + + + + + +

When complete, the chalice had a plain bowl slightly shallower than a hemisphere. This was attached to the cylindrical stem by a moulded collar. Two similar collars are above and below the knop midway down the stem. The knop is a flattened sphere with twelve vertical rounded segmental ridges. Above the foot is a further collar, moulded and stepped, with a frieze of small punched quincunx ornaments. The concave flaring foot has a stepped and moulded edge, shaped as six incurving arcs and a continuous frieze matching that on the collar.

The paten, when complete, was circular with a slightly moulded edge and a shallow slope to a depression with an incised motif in the centre. The motif is a circle containing four radiating cup shapes each filled with criss-cross matting.

+ + + + + + + + + + + + + + + +

The design of the chalice combines a knop shape which was very fashionable in the mid-13th century and becoming rather archaic a century later, with a hexagonal foot of the type adopted in Paris by 1286,[2] and popular by the 1360s in England.[3] Normally the hexagonal foot, whether its sides were straight or concave would have been combined with a facetted stem echoing its shape.[4] The curious combination on B6 of the segmental knop, the plain round stem and the foot shape is exactly paralleled on a chalice in the Danmarks Nationalmuseet bought in Copenhagen in 1835 and said to come from Eastern Iceland.[5] Similarly, a Galloway silversmith might have used elements from various sources without being too restrained by more metropolitan norms.

NOTES: [1] See C1, page 32, for details of the excavation.
[2] Paris 1996, no 27, 330-1. [3] Oman 1957, pl 9. [4] Ibid, pls 10-23. [5] Copenhagen 1996, no 282, 390-1.

ENAMELS III

The enamels catalogued here demonstrate Scotland's close connections and affinities with England, France and Scandinavia.

    The Whithorn Crozier is related stylistically to the Balfour Ciborium now in the Victoria and Albert Museum,[1] which also has a plausible medieval Scottish provenance[2] (fig 10, page 28). In the late 19th century it was said that the then Lord Balfour 'attaches no importance' to the obviously untenable family tradition that the ciborium had belonged to Malcolm Canmore.[3] Their other belief that it had been a gift from Mary, Queen of Scots, could also be pure romanticism, numerous probable and improbable artefacts having acquired such a pedigree down the centuries.

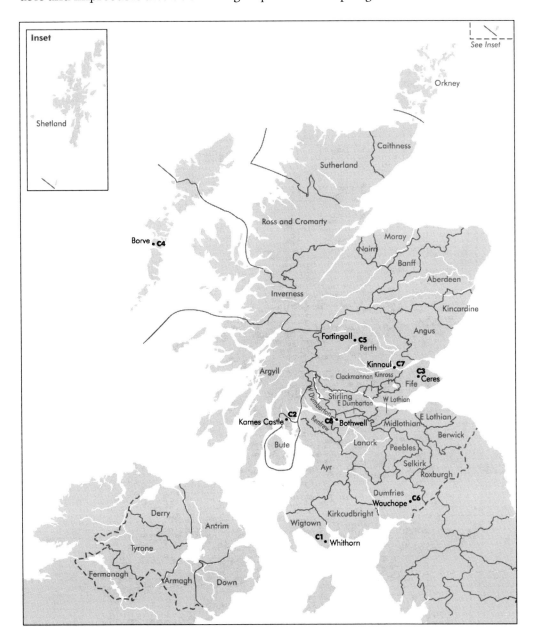

However, by the late 1550s much church plate and other valuables were being placed in private hands for safe keeping from the ravages of the iconoclasts and the invading English, including some of the treasure of Aberdeen Cathedral, which was sent to Huntly Castle.[4] In 1562, Mary's forces defeated George, Earl of Huntly at the battle of Corrichie and subsequently the queen acquired a splendid group of costly furnishings from the castle.[5] These circumstances have led one writer to suggest that the Balfour Ciborium may have come from there.[6] By 1565-66, James Balfour of Pittendreich was in high royal favour, holding the strategic post of Keeper of Edinburgh Castle, and might well have received such a gift.[7] Speculative as this may be, the object had been in the family for some centuries before 1890, there is no documentary evidence for it having been anywhere other than Scotland and it was very unlikely to have been imported by any Protestant family after the Reformation.

The Balfour Ciborium and the Whithorn Crozier are objects generally studied in the context of the most skilled Mosan craftsmanship and are part of a group which can be tentatively attributed to a 12th-century school of artists in south-west England. Along with the Morgan and Warwick Ciboria and the Bargello Crozier,[8] they represent the output of a workshop, or several closely related workshops, deriving their Romanesque style from that of the Master of the Stavelot Portable Altar of *c* 1150-60,[9] and by the period of the Whithorn Crozier evolving it into the forms characteristic of early Gothic art.

The Bute Mazer shows an indigenous goldsmith interpreting the norms of court circles in the rest of Europe. His approach to the structure of the object is cautious and conservative and his use of the fashionable translucent enamel rather tentative. The survival rate of enamelled Scottish silver of the early 14th century is particularly lamentable, but the existence of the Randolph Baldric in the British Museum[10] shows that a really grand client would use these expensive materials for even a fairly utilitarian object.

fig 10: BALFOUR CIBORIUM
Copper alloy and champlevé enamel, English,
1150-1175, V & A Picture Library.
H 180, DIAM 159 (bowl)

The Limoges imports are a tribute to the many students, clerics and pilgrims who travelled to France in the 13th century,[11] bringing back objects to enrich their churches and enhance their dwellings. So popular were Limoges enamels that inferior imitations were also acceptable, at least in outlying areas, as shown by the Borve crucifix plaque [C4].

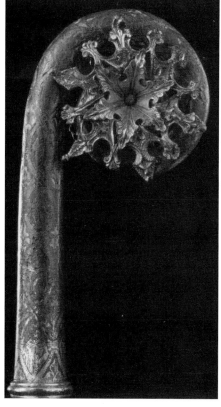

NOTES: [1] London 1984, no 279, 264-5, bibliography, 263. [2] Loc cit, Stratford says that no documentary evidence exists for associating the ciborium with earlier Scottish history. [3] Constable 1890, 14, 20. [4] McRoberts 1959, 139-40. [5] Wormald 1991, 123-4. [6] Edinburgh 1982, no B25, 19-20. [7] Wormald 1991, 165. [8] London 1984, 268 says of the Bargello Crozier that its iconography 'belongs to a specifically West Country series of the Virtues and Vices', citing sculpture at Malmesbury Abbey and two fonts in Gloucestershire and Wiltshire. [9] Lasko 1972, 191-2; Cologne 1972, no G13, 252. [10] Glenn 1998, 116. [11] Michel 1862, 2-25.

C1 (detail)

C1 (colour plates)   B26, 20-21
WHITHORN CROZIER
[H.1992.1833]

English (?), c1175
Copper alloy, gilt, enamel; raised, cast, engraved, champlevé
DIAM 92 (across crook), H 162, D 30

CONDITION
Widespread surface corrosion due to burial, most of the gilding worn away; cast blossom very brittle, three leaves broken off one side, central berry missing from the other. The crozier was subject to expert and extensive post-excavation conservation.

PROVENANCE
Found in a grave at the cathedral church at Whithorn with a copper alloy pinnacle [A9], a shattered 14th-century silver chalice and paten [B6] and some gold sequins.[1]

✢ ✢ ✢ ✢ ✢ ✢ ✢ ✢ ✢ ✢ ✢ ✢ ✢ ✢ ✢ ✢

A hollow tapering tube forms the spiral volute of the crozier head, with a lavish gilt blossom sprouting from each side. The tube is engraved and enamelled in four vertical bands of pointed ovals. The ovals are framed by a pattern of interwoven and loosely knotted ribands in plain gilt with pricked borders and a fine zigzag line engraved up the centre. The interstices are filled with enamelled flowers.

Most of the colours, white, yellow, light and dark green, turquoise, light and dark blue, lilac and red are in opaque enamel, but the backgrounds to some of the figures are translucent. The enamel is very worn and corroded, but the decoration is most legible towards the bottom of the shaft. Working upwards and starting at the side where the blossom has lost its central berry it is as follows:

TIER I

1 A bishop reserved in gilt, the drawing of his outline, features and vestments in red enamel. The background is mottled violet and blue. His face and mitre are indistinct, he wears an amice with scooping folds and decoration is indicated on his apparels.

C1

C1 WHITHORN CROZIER
During excavation, copyright Historic Scotland.

WHITHORN CROZIER
Partially conserved.

2 An abbot delineated in the same technique as I.1., with a deep red and dark blue ground. His beardless face and bushy hair are naturalistically drawn with a few flowing strokes, he wears a monastic habit with a cowl, holds a stole (?) in his right hand, which emerges from a wide sleeve falling in loose folds over his arm and showing a tight cuff to his undergarment. The left hand is indicated very summarily, but seems to be holding the folds of his habit. An arc above the right hand side of his mitre may be a halo.

3 Bishop saint with large round gilt halo, the figure drawn in the same technique as before against a deep red ground. He has bushy bobbed hair and his long face may be bearded, but is damaged. His mitre is low and triangular with a horizontal band at the brim, his alb has a square neck over a softly folded amice and apparels curving round his shoulders and falling in two vertical strips in front. He holds a book in his right hand.

4 Bishop or abbot in the same technique against a dark red and brown ground. He has a short rather shaggy beard and bushy wavy hair and wears a low triangular mitre with a horizontal band at the brim. His alb has a round neck outlined by an apparel, over a softly folded alb. Diagonally across his body is a simple spiral headed crozier held in his right hand with his forefinger raised in blessing. A book (?) is roughly indicated in his left hand.

All four half-length figures face forward and do not seem related to each other.

TIER II

1 The upper half of this oval is almost indecipherable, the lower part shows a figure in semi-profile, with clinging folds over its legs which are in vigorous motion, possibly a censing angel?

2 Even more damaged than II.1, there is a bareheaded standing figure in frontal pose with bobbed hair; arms raised to hold an object at shoulder level.

3 The gilt is worn away, but the red champlevé drawing and a burgundy red ground with green flecks remain. The figure is a standing female with long hair holding a book (?) at her left shoulder.

4 Also very worn, but traces of red drawing remain against a green and red ground. The standing figure is in semi-profile, raises its right hand up to its shoulder and holds a long scroll or (stole) in its left. The garments fall in looping folds.

The poses of these full-length figures suggest that they are linked in some kind of narrative.

TIER III

1 A seated female figure with long wavy hair, her head turned three-quarter face, looks down to her right hand raised on her breast and her left hand which holds a round object below her right elbow. Her costume has agitated criss-cross fold patterns. The ground is burgundy red with green flecks.

2 A three-quarter-length male figure with his head in profile to the right turns his body to that side. He has receding bobbed hair and a shaggy beard and holds a book (?) up to his left shoulder. The ground is very dark blue and green.

3 A seated female figure with long wavy hair shares the pose of III.1, but reversed to the left. They also have the same ground colours.

4 Almost indecipherable, a figure with a beardless face is shown against an opaque burgundy ground.

The four figures form a balanced composition, but the iconography is completely inscrutable.

TIER IV

1 A standing female figure with a veil over her head, bowing her head to the right and holding a book (?) above her left shoulder, is shown against a ground which is burgundy on one side and green on the other.

2 (Partly under the crook.) A three-quarter-length figure of a young person looking downward to the left is shown against a burgundy ground with some opaque white.

3 A female figure with long wavy hair kneels with her body in profile to her right and looks down to her left. She raises an object in both hands to her right. The ground is dark green with some burgundy.

4 A female figure in distinct secular dress wearing a head-dress and veil and long bodice with centre fastening stands with both hands raised in prayer against a dark green ground.

These four female figures probably form a coherent group, but their significance is unclear.

TIER V

1 A seated female figure turns three-quarters to her right using her left hand to play a portable organ (?) on her knees which is supported by her right hand at the top. The ground is mottled burgundy and green.

2 Is invisible under the crook.

3 The oval is very worn, but a seated female figure, with knees apart and feet together, wearing a coif on her head which is inclined to her left, rests her right elbow on her knee with her hand raised and pointing to (or plucking?) a large rectangular object balanced on her knee.

4 This very worn and corroded figure is seated and inclined to its right holding an object in both hands or a child reaching up to its face. There is possibly a halo.

V.1 and V.3 turn towards V.4, which is at the focal point of the curve of the crozier. Together they may represent the Virgin and Child flanked by musicians.

TIERS VI AND VII

Partly hidden by the crook and the blossom and in poor condition, the visible decoration is of grotesque creatures with serpent heads, wings and feet.

C1
(detail)

Tier I: 3

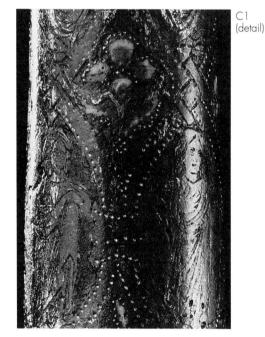

C1
(detail)

Tier II: 2 and 3

C1
(detail)

Tier II: 4

C1
(detail)

Tier VIII: 3

TIER VIII

Has one clear oval of an energetic galloping hare with long ears and tail against a green ground.

TIERS IX – XII

Are indecipherable except for a fish on IX.4 and XII.3.

The gilt blossoms attached to each side of the volute are similar, but not identical. One has a central peg in the form of a tall oval berry with cross-hatched engraving; piercing the centre of a flower with six pointed outward curving petals with slanting veins. Behind is a circle of openwork leaves originally sprouting twelve (three are broken off) semicircular fronds, the whole cast and engraved as scrolling foliage.

The other blossom has lost its central berry and has a flower of six pointed petals with serrated edges and a central vein. The leaves behind are long and pointed, six large alternating with six smaller fronds, the whole cast and engraved with an intricate pattern of scrolling foliage.

✚ ✚ ✚ ✚ ✚ ✚ ✚ ✚ ✚ ✚ ✚ ✚ ✚ ✚ ✚

The excavations leading to the discovery of the crozier, which have never been fully published, began accidentally in August 1957.[2] Workmen waterproofing the vault of the crypt at the east end of Whithorn Cathedral found three medieval stone coffins. The first contained an early 13th-century silver chalice and paten [B5], two bronze buckles, a fragment of gold braid, a handsome mid-13th-century gold ring with a large amethyst [D1] and the remains of a wooden crozier indicating that this was the grave of a bishop. The second yielded a lead chalice and paten, another bronze buckle and two plain bronze rings and a 13th-century silver finger ring with a small amethyst [D2]. The third grave had also a bronze buckle, a 13th-century gold finger ring and again fragments of a wooden crozier head.

Work continued sporadically at the site and in August 1960 a further three coffins were uncovered, two stone and one wooden. These contained a second lead chalice and paten and a silver penny of Edward II. In mid-September a 14th-century silver chalice [B6] was found by a workman digging at the side of the vault, between two of the stone coffins. Archaeological investigation immediately recommenced and this proved to be a seventh grave, with a wooden coffin, containing the crozier [C1] and a small gilded copper-alloy pinnacle [A9].

Excavations finally ceased in this area of Whithorn Cathedral in 1967. Fifteen graves had been identified altogether, but with no further finds.

It was common practice to use either base metals or out-of-date plate as grave goods in the most prestigious medieval burials. Even Hubert Walter, archbishop of Canterbury, had in his splendid Purbeck marble tomb in the cathedral an engraved silver chalice and paten which was over fifty years old by his death in 1205.[3] The Whithorn bishop who was buried with the enamelled crozier presumably died at least as late as the mid-14th century, judging from the chalice and paten [B6] and copper-alloy gilt pinnacle [A9] also found in his grave.

From the 12th century onwards, Whithorn was subject to the archbishop of York,[4] every bishop from John (1189-1209) until after the Wars of Independence also having duties in the English diocese.[5] It may have been John himself who brought the crozier back to Whithorn. The grave could have been that of any of the seven bishops who ruled between 1350 and 1450.[6] It remains impossible to say whether the crozier was part of the

Whithorn Cathedral treasury, or whether it had been the personal property of the interred bishop. The general consensus, based on comparisons with manuscript illumination, is that it is English perhaps with West country connections.[7] The decoration on the stem, with its oval lattice of ribands and its grotesques resembles quite closely that on a crozier in the Bargello in Florence, which can be grouped with other enamels like the Warwick and Balfour Ciboria.[8]

The Bargello Crozier (fig 11) is also damaged and repaired. The end of the scroll has been crudely replaced with a plain tube, larger in diameter than the rest, with an animal head terminal. This element probably dates from soon after the main crozier, but looks like a conjunction effected in the 17th or 18th century, probably for Saint-Père de Chartres where it was discovered in 1793. There is considerable wear and damage to the inside of the enamel crook, but it is clear that this area was never meant to be visible. The indication is that the Bargello Crozier also had a blossom which concealed parts of the scroll. There is evidence that it has been altered just above the knop, where unlike Whithorn, there are no mouldings at the bottom of the stem, although there is a band which is undecorated and ungilded where a collar obviously sat. However, four slots for fixings, similar to those on C1, are just visible.[9] By looking at the Whithorn and Bargello Croziers together, one can deduce the original form of both, including the fact that the decorative scheme of C1 would have continued on to a large round knop.

The technique of leaving the figures gilt against a coloured ground, the interwoven framing and the palette of colours used is common to both croziers and the Warwick Ciborium,[10] as are the large enamelled blossoms between the ovals. The condition of the Whithorn Crozier makes analysis of its drawing style difficult, but the artist of the Warwick Ciborium was a finer and more precise draughtsman, working in a monumental Romanesque style, while on C1 the pointed shapes of the trellis, the more jagged fold style and the very realistic fishes and the hare point towards a transition to the Gothic.

A prominent feature of both the crozier in Florence and the Warwick Ciborium is a series of engraved inscriptions identifying the subjects of the enamelled scenes. This was not done on the Whithorn Crozier, although some kind of iconographical programme was certainly intended.

The splendid cast gilt blossoms in the crook are the most striking feature of the Whithorn Crozier. Blossoms are used like this on some late 12th-century Limoges croziers but they are less elaborate, and enamelled, not gilt.[11] A copper-alloy crozier without enamel decoration found in a grave at St David's Cathedral, Pembrokeshire has features reminiscent of C1,[12] in particular sharing the leaf shapes and the berry-shaped ovary of the blossom (fig 12).

NOTES: [1] Hill 1997, 10. [2] National Archives of Scotland, DD/27/1582. I am grateful to David Breeze for allowing me access to this Historic Scotland file. [3] London 1984, no 324d and e, 294-5. [4] For the earlier history of Whithorn, see also J7, page 130. [5] Donaldson 1950, 129-34. [6] Ibid, 140-41. [7] Oman 1967, 299-300; London 1984, no 285, 269-70; Rome 1994, no 105, 413, 431. [8] Campbell 1979, 369; Florence 1989, no 210, 430-31 [9] I am most grateful to Beatrice Paolozzi Strozzi for giving me access to the Bargello Crozier. [10] Gauthier 1972, 157-62. [11] Paris 1995, no 23, 126-7. [12] London 1984, no 270a, 257-9.

fig 11: BARGELLO CROZIER
Copper alloy and champlevé enamel, English, 1160s, Soprintendenza Speciale per il Polo Museale Fiorentino, Gabinetto Fotografico.
H 224, W 90 (crook) DIAM 64 (knop)

fig 12: ST DAVID'S CROZIER
Copper gilt, English, c1150-1180, courtesy of the Dean and Chapter, St David's Cathedral, Y Deon a Cabidwl, Eglwys Gadeiriol Tyddewi, photo copyright Jerry Sampson.
H 180, W 107

THE BUTE MAZER
[QL.1979.11]

Scotland, after 1314, before 1330,[1] and early 16th century
Silver, gilt, enamel, maple; cast, engraved, punched, gilded, champlevé, basse taille, wood turning
DIAM 256, H 108

CONDITION
Gilding on the print very good, some losses to the enamel, a hole has been punched through the print and the flange in front of the lion's left forepaw and repaired with a crude silver and copper-alloy (?) patch underneath; there is a small crack in the wooden bowl directly behind the lion.

INSCRIPTION
* NINIAN * bANNACHTYN THE LARdOFYECAMIS * SOUNTOUMQHILRObART bANNACHTINO * YECAMISI (traditional black letter/Roman) [for NINIAN BANNACHTYN THE LARD OF YE CAMIS SOUN TO UMQHIL ROBART BANNACHTIN O YE CAMISI, 'Ninian Bannatyne the Laird of Kames son to the late Robert Bannatyne of Kames']

PROVENANCE
For many generations an heirloom of the family of Bannatyne of Kames on the Isle of Bute.[2] On loan to the National Museums of Scotland.

✛ ✛ ✛ ✛ ✛ ✛ ✛ ✛ ✛ ✛ ✛ ✛ ✛ ✛ ✛ ✛

The early 14th-century wooden bowl is held by a raised circular central silver-gilt print, to which is applied a cast figure of a lion with red enamel eyes and six armorial shields. A silver rim and foot, joined by six silver straps, have been added to the mazer in the early 16th century. The thin turned hemispherical wooden bowl is completely plain.

The upper side of the print, inside the bowl, has a plain flat border with a single line engraved at the circumference. An angled step rises to the central boss and another shallower step to the sexfoil within it. The whole area is punched and engraved, wyverns and cinquefoils alternating in the spandrels between sexfoil and framing circle, a strawberry plant

C2

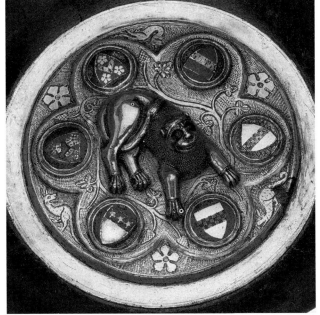

BUTE MAZER
Detail of Print

BUTE MAZER
Underside of print

trailing between the heraldic shields, the entire background matted with slightly irregular lines of blunt punch marks.

Six discs with enamel heraldry have been placed in low round settings in the lobes of the sexfoil. The shields are in silver, silver gilt and champlevé enamel, the circles around them in translucent enamel, now much darkened.

Moving anti-clockwise from between the lion's forepaws the heraldry is:

1 Or a fess chequy argent and azure (Stewart) against translucent green enamel over engraved trailing leaves.

2 Or a bend chequy sable and argent (Menteith) against a background engraved with lozenges and dots for translucent enamel now lost.

3 Gules, a fess ermine (Crawford) against almost black enamel over engraved scrolls.

4 Gules, a chevron ermine between three cinquefoils or (Gilbertson) against bluish-black enamel over an engraved scrolling plant.

5 Gules, three cinquefoils ermine (Walter son of Gilbert, later Hamilton) against very darkened enamel.

6 Argent, on a chief azure three stars of the field (Douglas) against very dark enamel over engraved diagonal hatching.

The lion couchant is in high relief, his forepaws splayed in front of him, both his hind legs resting to his right, his long tail curling up between them, its tuft lying across his back. His paws are represented by four long toes with large claws, below a horizontal ridge. Engraved lines are used to show tufted fur at the back of the rear and right forelegs. The legs and body are smooth and polished, contrasting with a mane covering his neck, chest and forequarters, indicated by rows of round punch marks. These are arranged in a more random pattern to give an effect of curls on the back of his head, between the prominent round ears. The animal's muzzle has bulbous red enamel eyes in deep sockets, a flat pug-like nose and a wide curving mouth and tongue.

The underside of the print is undecorated and shows clearly the method of construction. An irregular hole has been cut in the centre to allow the hollow casting of the lion to be pinned and soldered in place. Circular holes have also been cut to allow the insertion of the enamels into their settings; the central holes where pins held them during the fixing are visible and small extra patches have been applied around the edges for extra security.

The junction between foot and print is considerably mutilated. The original foot seems to have been cut away from the print and the plain flange which appears on the outer surface of the bowl. It may comprise the inner skin attached to the present foot; which has extensive remains of solder along the upper edge. There is a jagged vertical crack at one side which is echoed by a break in the outer skin.

The spreading foot is plain with a heavy round silver wire at the lower edge and a thick beaded wire covering

the join with the bowl. The straps which join the flange to the rim have hinged tabs at top and bottom; the tops engraved with feathery arrow heads, the bottoms plain rounded points. The edges of the straps are serrated and there is a raised central ornament consisting of a cast and engraved wavy line flanked by herringbone beaded borders.

The deep rim is completely plain inside. Outside it has a series of cast and engraved borders, lozenges imposed on squares, above a plain wire, over an inscription on a roughly cross-hatched ground. Below is beading between mouldings and a serrated edge of leaf shapes with engraved veins.

✦ ✦ ✦ ✦ ✦ ✦ ✦ ✦ ✦ ✦ ✦ ✦ ✦ ✦ ✦ ✦ ✦

The Bute Mazer is the only silver enamelled vessel of the period in the Museum of Scotland. The heraldry fairly firmly establishes its date to between 1314 and 1327 and shows that it was commissioned by a noble family, the Gilbertsons, whose arms appear twice, probably recording a prestigious marriage.[3] They were well established at the Scottish court, but did not quite rank with the great magnates Stewart, Crawford, Douglas and Menteith whose shields are also included.

The mazer is an ambitious concept constructed by a conservative and ultra cautious craftsman. Scientific analysis has shown that the entire print including the reinforcement patches, the discs containing the enamels, the main plate and the lion is made of silver which is virtually identical in composition. This unity was confirmed by X-ray examination which showed pins through the lion's paws securing him to the print and also round its double edge holding the wood in place.[4] Altogether, Stevenson appears to have been mistaken when he suggested that this area was a conglomerate of elements from different sources. Even the composition of the red enamel of the lion's eyes matches that of the red in the heraldry.

The enamels are skilfully and precisely applied, the opaque heraldic colours being clear and accurate. The spaces between the shields and their circular frames are filled with a not entirely successful attempt at translucent enamel which either fired to such a deep hue, or has darkened over the centuries to such an extent that the engraving beneath is barely visible. However, translucent basse taille of this type seems only to have been attempted from the 1270s onwards, whether its origins were Parisian[5] or Sienese.[6] The technique was transmitted to England from about 1300,[7] and the mazer demonstrates that it had arrived in Scotland just over a decade later.

Everything about the Bute Mazer suggests that it was made in Scotland. There is no doubt about who commissioned it or the circle of powerful courtiers to which they aspired. Between Bannockburn and the death of Bruce, relationships were such that it is unlikely they would have gone to an English goldsmith and the craftsmanship would have been quite outdated for a French *orfèvre* even outwith Paris. The conservatism, the belt and braces construction of the print (paralleled only on one of the bowls from the Dune hoard found in Gotland) and the apparent modelling of the lion on a late 12th-century prototype indicate the taste of a maker and patrons who were fashion conscious, but somewhat removed from the contemporary leading edge of court metalwork.

Three dimensional cast lions in this form continued to appear on Limoges enamel objects into the 1220s, an example notably close to that on the Bute Mazer decorating a crozier in the monastery of San Plácido in the archdiocese of Madrid.[8] The presence of Limoges enamels in medieval Scotland is demonstrated by finds such as C3-C8 and other lost pieces may have influenced the maker of the mazer. Alternatively, the archaic appearance of the lion may indicate that the drinking bowl was made to be incorporated into an earlier set of existing plate with similar features. The theory put forward by Stevenson that it represents Robert I is fanciful, as the lion is such a sprawling informal beast. If he were meant to symbolise the king, heraldry would have been used to make this obvious and the creature would have been an animal in a

fig 13: SAN PLÁCIDO CROZIER
Copper alloy and champlevé enamel, Limoges 1210-1220, Monasterio de San Plácido, Archidiócesis Metropolitana de Madrid, photo Institute de Patrimonio Histórico Español.
H 290, W 115

C2

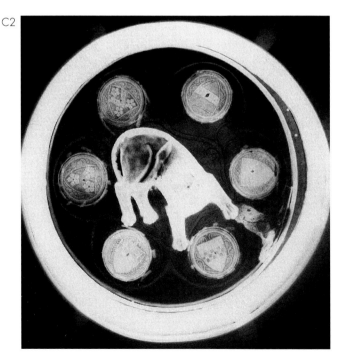

C2

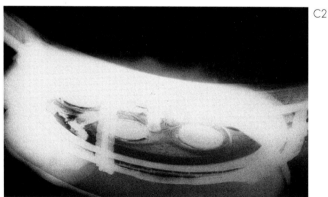

X-ray photographs of the print of the Bute Mazer from above and from the side, showing construction details like the pins through the lion's paws.

formal pose with a shaggy mane and legs in the normal early 14th-century style.[9]

Sadly, it is the only such object to survive and we can merely speculate about riches such as the sixty-nine silver items included in Isabella Bruce's trousseau as bride to the king of Norway in 1293.[10] What must the royal family themselves, the Stewarts, Douglases and Crawfords have owned? Their plate was almost certainly even more elaborate and more sophisticated than the Bute Mazer.

The rim and straps, which were probably added around 1500, are much coarser in style and heavier in construction. They were presumably necessary because nearly two centuries of use and handling had left the mazer in need of consolidation. A whalebone cover was made for the bowl at the same period [L11].

NOTES: [1] Barrow 1998, 122, 126-7. [2] Stevenson 1931, 220-21; see E21, page 67, for detailed provenance. [3] Barrow 1998, 122, 124-6. [4] Glenn 1998, 115. [5] Lightbown 1978, 83. [6] Middeldorf 1980, 57-63. [7] Campbell 1991, 126-31. [8] Madrid, Brussels, Silos, 2002, no 24, 137-9 [9] Barrow 1998, 126; Glenn 1998, 115-16. [10] CDS, 158.

fig 14: PROCESSIONAL CROSS
From Nävelsjö church, Småland, copper alloy and champlevé enamel, Limoges, 1190s, Statens Historiska Museum, photo Antikvarisk-topografiska arkivet, Stockholm. H 700

CERES CRUCIFIX FIGURE
[H.KE 7]

France, Limoges, c 1225-50
Copper alloy, enamel, gilt; raised, punched, engraved, champlevé
H 165, W 135, D 18

CONDITION
Generally good; missing eyes, much of the gilding and some enamel on the upper body.

PROVENANCE
Found in Ceres churchyard, Fife, presented to the museum by Dr Keith Macdonald of Cupar in 1883.[1]

✛ ✛ ✛ ✛ ✛ ✛ ✛ ✛ ✛ ✛ ✛ ✛ ✛ ✛ ✛ ✛

A figure in low relief of the crucified Christ in Glory from a processional cross stands with arms outstretched wearing a crown and long robes to his ankles. It was formerly attached by four nails, one through each hand and foot; only that in the left foot remains.

The hands, head and crown show traces of gilding. The crown has three flat-topped crestings and is decorated with pricked lines at the edges and in wavy

C3

horizontal bands. The eyes (presumably small gem stones) are missing, the long hair is flattened on the shoulders. From a horizontal neckband, vertical folds are indicated by broad flat areas of blue champlevé enamel on the long-sleeved tunic. It is held by a girdle with two semicircular loops below the waist and ends falling to mid-calf. The girdle and hem are plain metal with a double pricked wavy line. A green robe shows below. The bare feet have toes roughly marked by engraved lines.

The concave reverse is undecorated.

✛ ✛ ✛ ✛ ✛ ✛ ✛ ✛ ✛ ✛ ✛ ✛ ✛ ✛ ✛ ✛ ✛

This vision of Christ, fully robed and triumphant over death, was originally an early Christian and Byzantine ideal. Although the iconography was somewhat archaic, by the 13th century Limoges produced a number of these figures for altar and processional crosses. Similar examples are in the Ashmolean Museum, the Victoria and Albert Museum, the Musée de Cluny, Paris, the Walters Art Gallery, Baltimore and the Boston Museum.[2] Larger jewelled versions exist in the Louvre,[3] the Hermitage[4] and attached to a pair of tall crosses from the church of Nävelsjö now in the Statens Historiska Museum in Stockholm (fig 14).[5] A further example on a much altered cross comes from the church of St Hallvard in Oslo.[6]

NOTES: [1] Peddie 1883, 147, 151. [2] Swarzenski and Netzer 1986, no 23, 15, 80-81, list 14 examples, some now lost. [3] Paris 1995, no 49, 184-5 [4] Andersson 1980, fig 29, 60. [5] Andersson 1976, figs 4-5, 113, 115, 124. [6] Horgen 2000, 85.

C4 (colour plate)   C45, 43
BORVE PLAQUE
[H.KE 18]

Scandinavia or Scotland, mid-13th century
Copper alloy, gilt, enamel; engraved, gilded, champlevé
H 61, W 61, D 2

CONDITION
Gilding very worn, surface corroded, extensive losses to the enamel.

PROVENANCE
Excavated in 1943 from a grave at the east end of the Teampull Bhuirgh (Castle Chapel), Borve, Benbecula, Outer Hebrides by a member of the RAF stationed there; acquired by the museum in 1976.[1]

✛ ✛ ✛ ✛ ✛ ✛ ✛ ✛ ✛ ✛ ✛ ✛ ✛ ✛ ✛ ✛ ✛

A half-length figure of Christ stands in the centre, his head with cruciform halo inclined towards his right hand which is raised in blessing. He wears a belted robe with a cloak draped over his left shoulder, concealing his left arm. His features and the drapery folds are roughly

indicated by engraved lines. The background is carved out for champlevé, in large leafy shapes and a horizontal bar behind his head. A plain border of green enamel frames the plaque, further areas of green and blue decorate the background, with some traces of red. The outer edge is pricked with double dotted lines. The reverse of the plaque is completely plain.

There is a round hole, part of the original design, in the centre of each side and two later holes either side of Christ's head.

✛ ✛ ✛ ✛ ✛ ✛ ✛ ✛ ✛ ✛ ✛ ✛ ✛ ✛ ✛ ✛ ✛

C4

fig 15: PLAQUE
From Hova church, Västergötland, copper alloy and champlevé enamel, Scandinavia (?), 1250-1275, Statens Historiska Museum, photo Antikvarisk-topografiska arkivet, Stockholm.
H 62, W 64

Both the drawing and the application of the enamel colours is so crude that it is doubtful if this piece was actually made at Limoges, although it is strongly influenced by prototypes from the French centre.[2] It is true, however, that the production of the Limoges ateliers varied from carefully executed, specially commissioned works of art, to religious souvenirs carelessly produced for pilgrims and scholars to offer to parish churches on their return home. Therefore, quality cannot alone dictate either the origin or the date of an enamel of this type.[3]

Nevertheless, the disproportionately large right arm of this figure, the extremely sketchy engraved lines for features and folds and above all the blockish angular forms of the plants in the background do not seem to fit into the identifiable Limoges oeuvre at all. They are, on the other hand, very close to three plaques of Christ Blessing found in Gotland and south-west Sweden. Many of the drawing characteristics are shared with a circular plaque in Lund,[4] while almost identical designs and technical skills appear on two square enamels in the Statens Historiska Museum in Stockholm (fig 15, page 39). It is now believed that these were made in a Scandinavian workshop and it seems very likely that the Borve plaque was imported from that source. These square plaques probably originally decorated the reverse of a large crucifix.

NOTES: [1] Caldwell 1978, 379-80. [2] Thoby 1953, pls XXII, XXIV. [3] Nilsén 1998, 19. [4] Andersson 1980, fig 99.

C5
FORTINGALL DAGGER POMMEL
H.LC 106

C48, 44

French, late 13th century
Copper alloy, enamel; cast, engraved, champlevé
H 27, W 33, D 12

CONDITION
Very corroded, most of the enamel lost.

PROVENANCE
Found in a garden at Fortingall, Perthshire and acquired by the museum in 1974 through Mr A McAuley.[1]

+ + + + + + + + + + + + + + + +

The crescent-shaped pommel with inward curving tips (one damaged) has a vertical hole through the centre, smaller at the top than the bottom to take the tang of the dagger-hilt. A later hole has been driven into one curved side.

The two flat surfaces have central armorial shields between bifurcated leaf motifs, carved out to take champlevé enamel, traces of which remain in the red of the

heraldry. The charges on these shields are bendy of nine, although one is so corroded it is almost indecipherable. A further two shields, paly of seven, decorate the tips. The scheme is presumably purely decorative.

+ + + + + + + + + + + + + + + +

Although comparison with fitments from other daggers suggested a late 14th-century date,[2] the leaf motifs and the very simple fictive heraldry belong with Limoges enamel decoration of a century earlier.

NOTES: [1] Caldwell 1976, 322. [2] Ibid, 323.

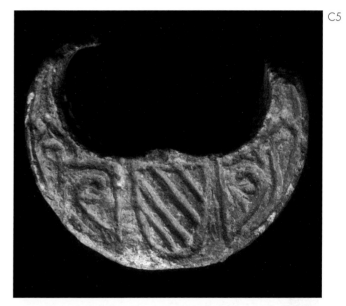

C5

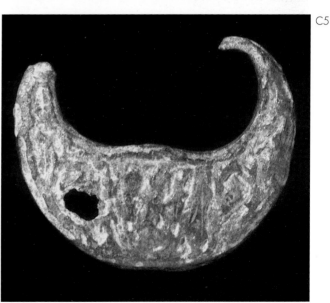

C5

WAUCHOPE CASKET HASP
[H.KJ 88]

France, Limoges, early 13th century.
Copper alloy, gilt, blue and yellowish green enamel, lapis lazuli; cast, engraved, gilded, champlevé
W 25, D 20 (max), L 350; 30 (pin)

CONDITION
Complete, but gilding worn, some losses to the enamel, particularly towards the tail of the largest serpent.

PROVENANCE
Found in the bank of Beck's Burn, between the graveyard of the old church of Wauchope and Wauchope Castle, near Langholm, purchased for the museum in 1895.[1]

✧ ✧ ✧ ✧ ✧ ✧ ✧ ✧ ✧ ✧ ✧ ✧ ✧ ✧ ✧ ✧

Four winged lizards with lapis lazuli gemstones for eyes form a hinged hasp for a casket. The upper part consists of a beast with a large square head, gilded and decorated on the neck with a central band of four engraved circles, between stripes of punched matting, holding the hinge in its wide bulbous jaws. Its wings, which are folded over its high convex back, are indicated by long stripes of blue champlevé enamel, with an oval panel of yellowish green on each shoulder. The serpent's body tapers to a gilt scrolled tail, the scales indicated by punching and enamel roundels (now lost).

From this emerges the gilt head of a smaller creature, similarly punched and engraved, curving to the right and holding in its jaws a scrolling three-petalled blossom, enamelled in yellowish green and red, with a central hole for a fixing to the casket.

The lower part has a broad-headed lizard facing downwards, its rectangular body ornamented with a lozenge pattern in blue enamel, its gilt head as before. It bites the tail of a longer slimmer serpent with wings as above and a small gilt head on a long neck, stretching below the fastening for the lock.

On the reverse of the upper part is a thick copper-alloy pin designed to lodge into the lid of the casket. The reverse of the lower part is gilt and has a rectangular loop to fit into a lockplate.

✧ ✧ ✧ ✧ ✧ ✧ ✧ ✧ ✧ ✧ ✧ ✧ ✧ ✧ ✧ ✧

Langholm was a remote Borders area virtually undocumented before the 1280s when the Lindsay family gained possession of the lordship, which they held continuously until 1707.[2] One glimpse of contact between the area and the outer world comes in 1333 when Edward III granted the locals a safe-conduct 'because they have frequent occasion to come to England to buy provisions'.[3] It is worth noting that Limoges and similar enamels have also been excavated around Carlisle, their nearest large town, perhaps indicating a merchant dealing in this material in the area.

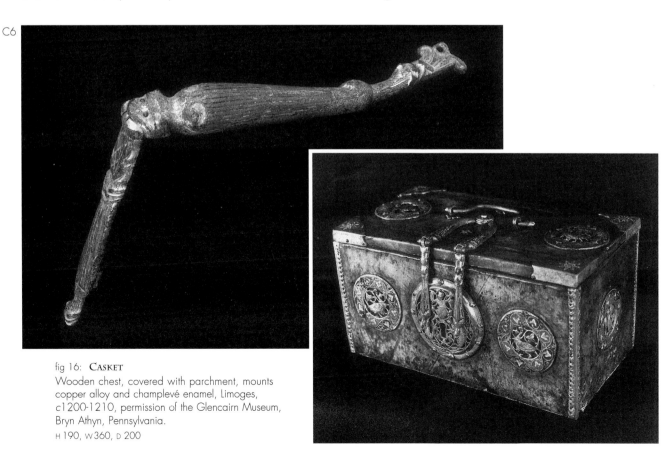

C6

fig 16: CASKET
Wooden chest, covered with parchment, mounts copper alloy and champlevé enamel, Limoges, c1200-1210, permission of the Glencairn Museum, Bryn Athyn, Pennsylvania.
H 190, W 360, D 200

A number of whole coffers survive with similar fittings. The nearest to C6 is in the Glencairn Museum at Bryn Athyn, Pennsylvania (fig 16, page 41).[4] Where these coffers are attributed to medieval owners, in some cases on convincing historical grounds, they were usually grand personages. For example, Cardinal Bicchieri's was preserved at his cathedral at Vercelli until the 19th century;[5] that of Richard of Cornwall, brother of Henry III of England, is still in the treasury at Aachen;[6] and another in the Louvre was formerly kept at the abbey church of Notre-Dame de Lys, where it contained relics of St Louis, king of France.[7]

Although they all have entirely secular ornament, they were happily incorporated into church furnishings and our hasp could have come from a coffer belonging either to a local or passing nobleman or an important cleric on church business.

NOTES: [1] *PSAS*, vol XXX, 7-9. [2] Barrow 1992, 186. [3] Ibid, 179. [4] Paris 1995, no 38, 158-60. [5] Ibid, no 89, 282-5. [6] Grimme 1972, no 52, 76-7, 254. [7] Paris 1995, no 124, 360-63.

C7   F24, 116
KINNOULL PRICKET CANDLESTICK
[H.KJ 22]

France, Limoges, early 13th century
Copper alloy, enamel; cast, engraved, champlevé
H 230, W 106, D 75

CONDITION
Very worn and corroded, all gilding removed and only traces of enamel remaining; one of the legs and possibly the tray replaced.

PROVENANCE
Donated to the museum in 1860 by Robert Mercer of Scotsbank; stated to have been found in digging the foundations of the parish church, Kinnoull, near Perth.[1] Kinnoull's new kirk, designed by William Burn, superseded its predecessor in 1826.[2]

+ + + + + + + + + + + + + + + + +

The candlestick has a tripod base on three tall flattened legs, a tapering tubular stem with a round knop half-way up and a circular dished tray below the spike. Originally, the base, the knop and possibly the rim of the tray were decorated with champlevé enamel.

The original legs are engraved with straight and wavy vertical lines and terminate in pad feet engraved with square lattice. At the top of each is a scrolling motif in relief, intended as a stylised animal mask. The shoulders of the tripod have identical triangular panels, carved for enamel, showing a pair of wyverns with long necks stretching upwards, spreading wings and long tails with

feathery ends curled behind them. They crouch on either side of a circle filled with four elongated leaves around a central quatrefoil flower motif.

The stem is decorated with a diagonal lattice pattern retaining some gilding in the engraving. The knop, which retains traces of enamel, has a plain band around its circumference, with borders of scrolling leaves above and below. The tray has a similar, but not identical, border with a small hole pierced at each side and may be a 19th-century replacement.

+ + + + + + + + + + + + + + + +

The candlestick has been so severely scoured and inexpertly repaired that its original appearance is difficult to visualise.

It has a similar foot design to a pair of candlesticks in the Metropolitan Museum in New York, although they have a more sophisticated decoration of lions around a leaping warrior in a roundel.[3] The lattice pattern on the stem is paralleled on a single tall candlestick in the same museum, where gilding remains in the engraving.[4]

NOTES: [1] *PSAS*, vol III, 1860, 339. [2] Macmillan 1986, no 9, 11. [3] Paris 1995, no 33, 146-7. [4] Ibid, no 37, 156-7.

C7

BOTHWELL CASTLE CANDLESTICK
[H.HX 506]

France, Limoges, last third 13th century
Copper alloy, gilt, enamel (lost); raised, engraved, gilded, champlevé
H 89, W 62, D 62

CONDITION
Object complete, but quite corroded; traces of gilding remain, no enamel is visible to the naked eye.

PROVENANCE
Found during pre-war excavations at Bothwell Castle, Lanarkshire by the Ministry of Works; presented to the museum in 1959-60 by the Earl of Home.[1]

+ + + + + + + + + + + + + + + +

The hollow tapering spike of the pricket candlestick rises from a hexagonal base, which slopes inward to a domed top and stands on three plain tab feet. The base has been carved to take champlevé enamel. Around the top there was a wavy riband roughly incised with a single line and a disc centred on the spike against an enamel ground. On each side of the hexagon there is an armorial shield with addorsed Z motifs below. The heraldry is very roughly executed, a shield with three billets fretty alternating with one with a bendy of nine (as on C5, page 40).

+ + + + + + + + + + + + + + + +

This little candlestick with its short spike was probably the smallest of a set which fitted on top of each other for travelling, like the splendid group now in the Louvre.[2]

The first building programme at Bothwell Castle began about the middle of the 13th century. Based on French prototypes with a massive round donjon and a vast fortified area it was designed by its builder, Walter Murray, to stand amongst the grandest secular structures in Scotland.[3]

The heraldic devices are difficult to decipher and have generally been dismissed as purely decorative. No Murray family connection suggests itself for the bendy device, but the three square motifs within an *orle* somewhat echo the arrangement of mullets on their arms.

NOTES: [1] *PSAS*, vol XCIII, 1962, no 32, 253. [2] Paris 1995, no 136, 380. [3] Tabraham 1986, 36-8.

IV JEWELLERY

In this collection we have only the most fleeting glimpse of what a court goldsmith might have provided in Scotland from the 12th to the 15th centuries. Both the gold Doune brooch [E15] and Queen Joan Beaufort's personal seal matrix [K3] (pages 140-41) hint at the taste and aspirations of royal circles in the early 15th century, but although very fine they are only two tiny items. The Iona gold fillet [G3] may have been associated with Bethag the first prioress, daughter of Somerled, or one of her ladies, suggesting that the western dynasty also led lives of considerable opulence and refinement at least as early as 1200. Families of middle rank meanwhile possessed carefully designed and well-made pieces of jewellery like the Kames [E21] and Islay brooches [E20].

Writing half a century ago, Dame Joan Evans in *A History of Jewellery 1100-1870* follows her remarks on medieval Scotland with the words 'In the more highly civilised countries ...', before proceeding to discuss French and English work. Perhaps it was her seminal influence which has led most recent writers to assert that all the above items, and indeed any other pieces of high quality, must have been imports. This cannot be proved either way, but seen in conjunction with some of the other material in this catalogue, for example the Bute Mazer [C2] and the cresting of the Quigrich [H6], there is no reason at all why highly skilled craftsmen should not have been operating in Edinburgh, Stirling or elsewhere.

The jewellery which survives from the later Middle Ages in Scotland is, on the whole, the day-to-day wear of the moderately prosperous. However, the supposition that most of the ring brooches, for example, were made by *ceardan* or travelling tinkers is perhaps unnecessarily dismissive, although some of them are quite crude in execution.[1] Similar brooches with more or less garbled inscriptions have been found at many sites in England, including the City of London.[2] At least in the less remote parts of Scotland normal dress and its accessories seem to have been much like those in England and northern Europe. Sketches representing ordinary working people just south of Hadrian's wall, probably drawn in the early 14th century,[3] depict them in quite carefully cut garments with rows of buttons, belts, hose, garters and shoes rather than the flowing shapeless drapery dear to the imagination of Hollywood (fig 17).

The frequent Latin inscriptions on the ring brooches mostly follow a very few well known formulae, notably *IHESVS NAZARENVS REX IUDAEORUM*, the titulus traditionally affixed above Christ on the cross. The craftsmen in many cases were clearly copying the words from other sources without understanding their meaning and the results vary from the quite accurate to the virtually unintelligible.

Eighteen of the 14th-century silver ring brooches were found as part of six groups of treasure, at least five of which were deliberately hidden. The concentration of these near to the English border and the dates of the associated coins, shows that they were hidden during the intermittent warfare of the early 14th century.

The handsome ring brooches with applied rosettes are characteristic of the Scottish Borders and the north of England and may have been made in either,

fig 17: LANERCOST CARTULARY
MS DZ 1, folio 28 recto, vellum, English-Scottish
border, 1252-1370, 'Gamelus de Walton',
reproduced by permission of Cumbria County
Archive, photo NMS.
(detail)

fig 18: NORHAM BROOCH
Silver, Scottish, c 1300, NMS H.NH 2
DIAM 76

fig 19: EFFIGY OF LADY CAMPBELL OF LOCHAWE
White sandstone, Scottish, 1440s, Argyll
Mausoleum, the parish church, Kilmun,
Crown Copyright, RCAHMS.
(detail)

although outlying examples have been discovered in Hereford[4] and Bohuslän in
south west Sweden.[5] The most impressive of these in NMS collections was found
near Norham Castle in Northumberland, one of the principal seats of the prince
bishops of Durham, an important medieval crossing point on the river Tweed and a
frequent meeting place for English and Scottish royalty and their emissaries.[6] It
could well have been lost there by a member of either party (fig 18).

Nor were all imports in the luxury class. The 'iconographic' rings are fairly
run-of-the-mill examples of their kind, except for the gold example from Tantallon

Castle [D13] which is rather more delicate. They were presumably made in England, where they occur with some frequency.

How this jewellery was worn and, for the most part, by whom, cannot be easily established from Scottish sources. Medieval tomb effigies which provide such valuable evidence in other countries have fared very badly in Scotland. Only one royal effigy, possibly the lower half of an early 14th-century monument to William the Lion (1143-1214), has survived.[7] Most extant medieval tomb carvings are so weathered or badly damaged that fine ornamental detail is erased.[8] Traces of a ring brooch or a decorated girdle occur here and there, but with a very few notable exceptions, for example at Kilmun and Houston, their condition is too poor to be successfully related to anything in this collection (fig 19, page 45). This gap in our knowledge makes the jewellery itself even more important as a signifier of lifestyle and social mores in the medieval period.

NOTES: [1] Finlay 1991, 42. [2] Egan and Pritchard 1991, no 1337, fig 164, pl 6C, 254-5. [3] Todd 1997, *passim*. [4] London 1987, no 652, 486. [5] Augustsson *et al* 1996, fig 740, 466. [6] Finlay 1991, pl 11 illustrates it in error as having been found at Canonbie. E10 is in fact the Canonbie find. The Norham brooch was purchased by the museum in 1871. [7] Gimson 1995. [8] Brydall 1895, *passim*.

ORDER OF THE JEWELLERY CATALOGUE ENTRIES

Rings – Listed by type:

1 Ecclesiastical
2 Probably secular
3 Fede rings
4 'Iconographic' rings

Brooches
Listed alphabetically by find site if known, then by donor if otherwise unprovenanced. Catalogue entries initialled JM are by Jackie Moran.

Pendants
Listed alphabetically by find site if known, then by donor if otherwise unprovenanced.

Fillets
Listed alphabetically by find site.

RINGS

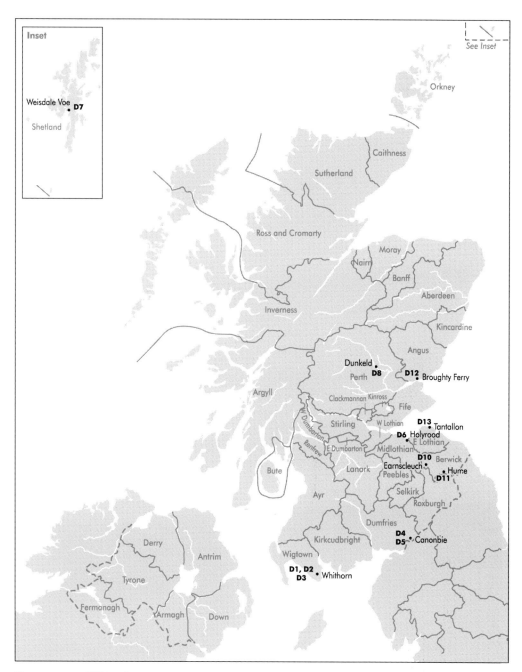

The provenance of D9 is unknown.

WHITHORN AMETHYST AND SAPPHIRE RING

[H.1992.1835]

Scotland (?), mid-13th century
Gold, amethyst, sapphires, iron (?); hammered, gems cut and polished
DIAM 23 (hoop), H 20, D 29 (with bezel)

CONDITION
Excellent, some cracks and losses inside, where the shoulders join the hoop.

PROVENANCE
Excavated from a bishop's grave at the cathedral church at Whithorn (see C1, page 32), with a silver chalice and paten, B5.

+ + + + + + + + + + + + + + + +

The thin flat hoop, which narrows at the back, has a central beaded ridge. The plain trapezoid shoulders are notched to meet this ridge. The bezel consists of an irregular table-cut amethyst in a slightly concave high plain setting surrounded by eight collets set with cabochon sapphires. The inside is undecorated. The ring is made of gold sheet and contains some other material possibly used as a repair.

+ + + + + + + + + + + + + + + +

Although this ring was declared by one writer to be purely decorative,[1] it is not always easy to distinguish a bishop's consecration ring,[2] and this handsome jewel, which is large enough to have been worn over a glove, may well have served a ceremonial purpose.

NOTES: [1] Oman 1974, 94, pl 16D.   [2] Cherry 1981, 58.

WHITHORN AMETHYST RING

[H.1992.1836]

Scotland (?), 13th century
Silver, gilt, amethyst; hammered, gem polished
DIAM 25 (hoop), H 11, D 31 (with bezel)

CONDITION
Good, silver slightly corroded, gilding worn.

PROVENANCE
Excavated from a grave at the cathedral church at Whithorn (see C1, page 32).[1]

+ + + + + + + + + + + + + + + +

The hoop of lozenge section is slightly stirrup shaped. The oblong bezel is plain behind and has an irregular amethyst cabochon in a high plain setting rising from a beaded border. A hole has been drilled horizontally through the gem.

+ + + + + + + + + + + + + + + +

It was not unusual for gems already pierced for another use to be set into rings in the 13th and 14th centuries.[2]

NOTES: [1] Oman 1974, 94, pl 16E. It is now known that this ring, D1 and another gold ring were all found in 1957, not 1962 as he was told.   [2] Campbell 1991, 136 n135; London 1987, no 634, no 637, no 639, 481-3. See also D4, page 49.

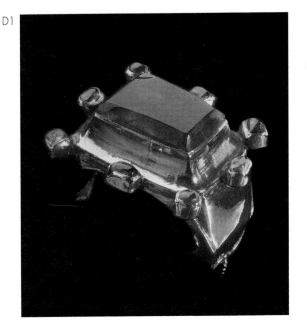

D1

D2

D3
WHITHORN SILVER RING

Scotland, 14th century
Silver; hammered, raised
DIAM 25 (hoop), H 14, D 27 (with bezel)

CONDITION
Poor, corroded, top edge of setting partly broken, gem missing.

PROVENANCE
Excavated from a grave at Whithorn priory (see C1, page 32).

✝ ✝ ✝ ✝ ✝ ✝ ✝ ✝ ✝ ✝ ✝ ✝ ✝ ✝

The large round hoop is lozenge in section. It broadens slightly to join the sides of a deep plain flaring triangular setting with rounded corners. Part of one small claw to hold a gem in place remains in the middle of one side.

CANONBIE SAPPHIRE RING
[H.KO 7]

Scotland or England, mid-13th century (hoard deposited *c*1292-26)[1]
Gold, sapphire, emeralds; hammered, gem drilled and polished
DIAM 22 (hoop), H 12, D 28 (with bezel)

CONDITION
Good, slight cracking at join on one side, four emeralds missing.

PROVENANCE
Found with coins of Alexander III, John Balliol, Edward I and II in ploughing a field at Woodhead, Canonbie, Dumfriesshire in 1861 with D5, E10, E11, E12 and E13.[2]

✝ ✝ ✝ ✝ ✝ ✝ ✝ ✝ ✝ ✝ ✝ ✝ ✝ ✝

The thin flat hoop widens to form solid shoulders behind a high moulded bezel holding a pale irregular cabochon sapphire surrounded by six collets containing small emeralds. A drilled hole pierces the sapphire longitudinally.

✝ ✝ ✝ ✝ ✝ ✝ ✝ ✝ ✝ ✝ ✝ ✝ ✝ ✝

It was not unusual for gems already pierced for another use to be set into rings in the 13th and 14th centuries.[3]

NOTES: [1] Thompson 1956, no 70, 22. [2] *PSAS*, vol V, 1864, pl viii, 216; Graham Callander 1924, 168. [3] Campbell 1991, 136 n135; London 1987, no 634, no 637, no 639, 481-3. See also D2.

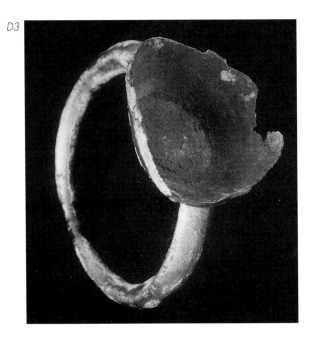

D3

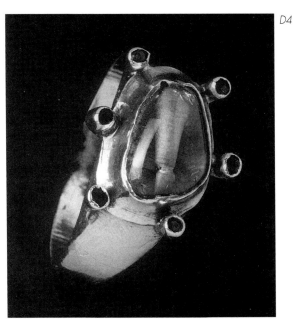

D4

CANONBIE RUBY RING
[H.KO 8]

Scotland or England, 13th century (hoard
deposited c 1292-26)[1]
Gold, ruby, cement core; hammered, gem polished
DIAM 21 (hoop), H 9, D 25 (with bezel)

CONDITION
Very good, horizontal hole in the gold behind the bezel.

PROVENANCE
Found with coins of Alexander III, John Balliol, Edward I
and II in ploughing a field at Woodhead, Canonbie,
Dumfriesshire in 1861 with D4, E10, E11, E12 and E13.[2]

+ + + + + + + + + + + + + + + +

The stirrup-shaped ring thins to a flat band at the back.
An irregular cabochon ruby is held at the front in a high
moulded bezel. The gold appears to be thin sheet on a
supporting core at the shoulders.

NOTES: [1] Thompson 1956, no 70, 22. [2] PSAS, vol V, 1864, pl viii,
216; Graham Callander 1924, 168.

HOLYROOD DIAMOND RING
[H.NJ 68]

Scotland (?), c 1300
Gold, diamond
DIAM 21 (hoop), H 7, D 28 (with bezel)

CONDITION
Excellent.

PROVENANCE
Found in the shrubbery in the south west angle of the
north gardens of Holyrood Palace, passed to the museum
about 1917 by the King's and Lord Treasurer's
Remembrancer.[1]

+ + + + + + + + + + + + + + + +

The plain stirrup-shaped ring has a square bezel set with
a natural octahedral diamond crystal. There is a small
square plug inside the hoop at the back of the gem
setting.

NOTE: [1] PSAS, vol LI, 1917, 128-9, fig 1.

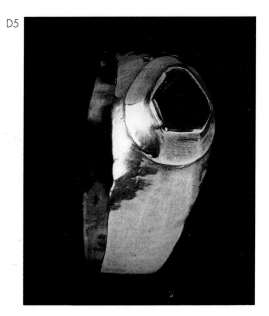

D5

D6

WEISDALE VOE RING
[H.NJ 124]

Scotland or Scandinavia, early 14th century
Gold; hammered, cast, engraved
DIAM 20 (hoop), H 15, D 23 (with bezel)

CONDITION
Fairly good, considerable wear to the hoop has made parts
of the inscription barely legible.

INSCRIPTION
AVE MARIA GRAC (Lombardic) [for *AVE MARIA GRATIA PLENA*,
'Hail Mary full of grace']

PROVENANCE
Found in Weisdale Voe, Shetland during road works before
1914, presented to the museum in the name of Dr George
Munro about 1955.[1]

+ + + + + + + + + + + + + + + +

The hoop is rectangular in section and has an engraved
inscription running round the outside, between the
raised moulded shoulders which join it to the high bezel
in the form of an eight-petalled rose. A line of beading is
punched at the edge of one petal on either side of the
shoulders and a Greek cross is engraved in the centre.

+ + + + + + + + + + + + + + + +

Fourteenth-century rings with similar bezels are in the
Bryggen Museum in Bergen[2] and the Nationalmuseet
in Copenhagen.[3] The former has a patriarchal cross
engraved in the centre, the latter is set with an amethyst.

NOTES: [1] Maxwell 1958, 193. [2] Bergen 1978, fig 22, 67. [3] Inv
no D2730, found at Ribe town hall.

DUNKELD RING
[H.NJ 73]

Possibly Italy, late 14th or early 15th century[1]
Gold, ruby, enamel (lost); cast, engraved, gem cut and
polished
diam 20 (hoop), h 9, d 24 (with bezel)

CONDITION
Good, except for the loss of the enamel.

PROVENANCE
Found outside the wall of the north aisle of the nave,
Dunkeld Cathedral, presented to the museum by HM
Office of Works in 1925.[2]

+ + + + + + + + + + + + + + + +

The hoop has a plain narrow back and flares towards the
shoulders where it is engraved with abstract leaf motifs
intended to be surrounded by enamel. The shoulders are
moulded fleur-de-lis with serrated edges. The bezel is a
scooped quatrefoil holding an irregularly shaped cabochon ruby. The interior is plain.

NOTES: [1] Cherry 1981, no 197, 84, illustrates an inscribed Italian
ring in the British Museum with a very similar bezel. [2] *PSAS*, vol
LX, 1925, 13.

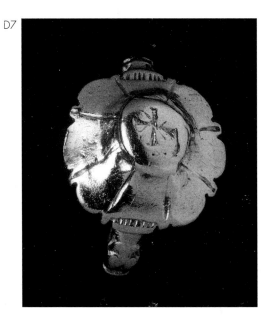

D7

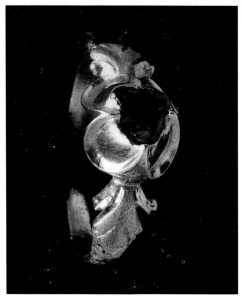

D8

FEDE RING
[H.NJ 61]

Scotland or England, late 15th century
Silver, gilt, enamel (lost); cast, engraved, champlevé
DIAM 24 (hoop), H 9, D 26 (with bezel)

CONDITION
Good, gilding worn.

INSCRIPTION
IESVSNA (black letter) [for IHESUS NAZARENUS, 'Jesus of
Nazareth']

PROVENANCE
Unknown.

+ + + + + + + + + + + + + + + +

The hoop is joined by the 'fede' or clasped hands device,
which is fully modelled on the inside and outside surfaces. An inscription is applied to the hoop, each letter in a
square silver block carved to take an enamel background.
The rest of the ring was gilt.

+ + + + + + + + + + + + + + + +

So called from the Italian *mani in fede* (hands in faith),
love or betrothal rings with this device were well known
in the Classical world and reappeared in both northern
and southern Europe in the 12th century (see also D10).[1]

NOTE: [1] Cherry 1981, 59, pls 114, 125, 195.

EARNSCLEUCH FEDE RING
[H.NJ 72]

Scotland or England, late 15th century
Silver, gilt; cast, engraved
DIAM 26 (hoop), H 12, D 25 (with bezel)

CONDITION
Fairly good, most of the gilding has worn away.

INSCRIPTION
Meaningless (black letter).[1]

PROVENANCE
Found at Earnscleuch Water, Lauder. Given to the museum
about 1921.[2]

+ + + + + + + + + + + + + + + +

The ring consists of a broad flat hoop vertically split
to take the 'fede' or clasped hands device. The hoop is
bordered with spirally beaded wire and has a roughly
engraved inscription against diagonal hatching. Cuffs are
indicated at the wrists by two vertical ridges and the
fingers are crudely cast and chased. All parts of the ring
have traces of former gilding. The interior is entirely
plain.

+ + + + + + + + + + + + + + + +

For Fede rings, see also D9.

NOTES: [1] The letter forms may be intended for 'u n i e i c n' and
were probably used purely decoratively by an illiterate craftsman.
[2] *PSAS*, vol LV, 1921, 14-20, part of a collection formed by Lady
John Scott of Spottiswood, mostly of Berwickshire archaeology.

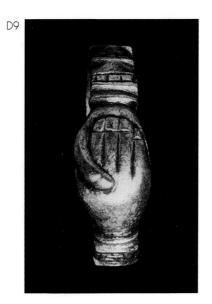

D9

D10

D11   E78, 92
HUME ICONOGRAPHIC RING
[H.NJ 90]

England, 15th century
Silver, gilt, iron (?); chased, engraved, gilded
DIAM 26 (hoop), H 13, D 28 (with bezel)

CONDITION
Gilt slightly worn, some splits and chips to edges of the hoop.

INSCRIPTION
M I (black letter)

PROVENANCE
Found at Hume Castle, Berwickshire during the life time of Sir Hugh Hume
Campbell, grandfather of the donor, Miss Eleanor Warrender, presented to
the museum about 1940.[1]

✦ ✦ ✦ ✦ ✦ ✦ ✦ ✦ ✦ ✦ ✦ ✦ ✦ ✦ ✦

The heavy silver-gilt iconographic ring seems to be built up on a core of
base metal, which is visible through damage at one edge of the bezel. The
hoop is a wide band, flat on the inner surface, slightly convex with lozenge
facets on the outer and flaring towards the two cell bezel.

The central ridge of the bezel is beaded, roughly engraved in one cell is a
standing figure of the Virgin and Child, in the other a saint (or angel?).
The hoop is chased with notched diagonal lattice, engraved rays radiating
from a central dot in each lozenge. The letters M and I are engraved, one
on each shoulder. The interior is entirely plain.

✦ ✦ ✦ ✦ ✦ ✦ ✦ ✦ ✦ ✦ ✦ ✦ ✦ ✦ ✦

It seems unlikely that the scene is the Annunciation, as has been suggested, since the Virgin is already holding the Child.[2]

The term 'iconographic' was coined by Victorian collectors to describe this
type of ring engraved with figures of the Virgin and or one of a small group
of saints, possibly chosen because they were the owner's name saint,
because they were the objectives of popular pilgrimage or because they
were saints particularly invoked against certain illnesses or misfortunes.[3]
The type is not found outside Britain and the discovery of these three
examples [see also D12 and D13] close to the east coast and its sea routes
suggests that they were probably imported from some centre of manufacture in England.

D11

NOTES: [1] *PSAS*, vol LXXIV, 1940, 150. [2] Oman 1974, 115 no 66D, pls 66C and 66D.
The catalogue is confused, '66C From Morayshire' does not exist and Oman has given
it the same museum number as D10. Pls 66C and D are back and front views of D10.
[3] Ibid 54-5.

BROUGHTY FERRY ICONOGRAPHIC RING

[H.NJ 54]

England, 15th century
Gold, enamel; engraved, champlevé
DIAM 21 (hoop), H 9, D 24 (with bezel)

CONDITION
Good except for the loss of some red enamel and most of the white.

PROVENANCE
Found in 1881 during the demolition of a cottage at Broughty Ferry.[1]

+ + + + + + + + + + + + + + + +

The gold iconographic ring has a hoop which is a plain band, flat on the inside, slightly convex on the outside, flaring to shoulders with five spiral bands of alternating translucent red and opaque white enamel. The two cell bezel is engraved with the Virgin and Child on one side of the plain central ridge and a standing figure of St John the Evangelist holding a chalice on the other, against a ground of black enamel.[2]

NOTES: [1] Hutcheson 1885, 156. [2] Oman 1974, 116, pl 66A. See also D11 and D13.

TANTALLON CASTLE ICONOGRAPHIC RING

[H.NJ 7]

England, 15th century
Gold, enamel; engraved, champlevé
DIAM 13 (hoop), H 8, D 20 (with bezel)

CONDITION
Good, except for lost and chipped enamel.

INSCRIPTIONS
j r / j r or i r / i r (black letter)

PROVENANCE
Found at Tantallon Castle, East Lothian in 1852 and presented to the museum in 1854 by Captain Henry James.[1]

+ + + + + + + + + + + + + + +

The gold iconographic ring has a hoop which is a plain band on the inside, slightly convex on the outside. It is engraved with feathery sprays of flowers and leaves and the monogram jr, used twice, different ways up. This decoration was probably intended to take enamel. The two-cell bezel is roughly engraved with three-quarter-length figures, probably of the Virgin on one side of the plain ridge and the Angel of the Annunciation on the other,[2] against a ground of black enamel (see also D11 and D12).

+ + + + + + + + + + + + + +

Tantallon Castle is an impressive fortress occupied by the Douglas family since at least 1374, soon after it was built. They had risen to prominence under Robert Bruce, married into his descendants and remained close to the royal family for the remainder of the 15th century.[3]

NOTES: [1] James 1855, 168; Caldwell 1991, no 1, 337. [2] Oman 1974, 115, pl 66B describes the flowers as lilies and identifies the scene as the Annunciation. [3] Tabraham 1986, 95-6.

D12

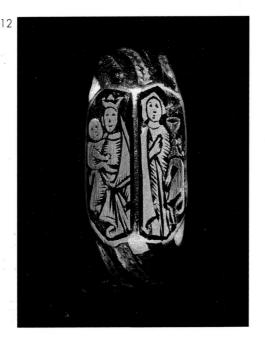

D13

BROOCHES

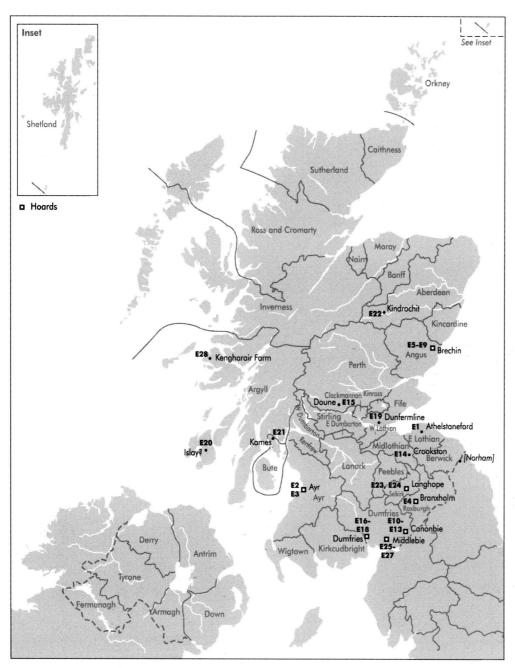

Inset

Shetland

□ Hoards

Orkney

Caithness

Sutherland

Ross and Cromarty

Moray

Nairn

Banff

Aberdeen

Inverness

Kindrochit

E22

Kincardine

E5-E9

□ Brechin

E28

Kengharair Farm

Angus

Perth

Argyll

Clackmannan Kinross

Doune E15

Fife

Stirling

E19 Dunfermline

E Dumbarton

E1

Athelstaneford

E21

Dumbarton

W. Lothian

E Lothian

Kames

Renfrew

Midlothian

E14

Crookston

[Norham]

E20

Islay?

Bute

Lanark

Berwick

Peebles

E23, E24

Langhope

Selkirk

E2

Ayr

E4

Branxholm

E3

Ayr

Raxburgh

E16-

E18

Dumfries

E10-

E13

Canonbie

Dumfries

□ Middlebie

Wigtown

Kirkcudbright

E25-

E27

Derry

Antrim

Tyrone

Fermanagh

Armagh

Down

The medieval provenances of E29-E37 are unknown.

ATHELSTANEFORD RING BROOCH
[H.NGA 23]

Scotland, 14th century
Silver; engraved
DIAM 21 (brooch); W 4, L 19 (pin)

CONDITION
Fair.

INSCRIPTION
X IhESVS NAZARE (Lombardic) [for *IHESUS NAZARENUS*, 'Jesus of Nazareth'].

PROVENANCE
Found whilst digging a grave in the kirkyard of Athelstaneford, East Lothian,[1] given to the museum in 1882 by Robert Whyte of Larbert.[2]

✛ ✛ ✛ ✛ ✛ ✛ ✛ ✛ ✛ ✛ ✛ ✛ ✛ ✛ ✛

The flat ring brooch complete with pin, has the inscription on the front between single marginal lines. The back is decorated with quatrefoils. The plain collar is mostly broken away.

NOTES: [1] Graham Callander 1924, fig 3, no 8, 164, no 6, 169.
[2] *PSAS*, vol XVI, 1882, 37.

JM

AYR RING BROOCH
[H.KO 19]

Scotland, second half of the 13th century (hoard deposited *c* 1280-1300)[1]
Silver; engraved
DIAM 34 (brooch); W 6, L 36 (pin)

CONDITION
Good, apart from an obvious repair to the ring.

INSCRIPTION
There is an illiterate attempt at letter forms, but they do not approximate to any recognisable inscription.

PROVENANCE
Found at the old fort at Ayr in 1862 in an earthenware pot with E3 and coins of Alexander III, John Balliol, Edward I and Edward II;[2] acquired by the museum in 1892 under Treasure Trove arrangements.[3]

✛ ✛ ✛ ✛ ✛ ✛ ✛ ✛ ✛ ✛ ✛ ✛ ✛ ✛ ✛

The flat ring brooch complete with pin has the inscription on the front. The pin is rectangular in section with a collar marked by a horizontal groove. The reverse is completely undecorated.

NOTES: [1] Thompson 1956, no 18, 6. [2] Graham Callander 1924, fig 3, no 12, 164, no 4, 169. [3] *PSAS*, vol XXVI, 1892, 60.

JM

E1

E1

E2

AYR OCTAGONAL BROOCH
[H.KO 20]

Scotland, second half of the 13th century (hoard deposited *c* 1280-1300)[1]
Silver, niello; engraved
DIAM 38 (brooch); W 7, L 40 (pin)

CONDITION
Excellent.

INSCRIPTION
IHS/SVS/NA (debased Lombardic) [for *IHESUS NAZARENUS*, 'Jesus of Nazareth']

PROVENANCE
Found at the old fort at Ayr in 1862 in an earthenware pot with E2 and coins of Alexander III, John Balliol, Edward I and Edward II;[2] acquired by the museum in 1892 under Treasure Trove arrangements.[3]

✠ ✠ ✠ ✠ ✠ ✠ ✠ ✠ ✠ ✠ ✠ ✠ ✠ ✠ ✠ ✠

The octagonal brooch is complete with pin and its eight sides are alternately flat and ridged. The inscription is on the flat panels on the front, with a tablet flower at beginning and end. The flat panels on the back are decorated with longitudinal wavy lines and the intervening ridges with oblique lines meeting at the crest, the spaces between them punched with small circles. Both the inscription and the engraved lines are filled with niello. The pin is oval in section with a projecting rectangular collar marked by a horizontal groove.

NOTES: [1] Thompson 1956, no 18, 6. [2] Graham Callander 1924, fig 4, no 2, 166, no 19, 171. [3] *PSAS*, vol XXVI, 1892, 60.

JM

BRANXHOLM OCTAGONAL BROOCH
[H.NGA 21]

Scotland, 14th century (hoard deposited after 1370)[1]
Silver; engraved
DIAM 19 (brooch); W 2, L 18 (pin)

CONDITION
Fair.

INSCRIPTION
Individual letters can be deciphered, but the surface is too worn for an intelligible inscription to be recovered.

PROVENANCE
Found at Branxholm, Roxburghshire with coins of David II and Robert II,[2] given to the museum by W W Hay Newton in 1860.[3]

✠ ✠ ✠ ✠ ✠ ✠ ✠ ✠ ✠ ✠ ✠ ✠ ✠ ✠ ✠ ✠

The octagonal brooch is complete with pin, the sides alternately flat and ridged. The inscriptions on the four flat panels on both sides are illegible. Each panel appears to have two letters on it. The ridged areas between the flat panels have sloping sides decorated alternately with oblique lines meeting at the crest and small circles. The pin, a flattened oval in section, has a rectangular collar with a horizontal groove.

NOTES: [1] Thompson 1956, no 53, 19. [2] Graham Callander 1924, fig 4, no 5, 166, no 21, 171, gives the inscription as I HE SV SN(front) AZ AR EN VS (reverse). [3] *PSAS*, vol III, 1860, 484.

JM

E4

E3

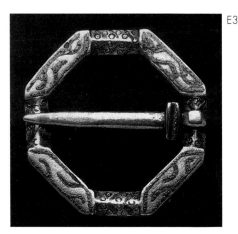

E3

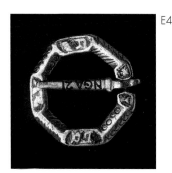

E4

E5
BRECHIN RING BROOCH
[H.KO 22]

Scotland, mid-13th century (hoard deposited *c*1280-1320)[1]
Silver; engraved
DIAM 60 (brooch); W 4, L 57 (pin)

CONDITION
Poor.

PROVENANCE
Found in a garden at Brechin, probably in 1891, with E6, E7, E8 and E9 and Edward I and II coins,[2] purchased by the museum in 1891.[3]

✦ ✦ ✦ ✦ ✦ ✦ ✦ ✦ ✦ ✦ ✦ ✦ ✦ ✦ ✦

A wire ring brooch with only two out of four complete knops and one other half remaining. It would originally also have had four rosettes. The pin is circular in section and is missing its point and collar.

NOTES: [1] Thompson 1956, no 56, 19. [2] Graham Callander 1924, no 25, 172. [3] *PSAS*, vol XXV, 1891, 417.

JM

E6
BRECHIN SILVER BROOCH
[H.KO 23]

Scotland, 13th century (hoard deposited *c*1280-1320)[1]
Silver; engraved
DIAM 48 (brooch); W 4, L 47 (pin)

CONDITION
Fair, inscription worn, part of the collar of the pin broken away.

INSCRIPTION
+IhESVS NAZ....VS REX IVDEORVM+ (Lombardic) [for *IHESUS NAZARENUS REX IUDEORUM*, 'Jesus of Nazareth King of the Jews']

PROVENANCE
Found in a garden at Brechin, probably in 1891, with E5, E7, E8 and E9 and coins of Edward I and II,[2] purchased by the museum in 1891.[3]

✦ ✦ ✦ ✦ ✦ ✦ ✦ ✦ ✦ ✦ ✦ ✦ ✦ ✦ ✦

The flat ring brooch complete with pin has the inscription on the front. The pin is a flattened oval in section and retains part of a heavy projecting oval collar. The letters AREN of the inscription have been worn away by the friction of the point of the pin. The first letter S in IHESVS is reversed. The reverse is completely undecorated.

NOTES: [1] Thompson 1956, no 56, 19. [2] Graham Callander 1924, fig 3, no 5, 164, no 14, 170. [3] *PSAS*, vol XXV, 1891, 417.

JM

E5

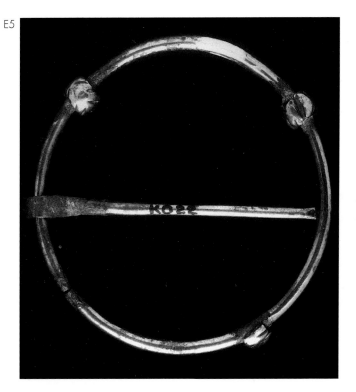

E6

E7
BRECHIN RING BROOCH
[H.KO 24]

Scotland, 13th century (hoard deposited *c* 1280-1320)[1]
Silver, niello; engraved
DIAM 43 (brooch); W 6, L 45 (pin)

CONDITION
Fair, niello mostly lost, inscription worn.

INSCRIPTION
IhESVS NA.V.OI. (front) ... IHESVS NVS (back) (debased Lombardic)
[probably for *IHESUS NAZARENUS* (twice), 'Jesus of Nazareth']

PROVENANCE
Found in a garden at Brechin, probably in 1891, with E5, E6, E8 and E9 and
coins of Edward I and II,[2] purchased by the museum in 1891.[3]

+ + + + + + + + + + + + + + +

The flat ring brooch is complete with pin. The inscriptions on front and
back with traces of niello are still visible, but are semi-literate, copied from
another object without clear understanding. The pin is a flattened oval in
section with a flattened rectangular collar, engraved with a horizontal
groove.

NOTES: [1] Thompson 1956, no 56, 19. [2] Graham Callander 1924, fig 3, no 4, 164, no
1, 169. [3] *PSAS*, vol XXV, 1891, 417.

JM

E8
BRECHIN HALF RING BROOCH
[H.KO 25]

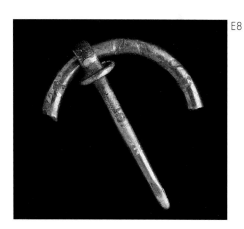

Scotland, 13th century (hoard deposited *c* 1280-1320)[1]
Silver, niello (lost); engraved
DIAM 36 (brooch); W 8, L 38 (pin)

CONDITION
Poor.

PROVENANCE
Found in a garden at Brechin, probably in 1891, with E5, E6, E7 and E9 and
coins of Edward I and II,[2] purchased by the museum in 1891.[3]

+ + + + + + + + + + + + + + +

This is the remaining half of a wire brooch with a pin. On the front of the
ring are transverse and oblique grooves. The pin is oval in section and has
a prominent collar. The reverse is completely undecorated.

NOTES: [1] Thompson 1956, no 56, 19. [2] Graham Callander 1924, no 35, 174.
[3] *PSAS*, vol XXV, 1891, 417.

JM

E9
Brechin Octagonal Brooch
[H.KO 26]

Scotland, 13th century (hoard deposited *c* 1280-1320)[1]
Silver; engraved

W 58 (brooch); W 9, L 61 (pin)

CONDITION
Excellent.

INSCRIPTION
O/I/HESV/SNAZA/VIXER (front) (debased Lombardic) [possibly for *IHESUS NAZARENUS REX*, 'Jesus of Nazareth King'] R (or B) MES IAEV MSD (?) IAN (back) (debased Lombardic) [meaning completely obscure]

PROVENANCE
Found in a garden at Brechin, probably in 1891, with E5, E6, E7 and E8 and coins of Edward I and II,[2] purchased by the museum in 1891.[3]

+ + + + + + + + + + + + + + + +

The octagonal brooch is complete with pin, the sides alternately flat and ridged. The inscription is on the flat panels of the front and back of the ring. It is largely illiterate with reversed letters S, E and H, the latter also upside down. The pin is flat and thick with chamfered corners and a flattened rectangular collar with a horizontal groove.

NOTES: [1] Thompson 1956, no 56, 19. [2] Graham Callander 1924, fig 4, no 1, 166, no 17, 171. [3] *PSAS*, vol XXV, 1891, 417.

JM

CANONBIE RING BROOCH
[H.KO 3]

Scotland, late 13th century[1] (hoard deposited *c* 1292-96)[2]
Silver; cast punched
DIAM 69 (brooch); W 6, L 51 (pin)

CONDITION
Good, except for the missing point of the pin.

PROVENANCE
Found in the course of ploughing a field at Woodhead,
Canonbie, Dumfriesshire in 1863 with D4, D5, E11, E12
and E13 and coins of Alexander III, John Balliol, Edward I
and II,[3] acquired by the museum in 1864 under Treasure
Trove arrangements.[4]

✝ ✝ ✝ ✝ ✝ ✝ ✝ ✝ ✝ ✝ ✝ ✝ ✝ ✝ ✝ ✝

The wire ring brooch is complete except for the point of
the pin. The ring has six rosettes of four large and four
small petals alternating with six tubular knops. The
knops are covered with small ring punch marks. The pin
is square in section with a prominent round collar and is
hinged in the centre of one rosette. The point of the pin
would have rested on the opposite rosette. The reverse is
completely undecorated.

NOTES: [1] Lightbown 1992, fig 75, 153, 154, dates this brooch as
early 14th century. [2] Thompson 1956, no 70, 22. [3] Graham
Callander 1924, fig 5, no 1, 167, no 26, 172. [4] *PSAS*, vol V, 1864,
pl viii, 216.

JM

CANONBIE RING BROOCH
[H.KO 4]

Scotland, late 13th century (hoard deposited *c* 1292-96)[1]
Silver, niello; engraved
DIAM 54 (brooch); W 5, L 54 (pin)

CONDITION
Good, niello mostly missing.

INSCRIPTION
+IHESVS NAZARENVS REX (Lombardic) ['Jesus of Nazareth
King']

PROVENANCE
Found in the course of ploughing a field at Woodhead,
Canonbie, Dumfriesshire in 1863 with D4, D5, E10, E12
and E13 and coins of Alexander III, John Balliol, Edward I
and II,[2] acquired by the museum in 1864 under Treasure
Trove arrangements.[3]

✝ ✝ ✝ ✝ ✝ ✝ ✝ ✝ ✝ ✝ ✝ ✝ ✝ ✝ ✝ ✝

The flat ring brooch is complete with pin and has the
inscription on the front within single marginal lines. The
lettering is crude but legible with the letters S reversed.
The pin is flattened oval in section with a rectangular
collar decorated with two horizontal grooves. The
reverse is completely plain.

NOTES: [1] Thompson 1956, no 70, 22. [2] Graham Callander 1924,
164, no 16, 171. [3] *PSAS*, vol V, 1864, pl viii, 216.

JM

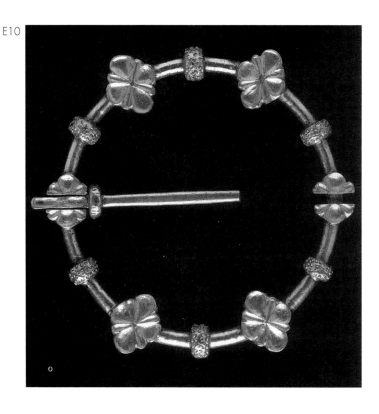

E10

E11

CANONBIE HALF RING BROOCH
[H.KO 5]

Scotland, late 13th century (hoard deposited *c* 1292-96)[1]
Silver, gilt; engraved
DIAM 49 (brooch); W 5, L 32 (pin)

CONDITION
Good, but incomplete.

PROVENANCE
Found in the course of ploughing a field at Woodhead,
Canonbie, Dumfriesshire in 1863 with D4, D5, E10, E11
and E13 and coins of Alexander III, John Balliol, Edward I
and II,[2] acquired by the museum in 1864 under Treasure
Trove arrangements.[3]

+ + + + + + + + + + + + + + + +

The surviving half of a wire ring brooch has three
remaining lozenge-shaped plates attached to the front.
The lozenges bear an engraved lattice design and traces of
gilding. The pin, which is missing its point, is a flattened
oval in section. The collar is round and is decorated with
small ring punch marks. The reverse is undecorated.

NOTES: [1] Thompson 1956, no 70, 22. [2] Graham Callander 1924,
fig 5, no 4, 167, no 32, 173. [3] *PSAS*, vol V, 1864, pl viii, 216.
JM

CANONBIE RING BROOCH FRAGMENT
[H.KO 6]

Scotland, late 13th century (hoard deposited *c* 1292-96).[1]
Silver; cast, punched
DIAM 58

CONDITION
Good, but incomplete.

PROVENANCE
Found in the course of ploughing a field at Woodhead,
Canonbie, Dumfriesshire in 1863 with D4, D5, E10, E11
and E12 and coins of Alexander III, John Balliol, Edward I
and II[2], acquired by the museum in 1864 under Treasure
Trove arrangements.[3]

+ + + + + + + + + + + + + + + +

The surviving half of a ring brooch originally with four
rosettes and four knops. Two eight-petalled rosettes and
one knop decorated with short punched lines remain.
The pin is missing, but would have hinged in the centre
of one of the rosettes. The reverse is plain.

NOTES: [1] Thompson 1956, no 70, 22. [2] Graham Callander 1924,
no 27, 172-3. [3] *PSAS*, vol V, 1864, pl viii, 216.
JM

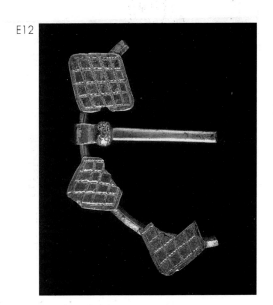
E12

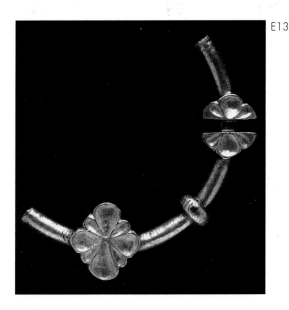
E13

CROOKSTON RING BROOCH

[H.NGA 242]

Scotland, 14th century
Silver, engraved
DIAM 56 (brooch); W 7, L 57 (pin)

CONDITION
Excellent.

INSCRIPTION
+IHESVISNA .... (front) debased Lombardic [possibly for *IHESUS NAZARENUS*, 'Jesus of Nazareth'] (back illegible)

PROVENANCE
Found in 1859 at Crookston, Midlothian, given to the museum in 1951 by Miss A B Greig.[1]

+ + + + + + + + + + + + + + + +

The flat ring brooch is complete with pin. It has an inscription on the front and back between single marginal lines, but it is virtually illiterate and copied without comprehension from another source. The pin is oval in section with a projecting oval collar which is decorated with oblique lines.

NOTE: [1] *PSAS*, vol LXXXV, 1951, 185

JM

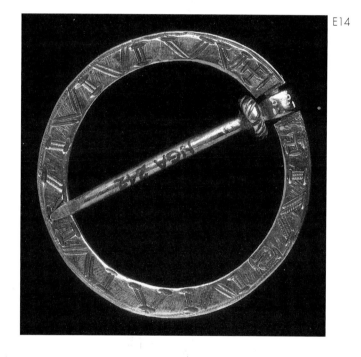

DOUNE BROOCH

[H.NGA 126]

Scotland or England, late 14th or early 15th century[1]
Gold; cast, engraved
DIAM 38, D 6

CONDITION
Excellent, almost no wear or damage, pin slightly bent.

INSCRIPTION
auri/de+moy/mercie/pite/moun/coer/en+vous/repoce
(black letter) [for *pite aura mercie de moy – moun cuer en vous repose*, 'Pity will have mercy on me, my heart reposes in you'].

PROVENANCE
Found by boys guddling for fish in the Water of Ardoch, near Doune Castle, Perthshire about 1830,[2] purchased by the museum in 1897.[3]

+ + + + + + + + + + + + + +

The heavy ring brooch with a plain hinged pin has elaborate spiral ornament alternately of rope twist and a broad engraved riband which continues across and conceals the hinge. The riband is engraved with sprays of four-petalled flowers and fernlike leaves and has a black letter inscription.

+ + + + + + + + + + + + + +

The very high quality of the workmanship entirely justifies the assertion that the brooch could have been made in France. Its lettering and the tiny flowers which punctuate it are very similar to those on a notably fine gold heart-shaped brooch in the Victoria and Albert Museum also assumed by Continental scholars to be French.[4] However, analysis of the wording of the inscription

shows that the language is certainly Insular rather than Continental. The use of 'auri' for 'aura', of 'coer' for 'cuer' and 'repoce' instead of 'repose' all indicate a Scottish or English artist.[5]

Doune Castle was built in the late 14th century by Robert Stewart, 1st duke of Albany.[6] Albany (1339-1420) was the third son of King Robert II and wielded enormous power in the later years of his ageing father's reign. Under his invalid, ineffectual brother, who took the name of Robert III on his accession in 1390, he virtually ruled Scotland. This elegant piece of jewellery indicates the lifestyle of such a courtly household. The duke had a very fine seal with a black letter inscription comparable in style and quality with E15.[7] Albany's political affiliations were such that he and his circle would have been unlikely to obtain precious items from an English source. There is no reason to suppose that E15 could not be a product of a native court goldsmith working for patrons very much in tune with French fashions of the period.

NOTES: [1] Paris 1956, no 24, 7, 'travail français du XIVe siècle'; Lightbown 1992, 154, pl 35, ascribes it to England (?) and dates it as *c* 1400. [2] Struthers 1870, 331. [3] *PSAS*, vol XXXII, 5. [4] Lightbown 1992, 408, 468, col pl 124. [5] I am indebted to Philip Bennett, School of European Languages and Cultures, University of Edinburgh, for his expert advice on these points. [6] Boardman 1996, 71-2. [7] Hutton *c* 1795, no 180.

E16   C34, 40

Dumfries Brooch
[H.KO 27]

Scotland, *c* 1300 (hoard deposited *c* 1310).[1]
Silver, niello; engraved, inlaid
DIAM 33, D 3

CONDITION
Poor, pin broken, some corrosion, most niello gone.

PROVENANCE
Found during demolition in 1878 as a mass of corroded
silver including E17, E18 and F2, in a purse in the wall of
an old house in Dumfries, with coins of Alexander III,
Edward I and Robert de Bethune, a length of chain and a
silver hook bow;[2] acquired by the museum by 1882; items
separated and conserved about 1920.[3]

+ + + + + + + + + + + + + + + +

The ring is round in section and decorated with notches
at each side containing some remnants of niello; it is
plain on the reverse. The pin is flat and tapering with a
disc collar and a loop hinge broken off.

NOTES: [1] Thompson 1956, no 139, 53. [2] *PSAS*, vol XVI, no 2,
144. [3] Graham Callander 1924, fig 1, no 2, 160-63, no 36, 174.

E17   C34, 40

Dumfries Brooch Fragment
[H.HO 28]

Scotland, *c* 1300 (hoard deposited *c* 1310)[1]
Silver, niello; engraved, inlaid
DIAM 34, D 3

CONDITION
Poor, fragment only.

PROVENANCE
Found during demolition in 1878 as a mass of corroded
silver including E16, E18 and F2, in a purse in the wall of
an old house in Dumfries, with coins of Alexander III,
Edward I and Robert de Bethune, a length of chain and a
silver hook bow;[2] acquired by the museum by 1882; items
separated and conserved about 1920.[3]

+ + + + + + + + + + + + + + +

Fragment of the ring of a brooch similar to E16.

NOTES: [1] Thompson 1956, no 139, 53. [2] *PSAS*, vol XVI, no 2,
144. [3] Graham Callander 1924, fig 1, no 3, 160-63, no 37, 174.

E18   C34, 40

Dumfries Brooch Fragment
[H.KO 29]

Scotland, *c* 1300 (hoard deposited *c* 1310).[1]
Silver, niello; engraved, inlaid
DIAM 34, D 3

CONDITION
Poor, fragment only.

PROVENANCE
Found during demolition in 1878 as a mass of corroded
silver including E16, E17 and F2, in a purse in the wall of
an old house in Dumfries, with coins of Alexander III,
Edward I and Robert de Bethune, a length of chain and a
silver hook bow;[2] acquired by the museum by 1882; items
separated and conserved about 1920.[3]

+ + + + + + + + + + + + + + +

Fragment of the ring of a brooch similar to E16.

NOTES: [1] Thompson 1956, no 139, 53. [2] *PSAS*, vol XVI, no 2,
144. [3] Graham Callander 1924, fig 1, no 4, 160-63, no 38, 174.

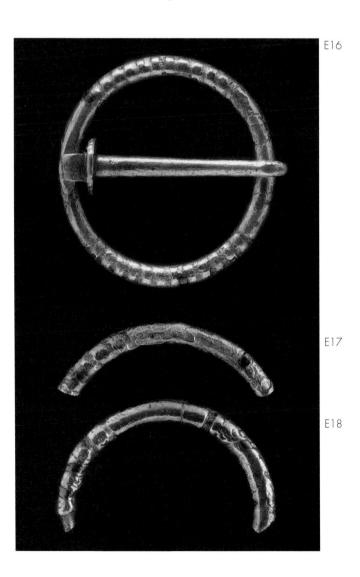

E16

E17

E18

E19
DUNFERMLINE ABBEY OCTAGONAL BROOCH
[H.NGA 24]

Scotland, 14th century
Silver, gilt; engraved
W 32 (brooch); W 6, L 32 (pin)

CONDITION
Excellent.

INSCRIPTION
ih/ESVS/NAZ/AR/E (Lombardic) (front) NVSR/EX IV/DEO/RVM (Lombardic) (back) [for IHESUS NAZARENUS REX IUDEORUM, 'Jesus of Nazareth King of the Jews']

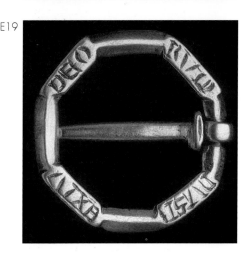

PROVENANCE
Found while excavating the tomb of Robert Bruce at Dunfermline Abbey in 1818,[1] given to the museum by D Douglas in 1849.[2]

✦ ✦ ✦ ✦ ✦ ✦ ✦ ✦ ✦ ✦ ✦ ✦ ✦ ✦ ✦ ✦

The octagonal brooch is complete, the sides alternately flat and ridged. The inscription is on the flat panels of the front and back. The pin is a flattened oval in section and has a rectangular collar with a groove on the front and back.

NOTES: [1] Graham Callander 1924, fig 4, no 4, 166, no 20, 171. [2] Wilson 1849, no 26, 92; Jardine 1822, gives a very detailed account of the excavations at Dunfermline, but does not mention this find although he refers to other material having been 'carried off at that time by some of the spectators' (page 441).

JM

E20   C40, 41
ISLAY BROOCH
[H.NGA 133]

Scotland, mid-13th century
Gold; chased, engraved
DIAM 27, D 3

CONDITION
Excellent, some wear to the inscription at the bottom of the pin.

INSCRIPTIONS
IASPER X MELD(?)HITR : ATROP/ IESVS n(?) NAZARENSVS RX (Lombardic) [for CASPAR MELCHOIR ATROPA / IHESUS NAZARENUS REX, 'Caspar Melchior Atropa Jesus of Nazareth King'] (see E21).

PROVENANCE
Said to have been found in Islay,[1] given to the museum in 1901 by Miss Sloan of Ayr.[2]

✦ ✦ ✦ ✦ ✦ ✦ ✦ ✦ ✦ ✦ ✦ ✦ ✦ ✦ ✦ ✦

A plain ring brooch with inscriptions back and front worked by leaving the lettering smooth and polished and carving into the surrounding surface, which may originally have been filled with niello or enamel. The pin is completely smooth and plain with a sharp point, simply hinged by curving its top into a loop around a notch in the ring.[3]

✦ ✦ ✦ ✦ ✦ ✦ ✦ ✦ ✦ ✦ ✦ ✦ ✦ ✦ ✦ ✦

The similarities in technique and wording of the inscriptions indicate that E20 and E21 were almost certainly made in the same workshop.

NOTES: [1] *PSAS*, vol LVIII, 268. [2] NMAS manuscript Register 1892-1914, 167-8. [3] Graham Callander 1924, 164, fig 3, no 11, 168, no 9, 170.

E21 (colour plate)   C32, 38-39
KAMES BROOCH
[H.NGA 437]

Scotland, mid-13th century[1]
Gold, pearls; cast, engraved, chased
DIAM 43, D 3

CONDITION
Excellent, apart from the missing gems.

INSCRIPTIONS
IhESVS : NAZARENVS : CRUCIFIIXVS : REX/IVDEORM : IASPER : MEL : PC hIOR : (Lombardic) A (on the ring) [for *IHESUS NAZARENUS CRUCIFIXUS REX IUDEORUM CASPAR MELCHOIR A*, 'Jesus of Nazareth crucified King of the Jews. Caspar Melchior A'] ATROPA (Lombardic) (on the pin) [for *ATROPA*]

PROVENANCE
Kept with the Bute Mazer [C2] by the MacGregors of MacGregor who inherited both from the MacLeods of Bernera, who had in turn acquired them through a marriage with the heiress of the last of the Bannatynes of Kames, on the island of Bute; bought by the museum in 1961 with assistance from the Pilgrim Trust, a special treasury grant and a contribution from the Special Purchases Fund of the Society of Antiquaries of Scotland.[2]

✝ ✝ ✝ ✝ ✝ ✝ ✝ ✝ ✝ ✝ ✝ ✝ ✝ ✝ ✝

The cast ring brooch is formed of a chain of six almost identical wyverns, each biting the back of the beast in front, while clutching it with its left claw and curling its long tail round the neck of the one behind. They have small skeletal heads with large eye sockets, only five of which retain their original gems, a spine marked by beading and scaly bodies indicated by heavy chasing. A narrow beaded border runs right round the wavy outer edge of the bodies. The plain polished pin has a rounded point and a band of beading below the top which is looped around the leg of one of the wyverns, forming a simple hinge.

The inscription is worked on the reverse of the ring by leaving the lettering smooth and polished and carving into the surrounding surface, which may originally have been filled with niello or enamel. The words are separated by pairs of small saltire crosses and a large Maltese cross marks the beginning of the inscription. A separate inscription is engraved on the back of the pin.

✝ ✝ ✝ ✝ ✝ ✝ ✝ ✝ ✝ ✝ ✝ ✝ ✝ ✝ ✝ ✝

Discussing ring brooches composed of dragons, Lightbown compares E21 with two silver examples in the British Museum which he dates to the mid-13th century and assigns to 'Northern Europe'. However, as far as the condition allows a judgement, they seem quite unlike the Kames Brooch, being chunky and asymmetrical, one made up of two dragons and one a dragon attacking a man.

The inspiration for this brooch, a unique survival in Scotland, may well have been manuscript illumination, rather than other metalwork. This kind of dragon with its pug-faced head, scaly body and a spine marked by a line of pronounced round beads was already to be seen in 12th-century English decorated books, such as a *Boethius* of *c* 1120-40 which appears to have been in Scotland

since soon after it was painted.[3] There two similar creatures with entwined tails and biting heads frame the circular lower part of an initial 'd'. The earliest known alphabet pattern book, produced in Tuscany in the mid-12th century, gives a design for a single dragon of this kind forming a comparable letter part by biting its own tail.[4]

The motif remained popular in the 13th century. A copy of Ptolemy's *Almagest* executed in Paris in 1213 has an elongated version forming the tail of a capital 'Q' and biting the main circle.[5] A serpent used in the same way on a Parisian psalter of 1235-55 is also close to those on the Kames Brooch.[6] The comparison between painting in the French capital and a piece of jewellery from Bute may not be so far fetched as it seems. Another book illuminated in Paris in the 1240s was clearly commissioned by patrons in the same area, almost certainly the Lamonts of Kilmun.[7]

After the mid-century, these dragon forms were used less and less in both English and French manuscripts, as more naturalistic and Gothic forms were adopted. Metalworkers in general tend to take up styles and devices rather later than they appear in monumental art and painting, but even allowing for that, a date closer to 1250 than 1300 seems more probable for E21. However, similar beasts entwined with foliage are carved on an *ex situ* boss at Elgin Cathedral apparently related to the rebuilding programme after the disastrous fire of 1270,[8] indicating that their period of popularity continued at least in Northern Scotland.

Caspar and Melchior were two of the three kings who brought gifts to the infant Jesus. Their shrine in Cologne was a popular place of pilgrimage. The names were believed in the medieval period to be a powerful charm against epilepsy, headache, fevers, the dangers of the road, sudden death and sorcery.[9] The combination with the name of Atropa, one of the Fates, is most unusual and thought to be peculiar to this brooch and E20, probably indicating a common origin for both in Bute or southern Argyll.

NOTES: [1] Lightbown 1992, 149, pl 30, dates the Kames Brooch to *c*1300 and describes it as English or French. [2] Stevenson 1931, 220-21; Stevenson 1962, 309, 315. [3] Thorp 1987, cat no 13, 61. [4] Alexander 1992, fig 154, 94. [5] Branner 1977, fig 24, 201. [6] Ibid, pl VII, 211. [7] Glenn 1998, 111-13. [8] Fawcett 2001, fig 68, 37. [9] Lightbown 1992, 99.

KINDROCHIT BROOCH
[H.NGA 153]

Scotland, late 15th century
Silver, gilt, translucent enamel; cast, engraved
DIAM 91, D 6

CONDITION
Fairly good, no losses apart from the enamel, gilding worn particularly on the pin.

INSCRIPTION
ami/i o/cue/ur[worn]/au/hi (black letter)
[for *ami o cueur* AU HI, 'friend of my heart' probably followed by the initials of the donor and recipient].[1]

PROVENANCE
Excavated in the pit prison, Kindrochit Castle, Braemar, Aberdeenshire during a supervised dig by Boy Scouts in 1925 and immediately presented to the museum by A H Farquharson of Invercauld.[2]

✦ ✦ ✦ ✦ ✦ ✦ ✦ ✦ ✦ ✦ ✦ ✦ ✦ ✦ ✦

The heavy ring brooch has a hinged pin and six rounded crescent-shaped lobes alternating with single cast spreading leaves, one of which forms the head of the pin. Thick spirally beaded wire runs right round the outer and inner edges of the ring and frames each of the lobes.

The lobes are engraved with long veined serrated leaves and the inscription. Originally they were covered with translucent enamel, a small bright green portion of which survives to the left of the pin. The pin bulges slightly in the middle and is engraved with an elongated lozenge-shaped leaf. The reverse of the brooch is undecorated and the whole, apart from the enamel panels, has been gilded.

✦ ✦ ✦ ✦ ✦ ✦ ✦ ✦ ✦ ✦ ✦ ✦ ✦ ✦ ✦

Lightbown again describes this brooch as English or French,[3] Graham Callander as a transitional Highland type coming between the flat 14th-century ring brooches and the elaborate 16th-century Lochbuy and Ballochyle brooches. The lettering composed of decorative ribands was widely fashionable in the late 15th and early 16th centuries. A rather more severe black letter inscription is engraved on the reverse of the Glenlyon Brooch in the British Museum, arranged in a strikingly similar manner in nine lobed shapes on the plain ring. Its Scottish origins have never been questioned, although Lightbown has redated it to the late 14th century as opposed to Evans' '? *c*1500'.[4]

NOTES: [1] Graham Callander 1926, 118, suggests it had talismanic or magical significance. It actually seems to be a courtly loving message, perhaps to mark a betrothal or marriage. I am indebted to Philip Bennett, School of European Languages and Culture, University of Edinburgh for confirming this conclusion. [2] Ibid, 118. [3] Lightbown 1992, 149, pl 31. [4] Evans 1953, 60, pl 14.

E22

E23

C33, 39-40

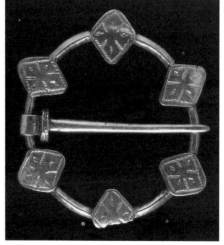

E23

LANGHOPE RING BROOCH
[H.KO 10]

Scotland, 14th century (hoard deposited 14th century)[1]
Silver, gilt; engraved
DIAM 42, D 3

CONDITION
Good, part of one of the lozenges missing.

PROVENANCE
Found at Langhope, Roxburghshire in 1882, in a brass tripod pot with a
hoard of objects including E24 and coins of Alexander I, II and III,[2] acquired
by the museum in 1892 under Treasure Trove arrangements.[3]

✛ ✛ ✛ ✛ ✛ ✛ ✛ ✛ ✛ ✛ ✛ ✛ ✛ ✛ ✛ ✛

The wire brooch is complete with pin and six lozenge-shaped plates
attached to the front of the ring. The lozenges are decorated with four long
and four intermediate short lines radiating from the centre and bear traces
of gilding. The pin, which is oval in section, has a projecting oval collar.
The reverse is undecorated.

NOTES: [1] Thompson 1956, no 229, 82. [2] Graham Callander 1924, fig 5, no 3, 167,
no 33, 174. [3] *PSAS*, vol XVI, 1881, 144.

Langhope Ring Brooch
[H.KO 13]

Scotland, early 14th century (hoard deposited 14th century)[1]
Silver, gilt; engraved, cast, punched
DIAM 56, D 4

CONDITION
Fair, part of one rosette broken off, gilding mostly gone.

PROVENANCE
Found at Langhope, Roxburghshire in 1882, in a brass tripod pot with a hoard of objects including E23 and coins of Alexander I, II and III,[2] acquired by the museum in 1892 under Treasure Trove arrangements.[3]

The wire ring brooch is complete with pin, four elongated rosettes and four depressed spherical knops. The rosettes have eight petals and three small ring punch marks in the centre. The knops are covered in similar markings. Both show traces of gilding. The pin is almost circular in section and has a heavy collar which is hidden by one of the rosettes attached to the head. The reverse is undecorated.

NOTES: [1] Thompson 1956, no 229, 82. [2] Graham Callander 1924, fig 5, no 2, 167, no 28, 173. [3] *PSAS*, vol XVI, 1881, 144.

JM

Middlebie Church Ring Brooch
[H.KO 16]

Scotland, 14th century
Silver; engraved
DIAM 47 (brooch); W 5, L 31 (pin)

CONDITION
Good.

INSCRIPTION
+IhESVS:NAZARENVS:REX IVDE (Lombardic) [for *IHESUS NAZARENUS REX IUDEORUM*, 'Jesus of Nazareth King of the Jews']

PROVENANCE
Found at Middlebie Church, Dumfriesshire, with E26 and E27[1] given to the museum in 1851 by the Rev. A E Macdonald Dawson.[2]

The flat ring brooch is complete with pin and has the inscription on the front. The half-length pin is a flat oval in section and has a projecting rectangular collar, with a horizontal medial groove between notched ridges. The front of the collar is decorated with small ring punch marks. The reverse is undecorated.

NOTES: [1] Graham Callander 1924, fig 3, no 6, 164, no 15, 170-71. [2] *PSAS*, vol I, 1854, 25-6.

JM

E24

E25

E26
MIDDLEBIE CHURCH RING BROOCH
[H.KO 17]

Scotland, 14th century
Silver; drawn, cast
DIAM 50 (brooch); W 8, L 38 (pin)

CONDITION
Good, one break in the ring.

PROVENANCE
Found at Middlebie Church, Dumfriesshire, with E25 and
E27,[1] given to the museum in 1851 by the Rev. A E
Macdonald Dawson.[2]

✛ ✛ ✛ ✛ ✛ ✛ ✛ ✛ ✛ ✛ ✛ ✛ ✛ ✛ ✛ ✛

The wire brooch is complete with pin. The ring is square
in section and decorated on each of the four sides with a
narrow longitudinal zigzag. One half of the ring is twisted
to produce spiral fluting. The pin is round in section with
a circular projecting collar.

NOTES: [1] Graham Callander 1924, fig 5, no 5, 167, no 40, 175.
[2] *PSAS*, vol I, 1854, 25-6.
                                                            JM

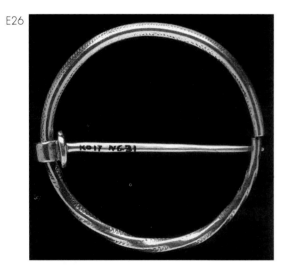
E26

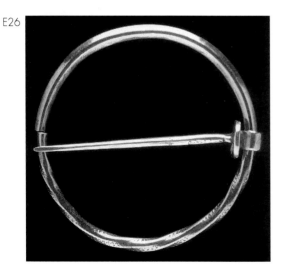
E26

E27
MIDDLEBIE CHURCH RING BROOCH
[H.KO 18]

Scotland, 14th century
Silver, gilt ; drawn, cast
DIAM 43 (brooch); W 8, L 46 (pin)

CONDITION
Good.

PROVENANCE
Found at Middlebie Church, Dumfriesshire, with E25 and
E26,[1] given to the museum in 1851 by the Rev. A E
Macdonald Dawson.[2]

✛ ✛ ✛ ✛ ✛ ✛ ✛ ✛ ✛ ✛ ✛ ✛ ✛ ✛ ✛ ✛

The wire brooch is complete with pin. The ring has four
eight-petalled rosettes and four round knops, the latter
are decorated with small punch marks and show traces of
gilding. The pin is circular in section and the projecting
collar is round and decorated with small ring punch
marks. One of the rosettes is attached to the front of the
pin. The reverse is undecorated.

NOTES: [1] Graham Callander 1924, no 29, 173.   [2] *PSAS*, vol I,
1854, 25-6.
                                                            JM

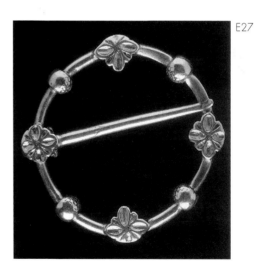
E27

MULL BROOCH

[H.NGA 116]

Scotland, mid-15th century
Silver, niello; hammered, engraved, inlaid
W 86 (max) 77 (min), D 1

CONDITION
Fair, considerable wear to the niello and engraving on the lower part of the
obverse, more extensive rubbing on the reverse where the engraving of the
lower part is almost erased, the tip of the pin is missing.

INSCRIPTION
an/an/ihcn/ihcn/ihcn (black letter) [for *ananizapta . ihesus christus nazarenus*
(thrice), 'ananizapta. Jesus Christ of Nazareth'].

PROVENANCE
Found at Kengharair Farm, Kilmore on Mull about 1833, purchased by the
museum in 1894.[1]

✚ ✚ ✚ ✚ ✚ ✚ ✚ ✚ ✚ ✚ ✚ ✚ ✚ ✚ ✚ ✚ ✚

The ring brooch is cut from silver sheet, a circle on the inner circumference, an octagon with concave sides on the outer edge. The engraved
decoration on obverse and reverse is divided into eight panels.

On the front, four sections of an elegant even inscription against a
dotted niello ground alternate with decorative engraving. This comprises
two kite shapes with cross-hatched and zigzag borders each divided into
four with a central dot and four diagonal crosses, divided by an elongated
reversed S; a trailing plant with pointed and round leaves; two four-

E28

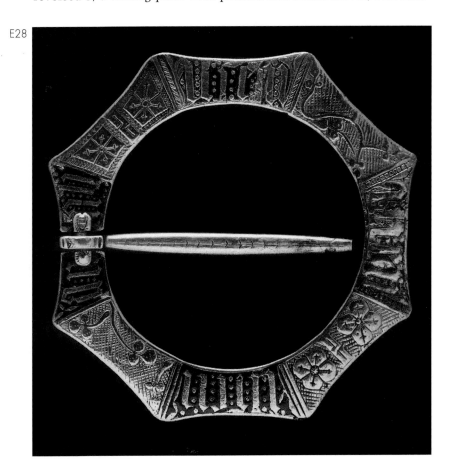

petalled flower heads with a central dot and four diagonal long veins, separated by an elongated reversed s; three trailing plant sprays with trefoil leaves; the three latter on hatched grounds.

On the reverse are engraved four panels of grotesque beasts with diagonally hatched borders against a niello ground alternating with more abstract engraving. This comprises two sections of four-petalled flowers as on the front; two sections with eight lozenges each with a central cross, arranged in two horizontal rows, against a hatched ground. The beasts in two cases have human heads looking forwards, in two cases reptilian heads with long tongues turned backwards. All have crouching bodies with long hind legs and tails which terminate in three large triangular leaves with serrated edges.

The pin is a flattened oval, a single line with short V-shaped branches engraved down the centre back and front. Its oval head is notched at the edge. The central loop hinges on two separate round tabs rivetted to the ring at back and front, bridging the gap cut to make way for the pin head.

✚ ✚ ✚ ✚ ✚ ✚ ✚ ✚ ✚ ✚ ✚ ✚ ✚ ✚ ✚ ✚

'Ananizapta' was a well known medieval charm against falling sickness and sudden or violent death.[2]

NOTES: [1] Duns 1883, 76-7, figs 1, 2; Graham Callander 1926, 121-2, fig 14; NMAS typescript Continuation Catalogue, brooches, 1892 onwards. [2] Lightbown 1992, 99, the initials stand for *antidotum Nazareni auferat necem intoxicationis sanctificet alimenta pocula trinitas alma*, 'may the antidote of Jesus avert death by poisoning and the Holy Trinity sanctify my food and drink'.

E28

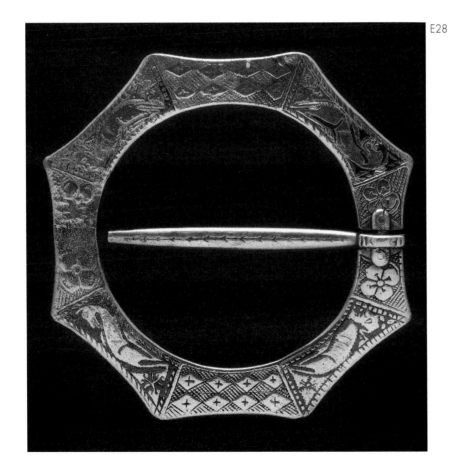

E29
ADVOCATES' OCTAGONAL BROOCH
[H.NGA 20]

Scotland, 14th century
Silver; engraved
W 33

CONDITION
Excellent, apart from missing pin.

INSCRIPTION
Letter forms are attempted, but indecipherable.

PROVENANCE
Purchased from the Advocates' Collection, presumably in 1873.[1]

✦ ✦ ✦ ✦ ✦ ✦ ✦ ✦ ✦ ✦ ✦ ✦ ✦ ✦ ✦ ✦

The octagonal brooch has alternately flat and ridged sides. The flat panels on the front bear illegible lettering while those on the back are engraved with three tablet flowers.[2]

NOTES: [1] Society of Antiquaries of Scotland *Minute Books* 1872-73 record the negotiations connected with the purchase, but do not itemise the collection. See also J3 and K6. [2] Graham Callander 1924, 166, no 19, 171.

JM

E30
ADVOCATES' RING BROOCH
[H.NGA 19]

Scotland, 14th century
Silver; engraved
DIAM 27

CONDITION
Fair, the pin and part of the ring are missing, the ring is also damaged at the hinge.

INSCRIPTION
A + G + L + A (Lombardic) (anti-clockwise) [for *ATHA GEBRI LEILAN ADONAI*, 'Thou art mighty for ever, O Lord'].[1]

PROVENANCE
Purchased from the Advocates' Collection presumably in 1873.[2]

✦ ✦ ✦ ✦ ✦ ✦ ✦ ✦ ✦ ✦ ✦ ✦ ✦ ✦ ✦ ✦

The flat ring brooch has the inscription on the front. On the back, the outer and inner edges have a rope twist moulding.[3]

NOTES: [1] Lightbown 1992, 99. [2] See E29, note 1. [3] Graham Callander 1924, no 7, 169.

JM

E29

E29

E30

E30
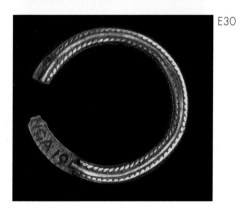

E31
ADVOCATES' RING BROOCH
[H.NGA 18]

Scotland, 14th century
Silver; engraved
DIAM 29 (brooch); W 5, L 30 (pin)

CONDITION
Excellent.

INSCRIPTION
IESVS NAZA (debased Lombardic) [for *IESUS NAZARENUS*, 'Jesus of Nazareth']

PROVENANCE
Purchased from the Advocates' Collection, presumably in 1873.[1]

✛ ✛ ✛ ✛ ✛ ✛ ✛ ✛ ✛ ✛ ✛ ✛ ✛ ✛ ✛

The flat ring brooch is complete with pin. The inscription is on the front between single marginal lines. The pin is a flattened oval in section, with the collar projecting slightly in front and at the sides. The reverse is undecorated.[2]

NOTES: [1] See E29, note 1. [2] Graham Callander 1924, 164, no 5, 169.

JM

E32
RICHARDSON OCTAGONAL BROOCH
[H.NGA 424]

Scotland, 14th century
Silver, niello; engraved
W 43, L 50 (brooch); W 2, L 53 (pin)

CONDITION
Excellent.

INSCRIPTION
+/IHES/VSN/AZA/R (Lombardic) [FOR *IHESUS NAZARENUS*, 'Jesus of Nazareth']

PROVENANCE
Bequeathed to the museum by Dr J S Richardson in 1970 as part of a large collection of varied medieval and later material.[1]

✛ ✛ ✛ ✛ ✛ ✛ ✛ ✛ ✛ ✛ ✛ ✛ ✛ ✛ ✛

The elongated octagonal brooch is complete with pin, the sides alternately flat and ridged. The inscription is engraved on the flat panels on the front of the brooch. The flat panels on the back of the brooch have foliage decoration. The pin is circular in section with a pincer loop.

✛ ✛ ✛ ✛ ✛ ✛ ✛ ✛ ✛ ✛ ✛ ✛ ✛ ✛ ✛

James Smith Richardson (1883-1970) trained as an architect and was appointed the first (part-time) Inspector of Ancient Monuments in Scotland in 1914. During his long and energetic career he brought many of the most important Scottish medieval monuments into public care and ownership. From 1925 until 1954 he was an honorary curator of the collection of the Society of Antiquaries of Scotland and thereafter a trustee of NMAS. Many objects were acquired under his guidance, others were presented by him and a large bequest from his personal collection came to the museum after his death.[2]

NOTES: [1] *PSAS*, vol 103, 1970, 245. [2] *PSAS*, vol 102, 1969, vii-x.

JM

E31

E32

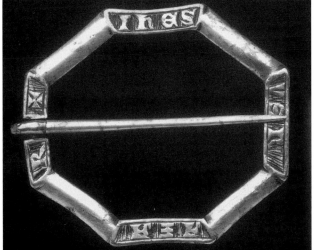

E32

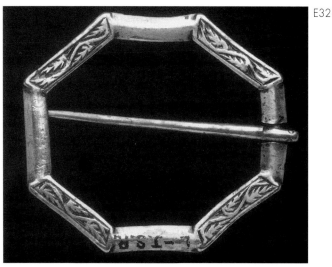

E33
Scott Ring Brooch
[H.NGA 22]

Scotland, 14th century
Silver; engraved
DIAM 57 (brooch); W 5, L 58 (pin)

CONDITION
Excellent.

INSCRIPTION
+IHESVS MAZAREMVS REX : NAZAE+ (debased Lombardic) [for *IHESUS NAZARENUS REX*, 'Jesus of Nazareth King']

PROVENANCE
Given to the museum by Mrs Scott of Edinburgh in 1872.[1]

❖ + + + + + + + + + + + + + + +

The flat ring brooch is complete with pin. The inscription on the front is bordered by single beaded marginal lines. The back is ornamented with reversed triangles alternately plain and hatched transversely. The pin, which is rectangular in section with a rectangular collar, is decorated on the front with similar triangles.[2]

NOTES: [1] *PSAS*, vol IX, 1872, 535-7. [2] Graham Callander 1924, 164, no 2, 169.

JM

E34
Whitelaw Ring Brooch
[H.NGA 183]

Scotland, 15th century
Gold; engraved
DIAM 57 (brooch); W 5, L 58 (pin)

CONDITION
Excellent.

INSCRIPTION
AVE MARIA PLENA D (Lombardic) (front) [for *AVE MARIA GRACIA PLENA*, 'Hail Mary full of grace'] +OM INVS TECVM* (Lombardic) (back) [for *DOMINUS TECUM*, 'The Lord be with you']

PROVENANCE
Bought in Glasgow, bequeathed to the museum by Charles Whitelaw in 1940.[1]

+ + + + + + + + + + + + + + +

The flat ring brooch is complete with pin. The ring is wedge-shaped in section. The first part of the inscription up to and including the letter D is on the front and the remainder on the back. The pin has no collar.

+ + + + + + + + + + + + + + +

Charles Whitelaw, a Glasgow businessman, was already taking an active interest in the museum by 1911, having previously made a loan on most generous terms to enable it to buy two 8th-century brooches. A large part of his collection of Scottish weapons and accessories on which he published major record contributions, was deposited with NMAS in 1929.[2]

NOTES: [1] Graham Callander 1924, no 13, 170; *PSAS*, vol LXXIV, 1940, 150. [2] Bell 1981, 174, 181, 195.

JM

E34

E34

E35
WHITELAW OCTAGONAL BROOCH
[H.NGA 182]

Scotland, 14th century
Silver; engraved
DIAM 48 (brooch); W 6, L 41 (pin)

CONDITION
Excellent.

INSCRIPTION
+/IhES/VSNA/ZARE/+ (front) NVS/RES/IXDI/EN + (debased Lombardic)(back) [for *IHESUS NAZARENUS REX IUDEORUM*, 'Jesus of Nazareth King of the Jews']

PROVENANCE
Bequeathed to the museum by Charles Whitelaw in 1940.[1]

+ + + + + + + + + + + + + + +

The octagonal brooch is complete with pin, the sides alternately flat and ridged. The inscription is on the flat panels on both the front and the back of the brooch. The ridged panels are blank. The pin is a flattened oval in section with a collar.

NOTE: [1] *PSAS*, vol LXXIV, 1940, 150. See E34.

JM

E35

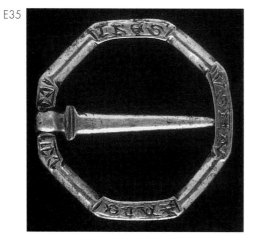

E35

 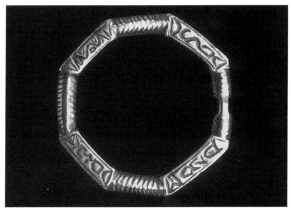

E36
UNPROVENANCED OCTAGONAL BROOCH
[H.NGA. 25]

Scotland, 14th century
Silver; engraved
W 47

CONDITION
Good, pin missing.

INSCRIPTION
Unintelligible.

PROVENANCE
Unknown.[1]

+ + + + + + + + + + + + + + + +

The octagonal brooch has alternately flat and ridged panels, back and front. It is engraved on the flat areas with curved lines which may form the letters D and C, but the inscription is virtually illiterate, probably copied without understanding from another object. The ridged panels are decorated with oblique lines meeting at the crest.

NOTE: [1] Graham Callander 1924, 166, no 22, 172.

JM

E37
UNPROVENANCED RING BROOCH
[H.NGA.26]

Scotland, early 14th century
Silver, hammered, engraved
DIAM 57, D 2 (brooch); W 9, L 67 (pin)

CONDITION
Good, ring slightly bent and broken (?) where it is held by the pin.

INSCRIPTIONS
+AVEMARIAGRACIALEMAPIVORA+ (Lombardic) (front) +IhESVSNAZARENVSREXIVDEORVN : A (Lombardic) (back) [for *AVE MARIA GRACIA PLENA PIU ORA/ IHESUS NAZARENUS REX IUDEORUM : A*, 'Hail Mary full of grace pray for us / Jesus of Nazareth King of the Jews']

PROVENANCE
Unknown.[1]

+ + + + + + + + + + + + + + + +

The flat ring brooch has a plain line border at each edge and an irregular crudely engraved inscription. The flattened, blunt ended pin has a thinner spear-shaped point and widens into an oval top with notched edges. The central hole takes the ring, which is waisted at this juncture, with a split reaching to the head of the pin.

NOTE: [1] Graham Callander 1924, no 3, 169.

JM

COMPOSITIONAL ANALYSIS OF SELECTED SCOTTISH BROOCHES

Katherine Eremin and Jim Tate

Twenty-eight late 13th- to 15th-century Scottish brooches were analysed to determine the alloy composition and the decorative techniques employed. The brooches had previously been divided into four types stylistically, shown in Table 1. The likely dates are shown in Table 2.

All brooches were analysed using non-destructive energy dispersive x-ray fluorescence (XRF), with several analyses from each artefact. Full results and analytical details are given in Eremin 2000c.[1] The surface compositions may, however, differ from those of the original alloys, as silver is often enriched in archaeological or historical silver artefacts. Surface enrichments of silver of up to 4% have been found in fairly pure silver (silver over 90%) and of up to 10% in more debased silver but surface enrichment was found to have little

Table 1: Types of Scottish brooch analysed

Type/Description	Brooch Number	
Type 1: Flat ring brooches, ring of rectangular section	H.NGA 18[E31]	H.NGA 19 [E30]
	H.NGA 22 [E33]	H.NGA 23 [E1]
	H.NGA 183 [E34]	H.NGA 242 [E14]
	H.KO 4 [E11]	H.KO16 [E25]
	H.KO19 [E2]	H.KO23 [E6]
	H.KO24 [E7]	
Type 2: Octagonal brooches, sides flat and ridged	H.NGA 20 [E29]	H.NGA 21 [E4]
	H.NGA 24 [E19]	H.NGA 182 [E35]
	H.NGA 424 [E32]	H.KO 20, 26 [E3,E9]
Type 3(a): Wire ring brooch with rosettes and knops on ring	H.NH 2 [fig 18, page 45]	
	H.KO 3 [E10]	H.KO 6 [E13]
	H.KO 13 [E24]	H.KO 18 [E27]
	H.KO 22 [E5]	
Type 3(b): Wire ring brooch with lozenge-shaped plates attached to front of ring	H.KO 5 [E12]	H.KO 10 [E23]
Type 4: Wire ring brooch	H.KO 17 [E26]	H.KO 25 [E8]

Table 2: Dates of analysed brooches

Date of Brooch		
15th century	H.NGA 183 [E34]	
14th century	H.NGA 18 [E31]	H.NGA 19 [E30]
	H.NGA 20 [E29]	H.NGA 21 [E4]
	H.NGA 22 [E33]	H.NGA 23 [E1]
	H.NGA 182 [E35]	H.NGA 424 [E32]
	H.KO 10 [E23]	H.KO 13 [E24]
	H.KO 16 [E25]	H.KO 17 [E26]
	H.KO 18 [E27]	
13th century (2nd half)	H.KO 3 [E10]	H.KO 4 [E11]
	H.KO 5 [E12]	H.KO 6 [E13]
	H.KO 19 [E2]	H.KO 20 [E3]
	H.KO 23 [E6]	H.KO 24 [E7]
	H.KO 25 [E8]	H.KO 26 [E9]
13th century (mid)	H.KO 22 [E5]	

effect on the minor or trace elements.[2] Ten of these Scottish brooches had no decoration on the back and were abraded and re-analysed to assess the extent of surface alteration.

Analysis of the surface indicated that most brooches had high levels of silver, with minor copper, minor to trace lead, and trace gold. The exceptions were brooches NGA 182 and NGA 183, the former being debased silver and the latter gold. These are discussed separately.

The surface composition of the brooches ranged from 81-98% silver and 2-16% copper, with up to 4% lead and trace gold (generally less than 1%). Comparison of analyses before and after abrasion showed an increase in copper and decrease in silver in all brooches. The surface silver enrichment varied from below 1% to 9%, showing that this can have a significant but unpredictable effect on the composition. There was less variation in trace elements, although some brooches showed a slight decrease in the gold to silver ratio and a slight change (both increases and decreases occurred) in the lead to silver ratio.

The highest silver levels occurred in brooches H.KO 10 and H.KO 19 after abrasion, with 15% and 16% respectively. The variable surface enrichment makes comparison of compositions difficult for brooches where abrasion was not possible. Variations in original copper content reflect variations in the extent of alloying with the cheaper metal, either for economy or to achieve materials with different working or decorative properties. The composition of brooches for which abrasion was possible are given in Table 3. The results indicate considerable variation in composition between brooches in a single stylistic group. Several brooches show a difference in copper to silver ratios for the loop and pin. In most cases, however, this could be due to the effects of differential surface alteration as pins were not abraded rather than an original feature.

Table 3: Levels below 0.5% are given as tr. and levels below the detection limit are given as nd.

Type	Brooch	Abrasion	Copper	Gold	Lead	Silver
1	H.NGA 18 [E31]	Before	5.9	tr.	1.6	92.0
		After	6.4	tr.	1.6	91.6
1	H.KO 19 [E2]	Before	6.9	tr.	1.4	90.9
		After	16.0	tr.	1.7	81.6
1	H.KO 23 [E6]	Before	4.3	tr.	2.3	91.5
		After	5.9	tr.	2.3	90.2
3a	H.NH 2 [fig 18]	Before	3.3	1.4	tr	95.0
		After	4.1	1.2	tr	94.0
3a	H.KO 3 [E10]	Before	4.3	tr.	1.7	93.2
		After	6.9	tr.	1.7	90.7
3a	H.KO 6 [E13]	Before	4.9	tr.	2.0	91.9
		After	6.8	tr.	1.6	89.9
3a	H.KO 22 [E5]	Before	4.3	tr.	1.6	93.6
		After	4.7	tr.	1.7	92.0
3b	H.KO 5 [E12]	Before	3.4	0.6	1.5	94.3
		After	4.2	tr.	1.8	92.3
3b	H.KO 10 [E23]	Before	10.3	tr.	1.9	87.2
		After	14.5	tr.	1.5	82.5
4	H.KO 25 [E8]	Before	3.1	tr.	2.7	93.2
		After	3.0	tr.	1.1	94.4

Medieval silver was often obtained from cupellation of lead ores[3] and Medieval craftsmen would have considered all the gold, silver and lead remaining as 'silver'.[4] However lead could also be added as a debasing element or to alter the working properties, making the alloy more fluid. The gold in the initial ore survives the cupellation process[5] and the ratio of gold per 100 parts silver hence provides an indicator of silver sources.[6, 7] Original lead and bismuth in the silver ore are not normally removed below 0.5% by processing, whereas original copper, tin and zinc are removed to very low levels.[8] None of the brooches analysed had significant bismuth, suggesting this was absent from the original ores. The lead content of the brooches varies from below the detection limit to around 4%. Levels above 1% can generally be taken as deliberate additions whilst levels below 0.5% suggest a lack of lead in the originals ores. All brooches in groups 1 and 3b had lead levels above 1%, whilst lead levels of brooches in the other groups ranged from below the detection limit to 4%.

The gold per 100 parts silver showed considerable variation for the brooches, ranging from 0.01 to 1.5 with significant variation within stylistic groups and between brooches with similar dates. The range of values suggests use of several silver sources and indicates that the silver stock had not been homogenised by frequent remelting. Some analyses of 14th-century Scottish coins indicate gold in silver levels of 0.1 to 0.3 for Robert I pennies (c1320-29), 0.2 to 0.4 for David II pennies (1351-57) and 0.3 to 0.5 for Robert III groats (1390-1400). There is hence a suggestion of an increase in the maximum gold contents with date, possibly due to introduction of a more gold-rich silver source or maybe from the re-melting of gilded material. Some of the brooches have gold in silver contents similar to the coins, but others have significantly higher or lower values.

There are few published studies of comparative material. Studies of Viking age Scottish and English silver showed most had over 90% silver with a range of gold in silver, indicating a variety of sources.[9, 10] The other trace elements were also varied with significant lead, zinc and/or tin in some artefacts, again suggesting there was no single silver source.[11, 12]

Several brooches have a black niello decoration as patchy inlay within engraved areas. These areas were analysed using XRF, scanning electron microscopy (SEM) and x-ray diffraction (XRD). The combined data suggests use of:

silver sulphide only – HKO 04, NGA 23, NGA 424

silver sulphide and lead sulphide – HKO 20

silver-copper sulphide and lead sulphide – NGA 21

An unidentified black material occurs on Brooch NGA 19.

Previous studies found silver sulphide for Roman and Byzantine niello, mixed copper-silver sulphide and silver sulphide for Anglo Saxon niello and copper-silver sulphide alone or combined with silver sulphide or lead sulphide for Medieval niello.[13, 14, 15]

Six brooches have decorative motifs attached to the loops: flat diamonds on HKO 10, flat diamonds and balls/rings on HKO 03, 'flowers' and balls/rings on NH 2 and HKO 18, balls on HKO 22 and ball/ring and 'flowers' on HKO 06. The balls/rings on HKO 03, HKO 06, HKO 18, HKO 22 and NGA 2 were formed by bending a small ring around the loop and attaching this with solder. The decorative features on HKO 22 and NGA 2 were attached with a grey solder whilst the decorative features on the other brooches were attached with a silvery solder which shows signs of smoothing. The grey solder has high levels of tin and traces of zinc and antimony, indicating use of tin-rich solder. In contrast, the silvery solder has high levels of silver with minor copper, lead and tin. The decorative features of brooches NH 2, HKO 05, HKO 10 and HKO 18 and decorated areas of brooch NGA 24 have high levels of mercury and gold, indicating use of amalgam gilding.

Brooch NGA 182 was composed of a debased silver alloy with a surface composition of around 71% silver, 2% lead and 26% copper. The pin has a higher copper content (34%) and hence a lower silver content (61%) but similar lead (3%). Both contain traces of gold and antimony. The difference in copper to silver ratios may be due to differential surface alteration or to deliberate use of different alloys.

Brooch NGA 183 has a golden appearance and is composed of a debased gold alloy with a surface composition of around 66% gold, 27% silver and 7% copper. There was no significant difference in the composition of the pin and loop.

NOTES: [1] Eremin 2000c, 8-10. [2] Kruse and Tate 1992, 298. [3] Hughes and Hall 1979, 323-4. [4] Metcalf and Northover 1986, 36. [5] McKerrell and Stevenson 1972, 197-8. [6] Metcalf and Northover 1985, 166-8. [7] Cowell and Lowick 1988, 70. [8] McKerrell and Stevenson 1972, 197-8. [9] Kruse and Tate 1992, 299. [10] P Wilthew 1995, 64-5. [11] Kruse and Tate 1992, 323-4. [12] P Wilthew 1995, 65. [13] Oddy, Bimson and La Niece 1983. [14] La Niece and Stapleton 1993. [15] La Niece 1983, 287.

BIBLIOGRAPHY:
EREMIN, K 2000c, Analysis of some 14th century Scottish brooches, Internal C&AR report, AR 00/42.

KRUSE, S E and TATE, J 1992, 'XRF analysis of Viking Age silver ingots', *Proceedings of the Society of Antiquaries of Scotland*, 122, 295-328.

HUGHES M J and HALL, J A 1979, 'X-ray fluorescence analysis of late Roman and Sassanian silver plate' *Journal of Archaeological Sciences*, 6, 321-344.

METCALF D M and NORTHOVER, J P 1986, 'Interpreting the alloy of the later Anglo-Saxon coinage', *British Numismatic Journal*, 56, 35-63.

McKERRELL, H and STEVENSON, R B K 1972, 'Some analyses of Anglo-Saxon and associated Oriental coinage' in D T Hall and D M Metcalf (eds) *Methods of Chemical and Metallurgical Investigation of Ancient Coinage*, London, 195-209.

METCALF, D M and NORTHOVER, J P 1985, 'Debasement in the coinage of southern England in the reign of King Alfred', *Numismatic Chronicle*, 145, 150-176.

COWELL, M R and LOWICK, N M 1988, 'Silver mines from the Panjhir mines' in W A Oddy (ed) *Metallurgy in Numismatics*, 2, London.

WILTHEW, P 1995, 'Appendix 1: Notes on the composition of Viking-age silver brooches, arm- and neck-rings from the Skaill (Orkney) hoard' in *The Viking-Age gold and silver of Scotland (AD 850-1100)*, J Graham-Campbell, National Museums of Scotland, Edinburgh, 63-72.

ODDY, W A, BIMSON, M and LA NIECE, S 1983, 'The composition of niello decoration on gold, silver and bronze in the antique and medieval periods', *Studies in Conservation*, 28: 29-35.

LA NIECE, S and STAPLETON, C 1993, 'Niello and Enamel on Irish Metalwork', *The Antiquaries Journal* 73 148-151.

LA NIECE, S 1983, 'Niello: an historical and technical survey', *Antiquaries Journal* 63, 270-297.

PENDANTS

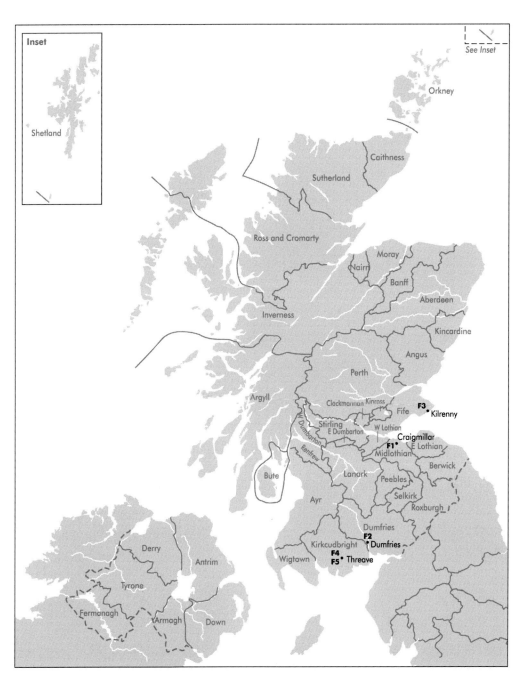

The provenance of F6 is unknown.

CRAIGMILLAR CRUCIFIX
[H.KE 16]

Scotland, 15th century
Silver; cast
H 60, W 48, D 5 (silver crucifix); H 77, W 58, D 6
(ebony); DIAM 6 (ring)

CONDITION
Fairly corroded, top of cross broken off.

PROVENANCE
Craigmillar Castle, Edinburgh (?),[1] presented to the
museum in 1960 by Miss C A Hamilton Bruce.[2]

✝ ✝ ✝ ✝ ✝ ✝ ✝ ✝ ✝ ✝ ✝ ✝ ✝ ✝ ✝ ✝

The small figure of Christ on the cross is crudely cast.
He wears the crown of thorns and a short pleated perizoma, held at the waist by a folded cummerbund with a
knot of three loops at his right hand side. His up-
stretched arms are at an angle of about 45 degrees, his
head slightly inclined to his right. The legs are widely
bowed and crossed at the ankles, where they are held
by a single nail. The crossbar of the crucifix has prominent fleur-de-lis terminals. A large inverted leaf shape
with channels radiating downwards from the centre top
supports Christ's feet.

The whole is attached by three pins to a 19th-
century plain ebony cross with a silver suspension ring
at the top.

NOTES: [1] A 19th-century silver plaque on the reverse of the ebony
cross reads 'Crucifix belonging to / Queen Mary of Scotland / found
in Craig Miller Castle'. [2] *PSAS*, vol XCIV, 1963, 328.

F1

DUMFRIES PENDANT CROSS
[H.KO 31]
Scotland, late 13th century (hoard deposited *c*1310)[1]
Silver, niello; cast, engraved
H 38, W 35, D 6

CONDITION
Fair, some corrosion, some niello missing.

INSCRIPTION
A G L A (Lombardic) (anti-clockwise) [for *ATHA GEBRI LEILAN ADONAI*, 'Thou art mighty for ever, O Lord'].[2]

PROVENANCE
Found during demolition in 1878 as a mass of corroded silver including E16, E17 and E18, in a purse in the wall of an old house in Dumfries, with coins of Alexander III, Edward I and Robert de Bethune, a length of chain and a silver hook bow;[3] acquired by the museum by 1882; items separated and conserved about 1920.[4]

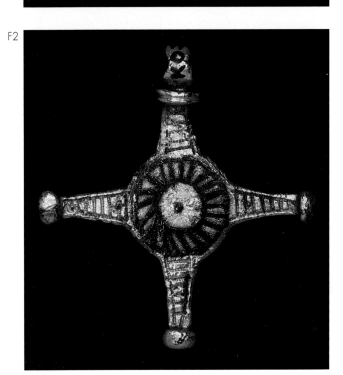

+ + + + + + + + + + + + + + +

The square cross has four short tapering arms, the top arm with a round collar and a suspension ring, the other three terminating in spherical knops. A single engraved line frames the central disc and the arms front and back. The disc is engraved with the reversed inscription on one side and radiating short lines on the other. The arms are decorated with parallel transverse lines. All the engraving was probably originally filled with niello.

NOTES: [1] Thompson 1956, no 139, 53. [2] Lightbown 1992, 99. [3] *PSAS*, vol XVI, no 2, 144. [4] Graham Callander 1924, fig 1, no 1, 160-63.

F3 (colour plate)
KILRENNY RELIQUARY PENDANT
[H.KE 10]

Scotland, late 15th century
Silver, gilt, glass; cast, engraved, raised
H 125, W 53, D 38

CONDITION
Good, some wear to the gilding

PROVENANCE
Donated by Robert Carfrae, curator of the museum in 1890, said to have come from Kilrenny in Fife.[1]

+ + + + + + + + + + + + + + +

The pendant is in two parts joined by a long silver strap at the back and hangs from a separate ring with fine rope twist decoration. Below a small thick suspension loop there are three cast domed elements with perfor-

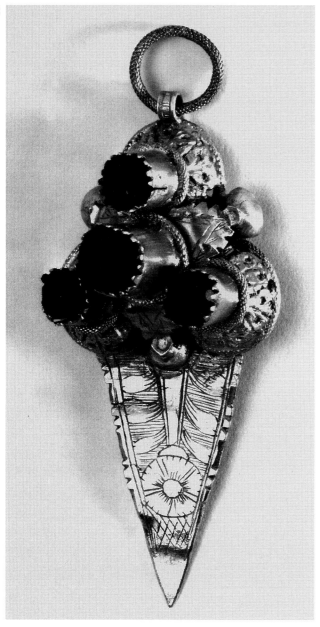

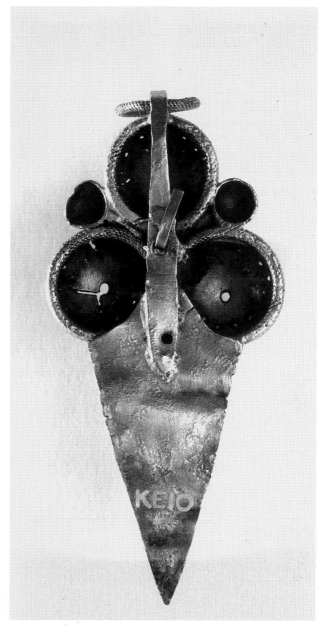

ated leaf decoration, framed at top and bottom with twisted wire matching the suspension ring. Between each dome is a smaller plain hemisphere and three engraved jagged triangular leaf shapes curve from the centre to rest a tip on each. In the centre a tall cylinder with a deckled top edge to form a gem setting stands on a further rope twist ring. It is surrounded by three shorter similar tubes, one on top of each domed feature.

The lower part is a long flat triangle with a notched edge engraved with a round formalised flower on a thick tapering stem which sprouts six plain leaves. The whole design points downwards. The ground is incised with

horizontal lines and the tip below the flower head with diaper cross-hatching. The decoration and some of the metal has been filed away to leave the point plain.

The reverse is undecorated, plainly showing the rather crude construction.

When acquired, the reliquary was fitted with glass tops to the cylinders, which contained scraps of paper from a Latin liturgical manuscript of about 1400, from some early 16th-century letters or notes and a fragment of a 16th- or 17th-century woodcut.

NOTE: [1] *PSAS*, vol XXIV, 1890, 412.

THREAVE LOCKET
[H.HXA 48]

England or Scotland, 15th century
Silver; raised (?), engraved
H 27, W 16, D 4

CONDITION
Good.

INSCRIPTION
ihs (black letter) [for *Ihesus*, 'Jesus']

PROVENANCE
Found at Threave Castle, Kirkcudbright in 1977, in a back-filled trench of 1920s excavations.[1]

✦ ✦ ✦ ✦ ✦ ✦ ✦ ✦ ✦ ✦ ✦ ✦ ✦ ✦ ✦ ✦

The rectangular locket has plain edges and suspension ring at the top. One side is engraved with an inscription on a cross-hatched ground. The other side, which slides up to reveal an undecorated compartment for a keepsake or relic, is engraved with a quatrefoil leaf motif with veins and serrated edges. The central dot and four elongated trefoils in the spandrels are cross-hatched.

The workmanship is so similar to F5 that they are probably by the same craftsman.

NOTE: [1] Caldwell 1981, no 14, 106-107, fig 9.

F5   E73, 90

THREAVE PENDANT CROSS
[H.KE 3]

England or Scotland, 15th century[1]
Silver, gilt; raised, engraved, gilded
H 42, W 30, D 6

CONDITION
Good, gilding slightly worn and discoloured on sides and back, ornaments missing as described.

PROVENANCE
Found at Threave Castle, Kirkcudbright, the precise find spot unknown, donated to the museum in 1880 by David Douglas.[2]

✦ ✦ ✦ ✦ ✦ ✦ ✦ ✦ ✦ ✦ ✦ ✦ ✦ ✦ ✦ ✦

The maltese cross is a silver-gilt hollow box, probably intended for a relic, with a suspension loop at the top holding a separate ring. The front is engraved with plain oval quatrefoil leaves set diagonally with double central veins around a cruciform shape of serrated leaves with double central veins radiating from a dot in the middle, the motifs centred on the reliquary. At each terminal is a trefoil of larger similar leaves. The sides and back, which is a separate detachable plate, are undecorated.

Small spikes protrude from the ends of the side and bottom terminals, possibly for gemstones or pearls. Single holes and discolouration suggest that there were also ornaments attached in the angles between the arms of the cross.

The workmanship is so similar to F4 that they are probably by the same craftsman.

NOTES: [1] Caldwell 1981, no 15, 106-108. [2] NMAS 1892, 287.

F6
SCALLOP PENDANT
[H.KH 5]

E77, 92

Spain or Scotland, 15th century
Silver, jet; jet carved, wire drawn, engraved
H 26, W 16, D 7 (pendant); DIAM 8 (ring)

CONDITION
Good, part of the lower edge missing, ring slightly squashed.

INSCRIPTIONS
ihs (black letter) [for *Ihesus*, 'Jesus']

PROVENANCE
Donated to the museum in 1890.[1]

✛ ✛ ✛ ✛ ✛ ✛ ✛ ✛ ✛ ✛ ✛ ✛ ✛ ✛ ✛ ✛

The scallop shell, carved from jet, is mounted in silver to form a pendant on a spirally beaded wire ring. The deep setting has a scalloped edge and is engraved with 15 vertical leaves with tapering central spines and V-shaped veins. At its base is a more closely spirally beaded wire behind which the finely scalloped edge of the back plate projects. The back plate has a skilfully engraved, decoratively embellished monogram.

✛ ✛ ✛ ✛ ✛ ✛ ✛ ✛ ✛ ✛ ✛ ✛ ✛ ✛ ✛ ✛

The inscription indicates that the scallop shell was not in this instance purely ornamental. Since at least the early 12th century it had been regarded as the symbol of St James the Great, one of the foremost of Christ's apostles, and closely associated with his shrine at Compostela in north west Spain.[2] A local cult had grown up there by the 8th century and had entered Christian literature by 865, maintaining that his relics had been brought to Spain from Jerusalem where he had been martyred.[3] Compostela was a major pilgrimage destination throughout the middle ages, second only to Rome and the Holy Land. In 1434 alone 2,310 pilgrims set sail from English ports to visit the shrine of St James.[4] From an early date the saint was venerated by the Scottish royal family, Malcolm IV having vowed to make the pilgrimage to Spain about 1164, which was prevented by his early death in 1165.[5] He was the patron saint of five successive Scottish kings between 1394 and 1542 and is shown standing behind the praying monarch in the Hours of James IV and Margaret Tudor.

F6

F6

In the Book of Hours St James is dressed as a pilgrim with a staff and a brimmed hat to which is attached a scallop shell. This had become his standard iconography, showing him in the same guise as one of his multitudes of followers. There are many fanciful legends about how the shell became his particular symbol, but it is known that actual shells and lead pilgrim badges in the shape of scallops were sold as souvenirs at Compostela from a very early period.[6] F6 may well have been a rather more superior keepsake and religious protective charm bought at the shrine.

NOTES: [1] Carfrae 1890, 411, no previous provenance is given. [2] Hohler 1957, 56. [3] Farmer 1992, 250. [4] Hohler 1957, 55. [5] Macquarrie 1997, 22. [6] Bruna 1996, nos 221-4, 152-4.

FILLETS

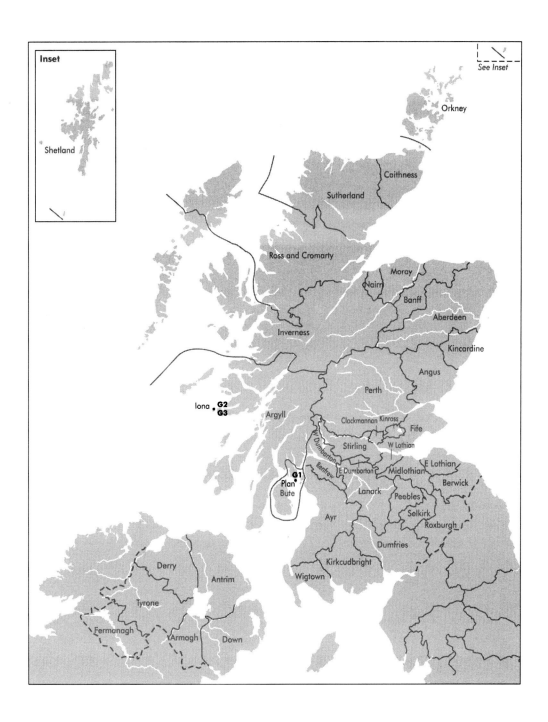

G1
H.FE 41

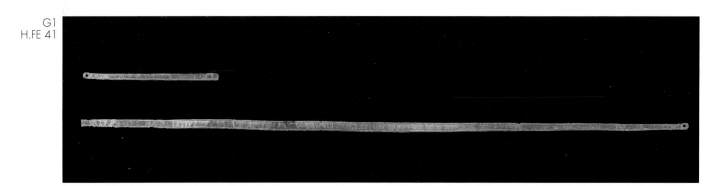

G1
H.FE 42

G1
H.FE 43

G1   B30, 22
Bute Gold Fillets
[H.FE 41-43] .

Scotland, c 1200.[1]
Gold; beaten, punched, engraved
w 6, L 237 + w 4, L 77 ; w 5, L 334 ; w 5, L 346

CONDITION
Surface unblemished, H.FE 43 is complete, H.FE 41 is
broken into two pieces, H.FE 42 is missing both ends.

PROVENANCE
Part of a hoard found in 1863 at Plan on Bute with two
rings and coins of David I, Henry I and Stephen of
England.[2]

✢ ✢ ✢ ✢ ✢ ✢ ✢ ✢ ✢ ✢ ✢ ✢ ✢ ✢ ✢ ✢ ✢

The three long narrow fillets are cut from thin flexible
gold sheet, a wider central band tapering to a round
terminal pierced with a hole. A border of punched dots
runs right along both edges of each fillet.

The middle of each is undecorated, with about a
quarter of the length at each end filled with zigzag
engraved lines with single dots between. The decoration
is faintly visible on the reverse which is otherwise plain.

✢ ✢ ✢ ✢ ✢ ✢ ✢ ✢ ✢ ✢ ✢ ✢ ✢ ✢ ✢ ✢

Generally accepted as hair ornaments which were held
in place by threads passed through the holes in the ends,
these fillets, along with G2 and G3, have been linked
with seven gold bands found at separate sites in Ireland.[3]
These have been dated to the 11th and 12th centuries and
in several cases were included in hoards with Scandinavian material. G1 and G2 were also excavated along
with finger rings of a Norse type. In spite of one author's
description of them as representations of the head-bands
worn by great ladies in 12th-century Scotland and
England and 'possibly elsewhere as well',[4] the find spots
of the only examples at present known are confined to
Ireland and the west of Scotland.

Plan is on the edge of the site of a monastery dedicated to St Blane, with a ruined 12th-century chapel
and burials dating back to the 6th or 7th century.[5]

NOTES: [1] Glenn 2001, 278. [2] Pollexfen 1864, 372-86. [3] Ó Floinn
1983, 6-7. [4] Lightbown 1992, fig 24, 109-10. [5] Glenn 1998, note
24, 119.

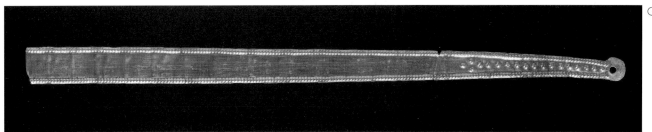

G2
IONA FILLET
[HX.39]

Scotland, second half of the 12th century.[1]
Gold; beaten, embossed, engraved
w 11, L 18

CONDITION
Good, but only a portion from one end extant.

PROVENANCE
Found by staff of HM Office of Works while removing loose earth from the south east corner of St Ronan's Church, Iona in 1923. It was folded up and wedged inside a gold finger ring of Viking type.[2]

+ + + + + + + + + + + + + + + +

The thin flat fillet tapers towards a round terminal pierced with a hole. It has a continuous embossed beaded border. A central spine of 16 tiny embossed flowerlets stretches from two flanking single motifs to the terminal.[3]

NOTES: [1] Glenn 2001, 278; Ó Floinn 1983, fig 2.3, 5. [2] Curle 1924, 109-10. [3] See G1 for purpose and dating.

G3 (colour plate) C37, 40
IONA FILLET
[H.HX 36]

Iona, late 12th or early 13th century[1]
Gold; beaten, punched, embossed
w 12, L 242

CONDITION
Good, completely severed in one place.

PROVENANCE
Discovered in 1922 during routine maintenance work, by HM Office of Works underneath a stone at the west corner of the base of the south respond of the chancel arch of the nunnery, Iona. It was wrapped in coarse linen with four silver spoons [B1, B2] (pages 19-23).[2]

+ + + + + + + + + + + + + + + +

The long band of thin gold sheet tapers towards its rounded ends, each pierced with a small round hole. A beaded border runs along each edge and round the ends, with a continuous embossed leafy scroll filling the entire surface between.[3]

NOTES: [1] Glenn 2001, 278, fig 25.5. [2] Curle 1924, 102; for the foundation of the nunnery see B1, page 20. [3] See G1 for purpose and dating.

G3

G3
(detail)

V WEST HIGHLAND METALWORK AND RELATED MATERIAL

The very practice of preserving books, bells and croziers as secondary relics of saints and holy men was characteristic of the Celtic church in Ireland and the Hibernian seaboard. Geraldus Cambrensis describes their use in 1191: 'The people and clergy of Ireland, Scotland and Wales, are wont to have in great reverence the hand bells, and staves curved in at the top and covered with gold, silver, and copper, and other relics of their saints, to such an extent that they are as much afraid of giving an oath

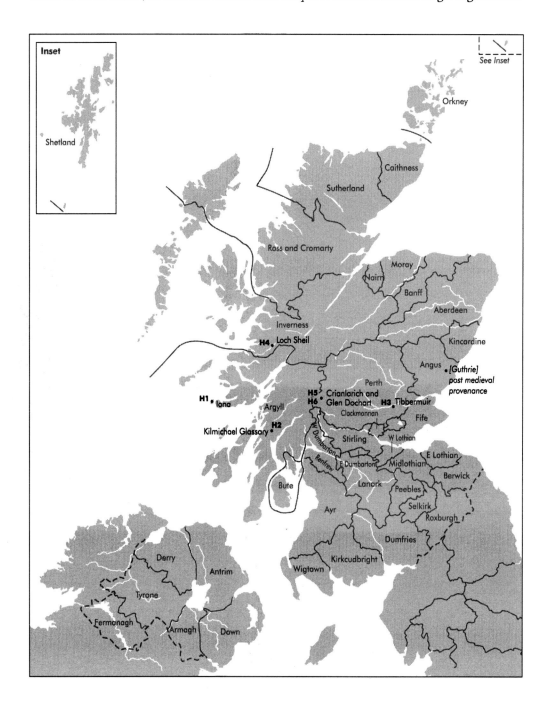

or violating one given on such relics than if taken on the gospels.'[1] Three of the most imposing pieces of metalwork in this catalogue, the Guthrie Bell Shrine [H1], the Kilmichael Glassary Bell Shrine [H2] and the Coigreach or 'Quigrich' [H6], were created to safeguard and venerate such sacred relics.

All three have a distinctively West Highland character, both in the shapes they take and in the detail of their decoration. H2 and H6 have early provenances in Argyll and the far west of Perthshire, while H1 can be convincingly argued to have come from Iona, founded by Columba himself. They are in marked contrast to most of the material from southern, central and eastern Scotland, where under the influence of the court – most of whose members were of Norman descent – the aspiration was towards the fashionable taste of contemporary western Europe and England.

However, in the medieval period these divisions were by no means watertight. If the imagery of the Dunkeld chapter seal is to be believed, they were quite happy to combine a crozier reliquary of entirely Celtic form with an up-to-date French *châsse*, in the cathedral which they were rebuilding in the 13th and 14th centuries in an unremarkable mainstream Gothic style.[2] The crucifix figures from graves in Tibbermuir near Perth [H3] and Dunfermline Abbey (fig 22, page 103) are closely related to that on the Kilmichael Glassary Bell Shrine and may indicate either direct connections with the west of Scotland or a shared influence reaching the east coast directly from Scandinavia. Equally, patrons with strong Irish and Norse family allegiances like the Lamonts are found commissioning smart illuminated manuscripts in Paris in the 1240s,[3] while a finely wrought gold brooch entirely free of Insular motifs can have a provenance in Bernera or Islay [E21, E20 pages 66-8].

It is surprising that although the qualities which make these West Highland objects distinct from other contemporary Scottish artefacts are inherently 'Hibernian', they do not very closely resemble surviving Irish material of the same periods. The Kilmichael Glassary Bell Shrine is a very Nordic reinterpretation of the type. At no stage can the Guthrie Bell Shrine have shared the glorious intricacy and technical virtuosity of St Patrick's Bell Shrine[4] or the Bearnán Cuileain,[5] while the composite cover made for the Bearnán Conaill at similar dates to the layers of H1 owes a great deal to English infiltration, which hardly seems to have reached these Iona metalworkers at all. If crozier reliquaries similar in appearance to the Quigrich were ever made in Ireland, they have not survived or are not identifiable in documentary sources.

The fact that Scotland had not only its own royal court but also, almost until the Reformation, the fairly separate ruling dynasties of the Lords of the Isles in the west as patrons, allowed a development which was on the one hand more cosmopolitan and on the other more resiliently traditional than in Ireland. This part of the collection presents a fascinating picture of a world which was deeply conservative, but strongly influenced not only by Ireland but also by Scandinavia, and acutely aware of contemporary taste in the rest of Scotland and further afield.

NOTES: [1] Itinerarium Cambriae, London 1804, 6, 7, 13, 14. [2] Glenn 2003, forthcoming. [3] Glenn 1998, 112-13. [4] Ó Floinn 1994, pl 2b, 19, pl 17, 32. [5] Ibid, pl 16, 31.

GUTHRIE BELL SHRINE
[H.KA 21]

Iona, mid-12th to late 15th century
Iron, copper alloy, silver, gilt (see detailed analysis, pages 98-99); cast, raised, repoussé, engraved, nielloed
H 198, W 144, D 124

CONDITION
Generally good, but much altered, gilding worn, losses to the strip framing the panels.

INSCRIPTION
iohannes alexan / dri me fieri feisit (black letter) [for *Johannes Alexandri me fieri fecit*, 'John son of Alexander had me made']

PROVENANCE
Bought by the museum in 1925 at the sale of the contents of Guthrie Castle, Angus. The Guthries are documented in the area from the 15th century onwards. Family hearsay credited Bishop John Guthrie (1577-1649) with the acquisition of the bell shrine, but a much more likely candidate is his kinsman Alexander who was appointed commissary to his cousin John Leslie, bishop of the Isles in 1628.[1] A further theory, that it had come from Guthrie collegiate church founded by the family in 1479, appears to be entirely speculative.[2]

✣ ✣ ✣ ✣ ✣ ✣ ✣ ✣ ✣ ✣ ✣ ✣ ✣ ✣ ✣ ✣

H1

The core is a plain, very corroded rectangular iron hand bell, the top of which is visible between the later decorative plates. A simple curved handle on the top is covered with plain bronze. The sides and the back are covered with thin sheets of bronze held in place by pins and vertical, reeded strips of brass at the corners. On the back is a small semicircular brass handle, its B-shaped terminals fastened with two large rivets at each end. It is placed horizontally on the right hand side 110 millimetres from the bottom, another alongside it having been broken off.

The front of the shrine is covered with a sheet of silver fastened at the sides and top with pins and a strip of beaded silver, parts of which have been lost. The embossed decoration of this sheet, which is partly obscured by the later figures, consists of a horizontal ridge with elongated fleur-de-lis terminals and trefoil sprigs, two rows of four square panels, each with four diagonal fleur-de-lis and a beaded square, and four vertical panels of foliate scrolls. A vertical panel of crude interlace has been engraved on the silver at a later date. The embossing is arranged around a central plain crucifix to which a cast bronze figure of Christ, partially gilt, is attached by a single nail through each hand and one through his crossed feet.

The corpus is very schematised, the hair in concentric swirls forming a flattened cap, the ears circular and protruding, the eyes large and oval, the short beard of formalised curls in a smooth curve on each cheek and the long straight hair falling on to his chest. The arm and leg muscles are naturalistically modelled, the rib cage indicated by simple curved lines. The perizoma falls to below the knees, clinging closely to the body. The whole figure is a rigid T-shape in a symmetrical frontal standing, rather than hanging, pose.

The cast bronze St John from this crucifixion group is now attached to the side of the shrine. Even more abstract than the corpus, it has an oval

fig 20: GUTHRIE BELL SHRINE ABOUT 1200
Reconstruction by J.S.Richardson, 1926, *PSAS*,
LX, 414, fig 4.
(detail)

H1
detail

FIGURE OF ST JOHN
Now attached to the side, copper alloy.

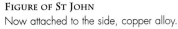

head slightly tilted to one side with projecting ears, the beard and features indicated by simple lines. The body is a flattened cylinder, the robes in vertical tubular folds on the torso, below a round collar and in horizontal crescent shapes on the lower body. The forearms and hands are in very low relief, the left clasping a book to the figure's chest, the right crossing the body beneath it. The feet and ankles are in profile, both pointing right. A rivet between the feet attaches the figure to the reliquary. Some traces of gilding remain in the folds of the garments.

A later figure, silver partially gilt, has been placed on the bell shrine above the Crucifixion. He is seated, embossed and roughly engraved in thick metal sheet, modelled in low relief. The reverse, where it is visible above the bell, is plain silver. He wears a crown with low fleurons, a wide collar with punched decoration over an open cloak hatched to represent fur, a deep belt engraved with round motifs and a flowing skirt falling in vertical folds from his knees, textured with cross-hatching. His shoulder-length hair turns outward at the ends and he has a short square beard. The left arm is outstretched, the right forearm missing. Two pins with quatre-foil heads hold the figure in place, one through the stomach, the other between the ankles.

Two further embossed silver figures of bishops or abbots have been added, one each side of the crucifix. Their low mitres have small round bosses either side of a plain vertical strip, high stiff apparels of their amices open at the front and long 'embroidered' chasubles (the left-hand figure with crude fleur-de-lis, the right hand with trifids and dashes; both with orphreys in triple splays top and bottom). The albs underneath are also decorated with irregular strips of cross-hatching. The figures have short bobbed hair and a beard is roughly indicated on the left-hand figure. Both raise their right hands in blessing and formerly held a crozier in their left hands. Like the seated king above, their arms are merely thick sheet metal cut and bent to shape and they are attached with similar pins.

A horizontal strip with a poorly formed niello inscription has been attached to the bottom of the front of the shrine, upside down. On the lower edge is an engraved rope twist border, at the left side a crudely engraved leaf motif, at the right a panel of interlace.

On the left-hand side of the reliquary, there is a third figure of a bishop, very similar to the two silver examples, but larger and made of bronze.

Two round silver-gilt ornaments resembling brooches have been added on either side of Christ's head. Within the alternately lobed and cusped circumference they have plain high settings for six small gems surrounded by a beaded border; in the centre a further larger setting. All the stones are now missing.

✛ ✛ ✛ ✛ ✛ ✛ ✛ ✛ ✛ ✛ ✛ ✛ ✛ ✛ ✛ ✛

Like many Irish bell shrines, for example the Bearnán Cuileain in the British Museum[3] and the bell of St Mura in the Wallace Collection,[4] this reliquary has been created by applying successive layers of decoration to the early hand bell itself over several centuries.[5] The differentiation of these layers by scientific analysis of the metal content is illustrated and fully discussed in the analysis, pages 98-9.

Stylistic comparisons argue that the figures of Christ and St John which combine features of Continental Romanesque art and Irish metal-work, for example St Manchan's Shrine now in the National Museum of Ireland, place them in the first half of the 12th century.[6] The embossed silver plate covering the front has distinctive Iona features in the vertical scrolls which are very close to a gold fillet found on the island [G2, page 91] and in the eight foliated cross heads, a frequent motif of Iona stone carvers.[7] Both motifs suggest an early 13th-century date. The two silver bishops and the crowned figure on the front are quite evidently by the same artist as the bronze bishop on the side. The bishops have been convincingly related to Iona effigies of the early 14th century.[8]

The position of the seated figure above the Crucifixion suggests he is intended for God the Father as he is shown, for example, on numerous English alabaster carvings of the Trinity. As the position of the cross with Christ was already fixed, it could not be placed in front of him in the usual way. It is possible that both his hands were outstretched holding a napkin of souls which would have covered the flat undecorated surfaces on his knees. The iconography with its detailed contemporary costume and covered feet did not, however, quite conform to the norm.

The niello inscription would fit neatly into its present position if it were the right way up, allowing for the flaring vestments on either side. A plausible identification of the donor as John MacIan of Ardnamurchan, whose family had styled themselves Iohannes Alexandri and Alexander Iohannis for generations, has been suggested.[9] Presumably this represents a refurbishment about 1500, when the silver-gilt ornaments were also probably added. Its re-attachment upside down, the stripping away of a cresting from the top of the shrine and the covering of the handle with plain bronze are likely to be a botched repair after the vicissitudes of the Reformation.

NOTES: [1] Glenn 2001, 276. [2] Guthrie 1855, 55. [3] Mahr and Raftery 1976, 57, 157, pl. 83. [4] Ibid, 157, pl. 81. [5] Eeles 1926, 411-17. [6] Ó Floinn 1994, 16. [7] Steer and Bannerman, 1977, 100, 145. [8] Ibid, 29-30. [9] Glenn 2001, 280, n 5, 284; Munro 1986, 284-6.

COMPOSITIONAL ANALYSIS OF THE GUTHRIE BELL SHRINE

Katherine Eremin and Jim Tate

Non-destructive x-ray fluorescence (XRF) analysis was undertaken on the Guthrie Bell Shrine to compare the composition of the various components. All analyses were of the unprepared surface, hence represent current surface values which, due to corrosion and cleaning, may differ from the original composition. The data can, however, be used to compare the different pieces and their possible construction sequence. The full results and analytical details are given in Eremin 2000a.[1]

Analysis of the copper components suggested the presence of at least three distinct compositional groups. All components are composed of a mixed copper alloy with variable amounts of lead, tin and zinc. Such mixed alloys are often termed gunmetal after the modern equivalent. Similar mixed alloys were used for Viking period artefacts produced at Scottish sites with Norse influence and for later Medieval artefacts found at Finlaggan.

The three groups are

gunmetal: copper alloy containing typically around 4% zinc, 2% lead and 5.5% tin and traces of iron, arsenic, silver and antimony

impure brass: copper with around 15% zinc, 2% tin and traces iron, lead and silver

zinc-rich gunmetal: copper with around 10% zinc, 1% lead and 4% tin

The figures of St John, Christ and Piece 1 are *gunmetal,* with Piece 1 having slightly higher surface levels of zinc (6.5%) and lower levels of lead (1%) than the figures but similar

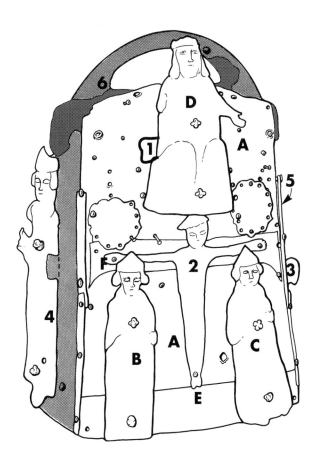

Drawing of the front of the Guthrie Bell Shrine by Marion O'Neil 1998

ANALYSIS OF THE METALS
Copper Alloy
1   is very similar, but not identical to 2 and 3 (St John);

2 and 3   match in both major, minor and trace elements;

4   and the sheets encasing the sides and back, the handle on the back and the framing strips (except 5) are a broadly similar type of zinc brass alloy;

5   differs from everything else;

6   differs from everything else.

Silver
A   has trace elements similar to B and C, but a lower copper content, which is possibly the result of surface depletion, but may be a genuine difference indicating a separate phase of workmanship;

B and C   are very similar and likely to be from the same batch of silver;

D   is not inconsistent with B and C, but the analytical results are clouded by the gilding;

E   has a high lead content due to the application of niello, is higher in gold than the rest of the silver parts and is definitely different in origin.

F   is very similar to A and likely to be from the same batch of silver.

tin. This piece may in fact be compositionally distinct from the figures but the differences probably are due to variable corrosion rather than true original variations. The possibility that this piece is part of the same compositional group is supported by the presence of antimony as a trace element in the two figures and in Piece 1.

The back, the left-hand side, the right-hand side, the two strips, the Bishop and the back handle are *impure brass*. This group lacks the traces of antimony found in the *gunmetal* group.

The top handle is composed of *zinc-rich gunmetal* and also lacks the traces of antimony found in the *gunmetal* group.

Analysis of the silver alloy components revealed remnants of mercury and gold on many areas, confirming that the shrine had been amalgam gilded. However, most pieces had areas of worn and missing gilding with no detectable mercury and here the trace levels of gold found may have come from the silver alloy.

The analyses suggested the presence of either 2 or 3 compositional groups of silver alloys, all with minor copper and traces of gold and lead. These are:

group 1A: copper around 2%, gold in 100 parts silver 0.6

group 1B: copper around 4-5%, gold in 100 parts silver 0.7

 group 2: copper around 5-6%, gold in 100 parts silver 1.1 to 1.3

It should be noted, however, that copper is often depleted in the surface of silver artefacts due to corrosion, hence care is needed in the interpretation of the surface data obtained in this study. Such enrichment has previously been found to vary from around 4% in artefacts with silver contents above 90% to around 10% in more debased silver alloys.[2] The amount of gold in silver alloys is not altered by processing of the ores[3] and the value of gold in 100 parts silver is often used to show differences in the silver source.[4, 5] In contrast, the lead content is altered by processing. If lead-bearing silver ores were used, traces of lead (0.5% to 1%) remain in the silver after cupellation and are inherited by the silver alloy whereas tin, copper and zinc are easily removed to very low levels.[6]

Pieces B, C, D and the silver strip on the right hand side of the Bell Shrine are *group 1B*. Pieces A and F are *group 1A*. However, since the main difference between these two groups is the copper content, they may originally have been compositionally identical. Piece E and the silver strip on the left-hand side are *group 2*. All the silver components had lead values between 0.5% and 1.0%, consistent with the use of lead-bearing silver ores.

Piece E is decorated with a lead-rich niello. X-ray diffraction analysis of a small sample of this niello indicated that this was a combination of silver sulphide and lead sulphide. There is little comparable data, but sulphides used for early Medieval niello included copper-silver sulphide, silver sulphide and lead sulphide, often combined on a single artefact.[7, 8, 9]

NOTES: [1] Eremin 2000a, 3-4. [2] Kruse and Tate 1992, 298. [3] McKerrell and Stevenson 1972, 197-8. [4] Metcalf and Northover 1985, 166-8. [5] Cowell and Lowick 1988, 70. [6] McKerrell and Stevenson 1972, 197-8. [7] Oddy, Bimson and La Niece 1983. [8] La Niece and Stapleton 1993. [9] La Niece 1983, 287

BIBLIOGRAPHY:

EREMIN, K 2000a, Analysis of the Guthrie Bell Shrine, Internal C&AR report, AR 00/40.

KRUSE, S E and TATE, J 1992, 'XRF analysis of Viking Age silver ingots', *PSAS*, 122, 295-328.

McKERRELL, H and STEVENSON, R B K 1972, 'Some analyses of Anglo-Saxon and associated Oriental coinage' in Hall, D T and Metcalf, D M (eds) *Methods of Chemical and Metallurgical Investigation of Ancient Coinage*, London, 195-209.

METCALF, D M and NORTHOVER J P 1985 'Debasement in the coinage of southern England in the reign of King Alfred', *Numismatic Chronicle*, 145, 150-76.

COWELL, M R and LOWICK N M 1988 'Silver mines from the Panjhir mines' in W A Oddy (ed) *Metallurgy in Numismatics*, 2, London.

ODDY, W A, BIMSON, M and LA NIECE, S 1983, 'The composition of niello decoration on gold, silver and bronze in the antique and medieval periods', *Studies in Conservation*, 28: 29-35.

LA NIECE, S and STAPLETON C 1993, 'Niello and Enamel on Irish Metalwork', *The Antiquaries Journal*, 73, 148-51.

LA NIECE 1983, 'Niello: an historical and technical survey', *Antiquaries Journal* 63, 270-97.

KILMICHAEL GLASSARY BELL SHRINE
[H.KA 5]

Argyll, mid-12th century
Copper alloys; cast, engraved, chased, probably formerly nielloed and gilded
H 148, W 95, D 85

CONDITION
Two feet missing, otherwise excellent

PROVENANCE
Presented to the Society of Antiquaries of Scotland in 1826 by John Macneill of Oakfield, on whose farm at Torbhlaren in the parish of Kilmichael Glassary, Argyll, it was found during the building of a dyke in 1814.[1] A counter tradition in the minister's family, that it was found at the back of the manse 'about the site of the old church', is recorded in a typewritten note of the early 20th century by J Graham Callander.[2]

✦ ✦ ✦ ✦ ✦ ✦ ✦ ✦ ✦ ✦ ✦ ✦ ✦ ✦ ✦ ✦

H2

The small plain 9th- or 10th-century rectangular iron hand bell for which the reliquary was made is now displayed alongside.[3] This was removed by Thomas Thomson about 1825, who discovered it wrapped in woollen cloth. He reported that the plain metal plate which forms the floor of the shrine had lost, since 1814, the four pegs which held it in place and had 'recently' been perforated by the circular hole in the middle.[4]

The main body of the shrine is formed of four tapering rectangular plates, the back and front wider than the two sides. These are of a darker, browner alloy than the yellowish brassy mounts which hold them, the vertical loop handles with leafy terminals on the sides and the crucifix figure attached to the front.

Each plate has a different scheme of engraved decoration. On the front the plain upright of a crucifix with a rectangular plinth and upper terminal is flanked by large symmetrical spiral leaf scrolls. There is a similar scroll in two tiers on the back. One side panel has two roughly engraved and pounced large triangles on either side of the loop handle, a frieze of triangular motifs and a frieze of palmettes below. The other side has scrolls either side of the handle and six square panels below

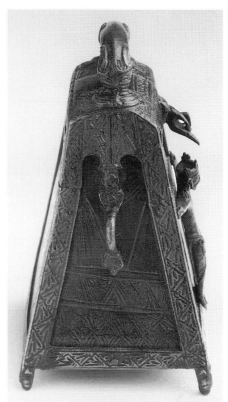

containing interlace patterns in four cases and a four-petalled flower and a saltire cross in the others.

The top plate is cast in one piece with the handle, the *Manus Dei* and the upper part of the four corner mounts. The corner mounts terminate in animal-head feet (two are missing) of dog-like form, with pointed backswept ears and bulging eyes, the muzzles resting on the ground. The mounts are joined by shaped foliate friezes at the top and a straight border along the lower edge of the shrine. The handle is cast and chased with two formalised long-eared animal-head terminals with prominent oval eyes. The two crooked fingers and the thumb of the *Manus Dei* form strong round loops. Deeply engraved leaf patterns, divided into triangles or lozenges, cover all the mounts except the lower edge of the back and the left-hand side, which have a pattern of saltire crosses in squares. All this decoration was probably originally filled with niello.

An applied strap engraved with a running Z-pattern forms the crossbeam of the crucifix. The figure of Christ has a tall crown with three prominent fleurons, slightly raised outstretched arms, and a perizoma to just above the knees in front and mid-calf behind the tapering joined legs, which part at the slightly splayed feet. The head is tilted to his right and looks downwards, with hair falling to the shoulders, a short straight beard, large protruding eyes, a long straight nose and small pursed mouth.

The upper chest is flat, the nipples indicated by stamped circles below a notch for the collarbone and a central depression for the breastbone. The lower ribcage is shown as curved engraved lines passing round the sides of the figure. The musculature of the arms is formed by a simple casting. The perizoma falls in a deep V below the navel; it is engraved with a fleck pattern over the left hip, where tightly bunched horizontal folds form the top edge and wavy zigzags the bottom. The right-hand side has an exuberant pattern of formalised scrolling drapery and a prominent knot at hip level.

Found near the bell shrine were a pendant cross and a long wire chain of figure-of-eight links. The pendant is a Greek cross with waisted arms and a central square, having suspension loops on three of its terminals. It seems unlikely that it was ever suspended from the shrine; it is too large in scale and would have obscured the decoration of the reliquary, particularly if attached to the *Manus Dei* as has been suggested.

✝ ✝ ✝ ✝ ✝ ✝ ✝ ✝ ✝ ✝ ✝ ✝ ✝ ✝

The angular shape of the Kilmichael Glassary Bell Shrine differs considerably from the Guthrie Bell Shrine [H1, page 94] and most of the surviving Irish examples.[5] Although the zoomorphic top handle and feet and the strapwork decoration are indebted to the Celtic tradition,

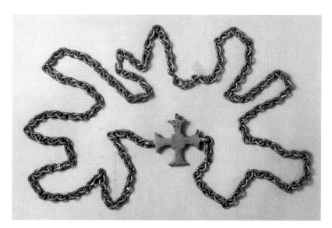

CROSS AND CHAIN
Copper alloy, found with Kilmichael Glassary Bell Shrine.
L 538, W 6 (chain)
H 36, W 48, D 4 (cross)

as is the very practice of venerating and enshrining bells as relics, the border decoration and the crucifix figure have their closest parallels in Scandinavian art.

Very similar leaf patterns in triangles and lozenges were used for the framework of the Eriksberg reliquary from Västergötland in Sweden, from the second half of the 12th century.[6] This still retains its gilding and some of the niello in the leaves (fig 21). The Kilmichael Glassary figure, a very similar Scottish example [H3, pages 104-105] and a lost piece from Dunfermline recorded in a late 18th-century drawing (fig 22, page 103) all compare closely with a damaged crucifix (fig 23) found during roadworks in Copenhagen in 1963.[7] Its Danish origins are in no doubt as it plainly derives many of its characteristics from large scale 12th-century crosses such as Åby,[8] Lisbjerg,[9] Odder[10] and Tirstrup.[11]

Just above the *Manus Dei* is a small rectangular panel of squiggles which at first glance looks like incompetent egg and dart. This is an incongruous motif in an object otherwise devoid of Classical references and surprising for a precise and well executed piece of metalwork. In the corresponding position at the back of the bell shrine, this area is left entirely blank.

The overriding effect of the squiggles in their rectangular panel, emphasised by bold horizontal borders, is that of some kind of label or inscription. The general appearance, at least, is evocative of cursive Arabic script, imitated by someone unfamiliar with its actual meaning.

This feature was first noticed by Daniel Wilson, who referred drawings of it to a number of eminent Orientalists.[12] With Victorian self-confidence, they reported that although the script did not quite conform to any specific inscription it might be read 'King of Kings and Lord of Lords', 'allah il allahu', 'There is no God but God', 'In the name of God' or 'In the name of God, the merciful, the gracious'. Wilson dismissed this out of

fig 21: ERIKSBERG RELIQUARY
Västergötland, side and end views, copper alloy, Swedish,
1150-1200, Statens Historiska Museum, photo Antikvarisk-
topografiska arkivet, Stockholm.
H 500, w 403, D 155

fig 22: DUNFERMLINE CRUCIFIX
Ink on paper, a 'brass' figure (now lost), from *Drawings in
Scotland*, an album collected by Francis Grose, late 18th
century. Society of Antiquaries MS 476, NMS Library. (detail)

fig 23: COPENHAGEN CRUCIFIX
Copper alloy, Danish, late 12th century, Nationalmuseet, photo
Antikvarisk Topografisk Arkiv, Copenhagen.
H 155

H2 'INSCRIPTION'
Detail, drawing by Marian O'Neil.

hand, unable to countenance the presence of an infidel inscription on a sacred Christian object. However, his theory that it represents formalised clouds from which the hand of God the Father is emerging does not quite hold water either. For a start the *Manus Dei* is firmly separated from the motif by three sets of borders and Wilson himself cannot quote any medieval representation of clouds which looks much like this.

Modern scholars of Near Eastern art more cautiously suggest that Arabic inscriptions were sometimes recognised by European artists as having a talismanic significance, which they copied without understanding their meaning.[13] If this was an attempt by a Scandinavian craftsman to do so, he would have had at his disposal the 250,000 Eastern silver coins imported by the Vikings[14] along with weights, jewellery and vessels from as far away as the Black Sea and Central Asia with Islamic motifs and inscriptions.[15]

All the previous literature has proposed systems for suspending the Kilmichael Glassary Bell Shrine from the chain found in the same area, none of them altogether convincing. In particular, the suggestion that the pendant cross, or anything else, should hang from the Hand of God would be a very odd, if not actually sacrilegious, piece of iconography.

As it was provided with four feet, it can be assumed that it normally stood on an altar and was not hung above it.[16] However, it is known that reliquaries were carried around in procession, to effect cures and for the swearing of oaths in both Scotland[17] and Ireland.[18] This would have been the purpose of the carrying handles on both the Guthrie and the Kilmichael Glassary Bell Shrines. Their wide flattened shape would have been more appropriate for thick leather straps than chains, as shown in the 17th-century drawing reproduced by Ó Floinn.[19]

NOTES: [1] Thomson 1827, 117. [2] Campbell and Sandeman 1962, 82. The typed note they quote postdates 1906 and, as it is based on family hearsay going back four generations, seems less reliable than the account of Thomson who had knowledge of the shrine from soon after its discovery. The two sites are less than 1 km apart. [3] Bourke 1983, 464, 467. [4] Thomson 1827, 118. [5] Mahr and Raftery 1976, 56-7, pls 68, 69, 79, 80, 81, 82, 83, 124. [6] Roesdahl and Wilson 1992, 212, 350, no 469; Langberg 1992, 56, figs 26-8; Karlsson, *et al* 1995, 297. [7] Bloch 1992, 209, no V A 13, pl 91. [8] Roesdahl and Wilson 1992, 348, no 460. [9] Ibid, 360, no 467. [10] Langberg 1979, pl 13 [11] Ibid, pl 14. [12] Wilson 1884, 86-93. [13] I am grateful to my colleagues Ulrike Al Khamis and Jennifer Scarce for their advice on this point. [14] Skaare 1976, 47-53. [15] Arne, 1914, 97, 113-203; Roesdahl and Wilson 1992, 74-8; Jansson 1996, *passim*. [16] Bourke 1997, 176. [17] Anderson 1910, 280. [18] Ó Floinn 1994, 11-14. [19] Ibid, 22.

H3 (colour plate)   B33, 25
TIBBERMUIR CORPUS
[H.1995.680]

Scotland, mid-12th century
Copper alloy, gilt; cast, engraved
H 124, W 106, D 40

CONDITION
Excellent, no missing parts, some wear to the nose and at knee level and to most of the gilding.

PROVENANCE
Bought from the estate of Sir James D Roberts in 1995; by family tradition found in a grave in Tibbermuir churchyard, Perthshire.[1]

✠ ✠ ✠ ✠ ✠ ✠ ✠ ✠ ✠ ✠ ✠ ✠ ✠ ✠ ✠ ✠

The figure of Christ Crucified has a tall crown with three prominent fleurons, slightly raised outstretched arms, a perizoma to the knees in front and mid-calf behind the straight joined legs; parallel down-turned feet. The head is slightly tilted to his right and looks downwards; with hair falling to the shoulders, a short straight beard, large protruding pointed oval eyes, a long straight broad nose and small pursed mouth. The eyebrows and lines either side of the nose are indicated by engraving, the ears small and cast.

The upper chest is plain and flat, below the V-shaped line of the collarbone. The lower ribcage is formed by curved engraved lines, and a pattern of horizontal lines continues up the sides to the armpits. The elbow joints and hands are simply cast. The hips and stomach are thrust forward and very slightly swung to his right, as are the bent knees. The perizoma falls in three deep rectangular pleats at each side below a wide waistband with notched edges; at the front there are three vertical double pleats below triangular drapery fastened in a large spiral knot on the right hip. There is a small hole in each hand, but none in the feet.

The back of the crown has a pattern of vertical lines, but otherwise the reverse of the figure is plain, with a deep irregular vertical cavity. Traces of gilding remain in the engraved lines and drapery folds and on the reverse.

✝ ✝ ✝ ✝ ✝ ✝ ✝ ✝ ✝ ✝ ✝ ✝ ✝ ✝ ✝

This figure closely resembles the corpus on the Kilmichael Glassary Bell Shrine [H2], where its date and stylistic affiliations are discussed. Both can also be compared with the mainstream of European Romanesque bronze crucifix figures.[2]

NOTES: [1] Archives of the Department of History and Applied Art, NMS. [2] Bloch 1992, 242,247, no VI A 17, pl 116; 323-6, X D 1-5, pls 162-3.

H4
LOCH SHIEL CROZIER DROP
[H.1993.634]

West Highlands of Scotland, mid-12th century
Copper alloy; cast, raised
H 78, W 22, D 25

CONDITION
Surface very corroded, but metal not misshapen or broken away.

PROVENANCE
Found using a metal detector on the shore of Loch Shiel, near St Finan's Isle, in 1992.

✝ ✝ ✝ ✝ ✝ ✝ ✝ ✝ ✝ ✝ ✝ ✝ ✝ ✝ ✝

The crozier drop is hollow, forming a relic compartment. A cast bald head of a king with a shallow wavy crown, prominent ears and long square jaw, projects from the top on a strong cylindrical neck. The shoulders of his robes, which are indicated by engraved lines, bulge out to form the top of the drop, with a slanting oval opening with serrated edge at the back. The remains of two pins

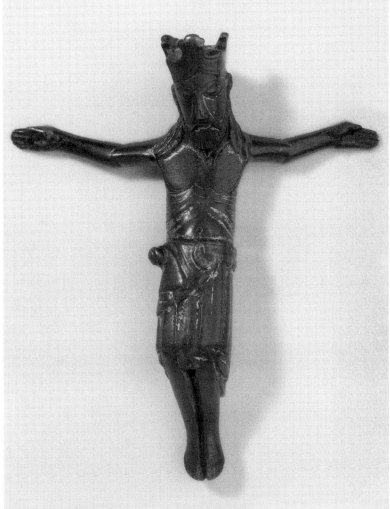

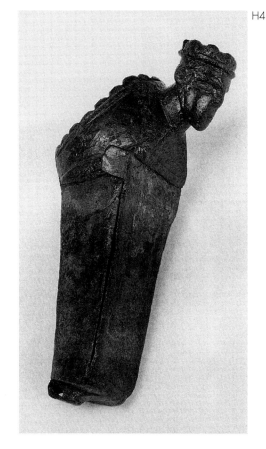

above and a small round hole below show where this was attached to the rest of the crozier.

The undecorated lower part is trapezoid in section, tapering towards the bottom and curving in behind to form the characteristic Celtic crozier shape. The front of this part of the drop is a separate sheet of metal, which originally was detachable. On the foot is a pierced tab from which to suspend a fine chain, probably with a crucifix.[1]

NOTE: [1] Bourke 1997, 175-6, fig 5.

H5

A7, 11

ST FILLAN'S CROZIER
[H.KC 1]

West Highlands, late 11th or early 12th century
Copper alloy, niello (see detailed analysis, page 115);
raised, brazed, inlaid
DIAM 25 (tube), H 151, W 168 (crook)

CONDITION
Deliberately removed elements, some niello chipped, severed and rejoined above drop, vertical joins parted and slightly buckled at back and front.

PROVENANCE
Discovered inside H6 in 1876.[1]

✝ ✝ ✝ ✝ ✝ ✝ ✝ ✝ ✝ ✝ ✝ ✝ ✝ ✝ ✝ ✝ ✝

The crozier is of the Irish or West Highland type. The shape of the characteristic crook has been altered from a pronounced horseshoe to a more angular profile by the removal of a triangular wedge above the drop. It is composed of a tapering round tube in two vertical sections curving towards a separately constructed drop with a sloping triangular top and flat front panel. The crook sections are decorated with a diagonal lattice of applied straps, with central lines of niello. At each intersection, a pin passed through the tube, attaching it to the original wooden core. Regular round holes pierce the lozenges and triangles of the lattice for pins which held the filigree ornament, which has all now been removed and attached to H6.

A fitment, probably a casting of a human head (cf H4), has been removed from the top of the drop. Comparison with Irish examples suggests that the vertical joins at back and front were concealed by a cresting and a decorative moulding respectively.[2]

The drop has similar bands decorating its inner surface in rectangles and triangles, and plain flat panels on the outer faces from which further ornament has been removed. It forms a thick bronze box, D-shaped in section, from which the bottom cover is missing.[3]

NOTES: [1] Stuart 1877, 166. [2] Mahr and Raftery 1976, pls 72, 77, 86-93. [3] For commentary and a full bibliography, see H6.

H5
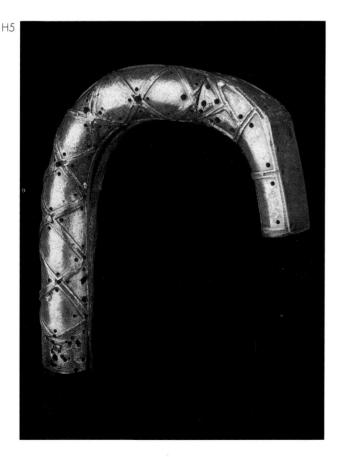

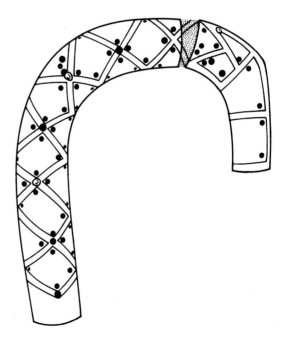
H5 Probable shape before 12th- or early 13th-century breakage, drawing by Marian O'Neil.

The Coigreach or 'Quigrich'[1]

[H.KC 2]

Scotland, 13th, 14th and 15th centuries with 12th-century filigree.
Silver, gilt, rock crystal, copper-alloy inner reinforcement, (see detailed analysis, page 115); cast, engraved, pierced, repoussé, filigree
DIAM 63 (KNOP), H 236, W 200

CONDITION
Generally excellent, some wear to the gilding,[2] the filigree flattened and distorted in places; impact damage on the side of the crook

PROVENANCE
Acquired by the Society of Antiquaries of Scotland for the National Museum of Antiquities in 1876 from its ancestral keepers, the family of Dewar.[3]

✛ ✛ ✛ ✛ ✛ ✛ ✛ ✛ ✛ ✛ ✛ ✛ ✛ ✛ ✛ ✛

This elaborate reliquary made for St Fillan's Crozier [H5] reflects the altered form of the earlier crook and incorporates panels of filigree taken from it.

The main part is a round tube made in two vertical sections, descending from the straight-angled drop in a curve to the depressed spherical knop. The inner join is flanked by a flat band of metal with an engraved border of truncated lozenges against a finely cross-hatched ground, held by a moulded metal strap with a prominent central line of beading. The bands of metal framing the outer join are finely engraved with a border of rope twist and a frieze of pointed leaves against cross-hatching and are joined to the cresting by a vertical strap with a prominent line of beading.

Each side of the crook is covered by a single sheet of metal with triangular and trapezoid apertures, the resulting lattice slightly roughly engraved with stripes of cross-hatching and simple line borders. The apertures all contain panels of filigree, of several different types. The large trapezoid panels mostly contain patterns of spirals, some arranged symmetrically, some not. The wires are plain, flattened and of even thickness, the centres of the spirals marked by silver granules, also flattened. The same technique is used for some of the triangles of spiral filigree and for one with a triangular knot motif. Where the framing wires are extant, they are spirally beaded wire.

The other triangles, part of the bottom trapezoid on one side and the smaller panels nearest the drop contain scrolled filigree carried out in finer spirally beaded wire with plain silver granules. The scroll patterns are more wandering and informal than the larger panels.

Straps with central lines of prominent beading are used to outline panels with concave tops above the knop on each side, the knop itself, semicircular panels on its

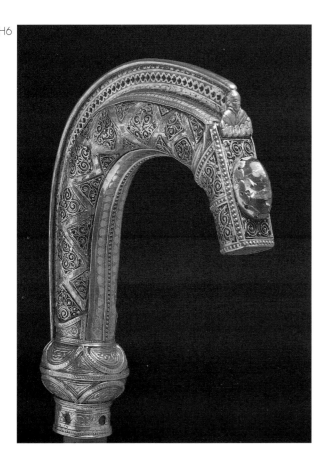

upper and lower halves and the collar below. All these areas have embossed ornament; the upper panels and collar of foliate scrolls, the knop of interlace and triangular knots. All the interlace and knot patterns differ subtly from one another.

The whole crook has a heavy cresting, perforated with a continuous band of quatrefoils against an engraved cross-hatched ground, between engraved bead borders. The outer edge is a plain flattened tube with a rounded end at the top and a decorative moulded double terminal, below two triangular notches at the bottom.

The drop has a flat rectangular outer face and a rounded inner surface. It is articulated by straps with central lines of prominent beading, larger than those on the knop and collar. The centre back has a vertical strap engraved with a line of tablet flowers. Filigree fills two squares and two trapezoids behind the front surface, which has a large oval rock crystal in a high crested setting, with faint punched outlines, surrounded by spiral filigree of twisted wire studded with silver granules.

A small cast bust-length figure of a tonsured monk in a simple habit, rising from formalised clouds conceals the join between the crest and the top of the drop. The shield-shaped bottom end has an engraving of Christ on the cross against a cross-hatched ground, between two five-pointed stars. A hole pierces this panel and the moulded beading behind, presumably to take a pendant cross.

✣ ✣ ✣ ✣ ✣ ✣ ✣ ✣ ✣ ✣ ✣ ✣ ✣ ✣ ✣ ✣

St Fillan's crozier and the 'Quigrich' come with a greater accretion of medieval and later documentation, tradition and folklore than any other object covered by this catalogue.

The spelling 'Quigrich' became established and familiar to scholars in 19th-century usage. Presumably it was a spontaneous attempt to render phonetically for an English readership what was heard when the St Fillan's Crozier was acquired. Given that, strictly speaking, this is neither

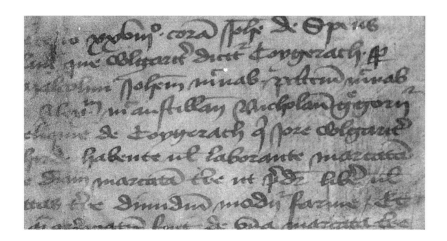

fig 24: Inquest Relating to the 'Quigrich'
Vellum, Scottish, 1428, NMS, the word *coygerach*
highlighted.
(detail)

English nor Gaelic, it seems appropriate to reconsider this. The term attached to the crozier was almost certainly Coigreach or a dialect version of it, a familiar Gaelic word meaning approximately 'stranger' or 'traveller'. The use of a descriptive term or name of this sort reflects a pattern of naming well established in the Gaelic of Ireland and Scotland. For example, surviving Irish relics almost invariably have familiar names. An original name is evident for the crozier, for example as 'coygerach' in the 1428 Inquest, representing what we may assume the scribe heard and wrote down (fig 24). The only difference is the addition of the feature of a typical epenthetic vowel in the middle of the word which renders it in three rather than two syllables. In adopting therefore 'Coigreach', we have followed the spelling in Alexander Macbain's *Etymological Dictionary of the Gaelic Language* (Inverness 1896) and the evolution of the term as indicated in the Royal Irish Academy's *Dictionary of the Irish Language*.

The saint himself, according to the Aberdeen Breviary, was the grandson of a prince of Leinster, who came as a missionary to Scotland with his mother St Kentigerna and his uncle St Comgan in the early 8th century. After a period in the community of St Mund on the Holy Loch, Fillan joined Comgan in upper Glendochart, where he founded the monastery and church in which he was subsequently buried.[4] There are dedications to St Fillan (Fáelán of Cluain Moesena) in Loch Alsh, Galloway, Kintyre and Renfrewshire, but he was particularly venerated in west Perthshire, from Strathfillan, through Glendochart, to Killin.[5]

By the reign of William the Lion the abbot of Glendochart, probably a secular figure, represented the community, about which little else is known.[6] A century later, Robert Bruce appears to have had a personal devotion to Fillan. Whether or not Boece invented the story of the miraculous appearance of the saint's armbone on the eve of Bannockburn, the king certainly granted land forfeited to the crown to the monastery or chapel of St Fillan and in 1318 donated the patronage of Killin to Inchaffray Abbey on condition the abbot and convent provided a canon for the church in Strathfillan in perpetuity.[7] This devotion on the part of Bruce possibly dates back to his hard-won victory at the battle of Dail Righ near St Fillan's Church in 1306.[8] That it continued to the end of his life is demonstrated by a donation of £20 to the fabric of the church in 1329.[9]

Like most Irish and West Highland religious communities of its period, Glendochart seems to have been run by a secular and ecclesiastical partnership, where the relics were commonly held by one family who passed them from generation to generation.[10] The Gaelic term for the keepers of such relics was *deòradh* which, anglicized as 'Dewar', evolved

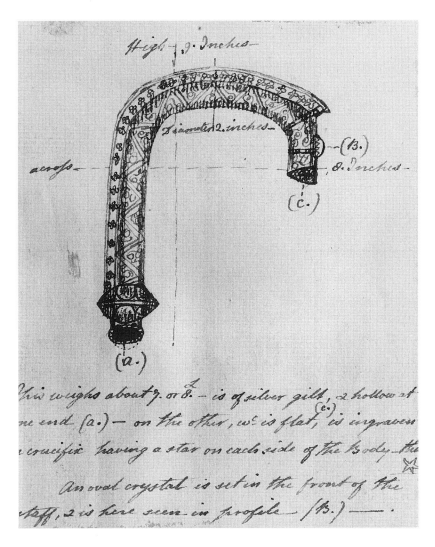

into the surname of the guardians of the Quigrich during the 14th century.[11] The privileges and obligations of the office were specified in an inquest of 1428 which stated that an annual levy of grain was to be paid to the bearer of the Quigrich; that the keepership was given to an ancestor of Finlay Dewar the present holder by the ecclesiastical successor of St Fillan and that all this had been recognised since the time of Bruce (fig 24, page 109). In return, with the aid of the miraculous powers of the relic, for a small fee the Dewars were to retrieve stolen goods or cattle within the kingdom of Scotland.[12]

These provisions were confirmed in a letter of James III in 1487, particularly emphasising the legitimate possession of the Quigrich by the Dewar family, their liberty from all interference except from the king and his heirs, and their right to pass through the country with it without impediment.[13] James IV confirmed it again in a charter of 1498, preceded by an account of his own devotion to St Fillan. Indeed, he paid eighteen shillings to a man who brought St Fillan's Bell, another relic held in Glendochart, to his coronation in Stirling in June 1488.[14]

After the Reformation, the belief that water in which the Quigrich had been dipped would cure fever, scrofula and ailing cattle, plus the conviction that an oath sworn upon it was dangerously binding, became part of local superstition and probably accounted for its careful preservation by the Dewars. During the reign of Charles II the keepers, who had become Presbyterians, relinquished the relic to a Catholic branch of the family but subsequently suffered such bad luck that they managed to get it back again.[15]

However, they still did not prosper and when William Thomson, an Oxford student of mineralogy travelling the Highlands, saw it and made his drawing in 1782 (fig 25), the owner Malice Doire was a mere day labourer with a son and heir dying of consumption. Thomson was so concerned about the fate of the Quigrich that having become a corresponding member of the Society of Antiquaries of Scotland, he wrote in 1784 to the earl of Buchan, its president, urging that they should try to acquire it before its impoverished owner sold it to 'find a ready passage to the melting pot'.[16]

Dewar fortunes did not recuperate and they emigrated to Canada after the Napoleonic Wars on an assisted government scheme taking the Quigrich with them. In Ontario, other Highland settlers continued to come to their clearing for water blessed by the crozier to treat their cattle.[17] When Daniel Wilson became Professor of History and Literature at University College, Toronto, in 1852 he tracked it down and managed to negotiate its return to Scotland, concerned about its fate as family links with their native country faded.

Alexander Dewar and his sons Malcolm and Alexander valued it at $700, but asked the Society for only $500. A descendant, Mrs Nilo Wilson of Toronto, handsomely repaid appreciably more than this sum to the Museum of Scotland in 1992 feeling that it was a part of the national heritage which was beyond price.

It is with all these vicissitudes in mind that the present state of H5 and H6 has to be examined.

✣ ✣ ✣ ✣ ✣ ✣ ✣ ✣ ✣ ✣ ✣ ✣ ✣ ✣ ✣ ✣

The most recently recorded interference with the Quigrich was the removal in 1876 of the earlier crook, which it then still encased.[18] John Stuart does not say how this was accomplished, but a slit has been cut through the silver from top to bottom at the base of the cresting at one side in the angle where its border spreads out over the tube of the crozier. This side of the Quigrich must then have been bent back to release its contents, leaving it with uneven bulges. Clearly it proved impossible to get this panel back exactly into place. At the central inner border, particularly the lower section, there is now an irregular gap between the edges of the filigree panels and the silver strip which is intended to cover them. Comparison with the other side of H6 shows that this originally fitted neatly and smoothly together. Finally, the sides of the empty Quigrich were secured together again by filling the cavity with resin, some of which has seeped out of the incision along the cresting. Further damage between cresting and knop probably also dates to this operation.

The intervention previous to that appears to have been the addition of the present knop and the collars above and below, which replace earlier features. On the undamaged side of the cresting, the quatrefoil piercing and engraved decoration stops short above the knop, presumably to accommodate a larger, more spherical, predecessor. When the panels of scrollwork above were fitted, this necessitated the removal of a vertical section of the framing of the cresting on both sides.

One writer has suggested that the interlaced ornament was copied from an earlier knop removed from H5.[19] However, it is just as likely that it is part of the same late survival and revival of Insular motifs in the West Highlands as numerous sculptured crosses, grave slabs and ivory caskets (for example L9 and L10, pages 186-191). Two panels on the lid of the

Eglinton casket [L9], are particularly close in their combination of arcs, points and straight lines. The scrolls above and below the knop can be paralleled in stone carving from Kintyre and Iona.[20] Together, these comparisons suggest a 15th-century date, perhaps as late as 1488, when St Fillan's Bell was taken to the coronation and the crozier may well have gone too. Apart from the shape of the whole, this is the only section with a distinctively Celtic character.

The cresting, by contrast, with its quatrefoil apertures is a motif which was established in Northern French and Flemish metalwork design by the 1270s when the shrine of Sainte Gertrude of Nivelles was commissioned and it was used for the parapet of the *châsse*.[21] It remained a favourite device for the edges of chalice feet and reliquary bases in France until the mid-14th century.[22] English goldsmiths also used it at the same period for large and small objects.[23] These stylistic considerations imply that this cresting may have been added during or soon after the period of enthusiasm for St Fillan at the end of Robert I's reign.

A fitment which sits rather uneasily on the Quigrich is the half-figure at the top of the drop (page 108). It is curiously flat and has an unfinished vertical area in the middle of the back, clearly not meant to be seen. It has been rather roughly attached and quantities of solder have been used to cover traces of alteration just behind it. Again, the decoration of the cresting stops distinctly short.

Whether this means that the figure represents yet another unrelated refurbishment or whether it is simply a clumsy piece of design by a craftsman unfamiliar with this type of object is difficult to say. Perhaps the latter, in view of the figure's probable date. Anderson pointed out the similarity of the formalised cloud formation under the bust to the privy seal of David II, who succeeded in 1329.[24] Although schematised clouds had been

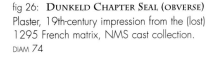

fig 26: DUNKELD CHAPTER SEAL (OBVERSE)
Plaster, 19th-century impression from the (lost)
1295 French matrix, NMS cast collection.
DIAM 74

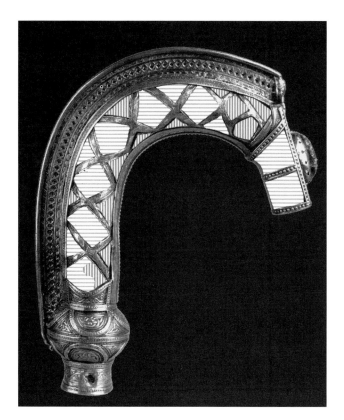
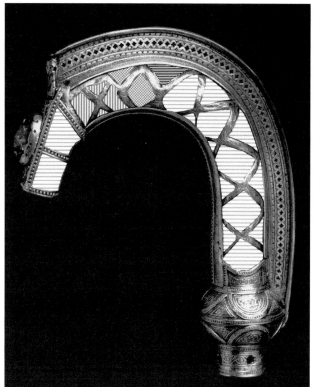

shown in manuscript painting for centuries, they took this particular frilly form in the first half of the 14th century. There is a strong resemblance to those on the Ascension page of the East Anglian Psalter of Robert de Lisle, datable to before 1339;[25] on the donor page of the early 14th-century Taymouth Hours, ascribed on purely circumstantial evidence to the patronage of Joanna, wife of David II, which is also East Anglian[26] and in the scene of St Peter in his boat on folio 37 of the Parisian Belleville Breviary painted in the 1320s.[27] The small engraved crucifix scene on the end of the drop (page 108) is also consistent in style with this period.[28]

The fine precise engraving on the cresting and the strips covering the vertical inner join is in such marked contrast to the fairly rough cross-hatching on the sheets of metal framing the filigree panels that it is difficult to believe they came from the same workshop. If the cresting was added in the first half of the 14th century, the Quigrich before that may have looked very much like the crozier reliquary depicted on the Dunkeld Chapter seal (fig 26, page 112) – a simple crook with decoration in diaper lattice patterns.

The lattice has been copied directly from H5, including the irregular shapes produced by the alteration. This could have been achieved fairly easily by hammering the thin silver sheet on to the copper alloy to produce the resulting pattern. The filigree panels from the earlier crook were then transferred with a small amount of trimming. As the filigree is still in the same sequence of distribution as on H5, which can be established by tracing the panels and matching them, this reveals a little about the history of the earlier crook. As shown in the figures above, a type of filigree different from the majority fills the area above the drop on both sides and down most of the inner border and part of the upper border on the other side. This indicates that not only did H5 have a wedge-shaped section removed and patched over (see the drawing on page 106), but very possibly it too was opened, damaging the edges and making replacements

fig 27: **WATERFORD KITE-BROOCH**
Silver, gold, glass and niello, Irish, c1100, Waterford
Museum of Treasures, photo Niamh Whitfield.
L39, W27, D6

necessary. What its appearance was before these events can only be guessed at by analogy with Irish croziers of the late 11th and early 12th centuries,[29] for example those from Dysert O'Dea and Lismore. Both types of filigree relate in design to work on the Cross of Cong datable to about 1123[30] and the shrine of St Lachtin's arm made between 1118 and 1121,[31] but the scale is much larger and the execution coarser. In this respect, the filigree on H6 resembles the mask on the tip of a brooch found in an early 12th-century context in Waterford (fig 27).[32]

NOTES: [1] Hugh Cheape provided the paragraph (pages 108-109) on the naming of this object. [2] Wilson 1877, 126: 'The only fact worthy of note is, that in the zeal of the late custodiers to make it look its best, it appears to have been rubbed or rather scoured, till traces of gilding which I remember to have noted when I first saw it 18 years ago, are now very slightly traceable.' [3] Ibid 122-31. [4] Breviarum Aberdonense pars. hyem. f. xxvi. [5] Watson 1926, 164, 171, 193, 264, 265, 284, 429. [6] Anderson 1881, 231. [7] Stuart 1877, 141. [8] Gillies 1938, 78-80. [9] Barrow 1988, 317-19. [10] Anderson 1881, 235-9. [11] Stuart 1877, 160; a letter of 1336 is addressed to 'Donald M'Sobrell dewar Cogerach' but by 1428 the bearer of the Quigrich is called simply 'Jore' another form of 'Dewar'; Anderson 1889, 112-13. [12] The original charter was presented to NMS by Hilary Kirkland in 1999. Anderson 1881, 229-30 gives full text and English summary of the document. [13] Ibid. [14] Stuart 1877, 147. [15] Wilson 1877, 122-3. [16] The drawing is bound in with 'Communications to the Society of Antiquaries', vol II, 1785-99 (unpaginated). Unpublished papers of the Society of Antiquaries of Scotland, National Museums of Scotland Library. Thomson writes 'I intreat the Society to excuse the rudeness of the representation annexed, it being the hasty sketch of a Traveller ....' A rather poor engraving and the full text of his letter finally appeared in 1862, *Archaeologia Scotica*, vol III, 289-90. [17] Lockwood 1989, 40-41. [18] Stuart 1877, 'Since the Coygerach came into the possession of the Society, a discovery has been made, which greatly enhances its interest. The great weight of the crozier led to a careful examination of the structure and internal fitting, the result of which was that an earlier crozier of bronze (see plate VI) was found enclosed within the present one.' There are two otherwise inexplicable holes bored in the covering of the inner join of the Quigrich, which may have been an exploratory part of the 'careful examination'. [19] Michelli 1986, 385. [20] Steer and Bannerman 1977, pls 8C, 11. [21] Paris 1996, 220-21, figs 12-13. [22] Ibid 330, cat no 27; 334, cat no 29; Paris 1998, 193-7, cat nos 120-21; 204-5, cat nos 128-9. [23] London 1987, 458-9, cat no 581. [24] Anderson 1881, 222. [25] Rickert 1965, pl 134 (A). [26] Harthan 1977, 48-9; Backhouse 1985, 56, pl 48; for further examples see Sandler 1986, I, illus 161, 163, 240, 241, 243, 248, 249. [27] Avril 1978, 63, pl 12. [28] The suggestion (Edinburgh 1982, cat no D12, 55, 56, 58) that the stars either side of the Crucifixion represent the mullets of the Murray arms and date this section of the Quigrich to around 1500, when John Murray was prior of Strathfillan, is improbable. To make armorial sense there should be three stars, a heraldic device which the Murrays acquired through their Douglas connections (see C2, page 35). Although a crescent moon and a sun are the usual symbols shown flanking the Crucifixion, the stars are likely to have had a religious significance to an artist possibly not entirely familiar with the normal iconography. [29] Mahr and Raftery 1976, 59, 158, 159f, pls 92 and 94. [30] Stalley 1977, 214-15. [31] Ó Floinn 1987, 181-7 [32] Whitfield 1997, fig 15: 18A, 5, 492, pls 37 and 43, 490-4, 507.

COMPOSITIONAL ANALYSIS OF THE ST FILLAN'S CROZIER AND THE QUIGRICH

Katherine Eremin and Jim Tate

The St Fillan's Crozier and the Quigrich were analysed using non-destructive x-ray fluorescence (XRF) to compare the composition of the different components. As all analyses were of the unprepared surface, the original composition may differ from the current values and the data can only be used to suggest possible links between components. The full results and analytical details are given in Eremin 2000b.[1]

The St Fillan's Crozier is composed of copper alloy containing minor zinc (6-8%), tin (3-4%) and lead (around 1%). This mixed alloy is best termed *gunmetal* by analogy with the modern equivalent (see report on the Guthrie Bell Shrine elsewhere in this publication). There were no significant differences between the compositions of the left-hand side, right-hand side or the front piece. All three pieces contained trace levels of antimony and silver, consistent with a common source. Similar mixed alloys were used for Viking period artefacts produced at Scottish sites with Norse influence and for later Medieval artefacts found at Finlaggan.

X-ray diffraction analysis of a small sample of niello from the bands indicated the use of a mixture of lead sulphide and copper-silver sulphide. Copper-silver sulphide, silver sulphide and lead sulphide were used for medieval niello, with more than one variety on a single artefact.[2, 3, 4] Of the Irish artefacts, silver sulphide occurred on an 11th-century bronze mount, copper-silver sulphide on the 11th-century St Cuilleann Bell Shrine, copper-silver sulphide and silver sulphide on the 12th-century Inisfallen Crozier, and copper-silver sulphide and lead sulphide on the 13th-century Hugo Crozier.

One white metal pin was analysed and had high levels of silver and copper with minor zinc and traces of lead, gold, tin and bismuth. The composition of the alloy cannot be determined accurately due to overlap of the x-ray beam with the surrounding copper alloy but was probably around 90% silver.

A copper alloy pin was also analysed and appeared to contain minor amounts of zinc, tin and lead. The analyses again include some of the surrounding copper alloy, hence the exact composition can not be determined.

Most areas of the Quigrich had high levels of gold and mercury, indicating the use of amalgam gilding. This gilded layer meant that no accurate measurement of the underlying original alloy composition could be made without sampling. Although some areas on the base and crest lack visible gilding, mercury was also detected here suggesting former gilding. The fact that only gold, mercury, copper, lead and silver were detected, may either be due to the absence of other elements at detectable levels or, more likely, to the masking of trace elements by the overlying gilding. Lower levels of copper in comparison to silver were found in areas with strong gold and mercury (*ie* thicker gilding). In contrast comparatively more copper was found in areas where the gilding was thinner or patchy. This is due to the greater absorption of the copper x-rays than the silver x-rays by the gold layer. This hinders use of the copper to silver ratio to assess variations in the composition of the underlying silver alloy.

The figures of the monk and Christ, the surround at the closed end of the crozier and the bands around the filigree appeared to be compositionally similar to each other. The rim and underside edge of the open end of the crozier had slightly higher levels of copper and lead than the other components. The open end may hence be compositionally distinct from the other components, although the possibility of variable surface alteration must be remembered. An area of the open end with no detectable mercury, hence presumed to be free of gilding, had a surface composition of 94.5% silver, 3% copper, 2% lead and 0.5% gold (0.5 gold in 100 parts silver). The lead may have been added to the silver alloy to alter the working properties.

Both sets of filigree panels appeared to be composed of silver with minor amounts of copper and only traces of lead, suggesting use of silver with a higher purity than that used for the other components. There was no significant difference in the composition of the two sets of filigree panels. The use of purer silver is normal for filigree work as the purer alloy has greater ductility than the more debased alloy.

NOTES: [1] Eremin 2000b, 3. [2] Oddy, Bimson and La Niece 1983. [3] La Niece and Stapleton 1993. [4] La Niece 1983, 287.

BIBLIOGRAPHY:

K EREMIN 2000b, Analysis of the St Fillan's Crozier and the Quigrich, Internal C&AR report, AR 00/41.

W A ODDY, M BIMSON and S LA NIECE 1983, 'The composition of niello decoration on gold, silver and bronze in the antique and medieval periods', Studies in Conservation, 28: 29-35.

S LA NIECE and C STAPLETON 1993, 'Niello and Enamel on Irish Metalwork', *The Antiquaries Journal*, 73 148-51.

S LA NIECE 1983, 'Niello: an historical and technical survey', *Antiquaries Journal*, 63, 270-97.

VI

SEAL MATRICES

It is very fortunate that as many as twenty Scottish seal matrices from the 12th to the early 16th centuries survive in the museum collections. In this period personal signatures were uncommon and wax impressions of the images on such matrices were attached to documents to authenticate them as the responsibility of the seal's owner. These seals were used on legal and financial documents and consequently were securely guarded in the same way as a modern bankers card. On the death of an individual owner they were normally destroyed so that they could not be put to

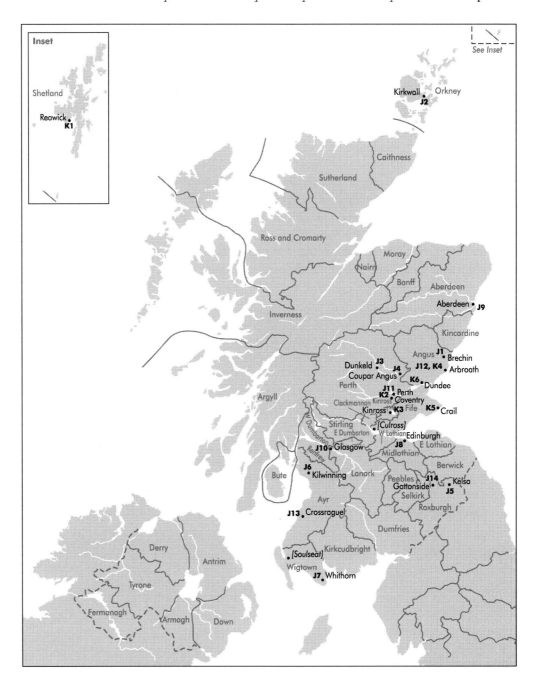

any fraudulent use. As a result corporate seals of cathedral chapters, abbeys, burghs and trade guilds, which were in use for several generations, were more likely to be preserved or simply put away and forgotten about; twelve of those catalogued here fall into this category. More than half of all the matrices have never been buried or exposed to high levels of damp, which means that they are in very good, uncorroded condition.

This makes them very important as evidence of the quality of metalwork available in Scotland during the period, something not easily deduced from many archaeological finds. Their other great value is that most of them have religious imagery of the kind which was ruthlessly destroyed in the Reformation and its aftermath. Scottish medieval churches must have had an abundance of stone and wooden sculpture, but so little is left that we must turn to the Brechin Chapter Seal [J1] to see how magnificent a 13th-century group of the Trinity might have been, or to J4, J5, J6 and K5 to visualise an undamaged Virgin and Child of the 15th or early 16th century. These small objects were sufficiently insignificant to escape the wholesale iconoclasm. With the development of antiquarianism in the 17th century they came to be collected in much the same way as coins and by the 18th and 19th centuries both matrices and impressions were systematically studied, particularly by heraldry enthusiasts.

These twenty matrices cover a wide spectrum of skill and sophistication as their original owners ranged from royalty and great cathedrals to comparatively obscure laymen and monks. The delicate gold personal seal of Queen Joan Beaufort [K3], with its intricate heraldry, is akin to a piece of exquisite jewellery, whereas the monk H de Carrick had a roughly cast copper-alloy matrix of a common standard pattern [J13]. Not only Brechin, but Kirkwall [J2] and Dunkeld [J3] had distinguished chapter seals indicative of international connections. Coupar Angus Abbey was rich enough to have a skilfully engraved silver matrix [J4], but less well endowed or less worldly religious houses like the Dominicans of Edinburgh [J8] or Perth [J11] used simpler devices with rudimentary images. Burgh seals could be very crude and made of lead, for example Arbroath [K4], or large, exuberant and probably imported as in the case of Crail [K5].

Although they are random finds or survivals, the distribution map of these seal matrices adheres closely to the known historical centres of political and diocesan power in the east of Scotland and the central belt, with the exception of J2 and K1 which properly belong in a Scandinavian context.

Normally, seal designs are particularly useful indicators in the history of medieval art as impressions are so often attached to dated documents. Although the Scottish collections in Durham and the British Library are well published and there is an adequate card index in the Public Record Office at Kew, lack of resources has so far prevented the production of any catalogue of the seals in the National Archives of Scotland, which might provide important clues to the dating of the matrices catalogued here. Stevenson and Wood provide notes in many cases, but these are incomplete and not wholly accurate, the principal author having died while the publication was in preparation. Apart from J4, they cite no charters bearing impressions of matrices in the Museum of Scotland earlier than 1500.

+ + + + + + + + + + + + + + +

The seal matrices have been catalogued as religious institutions followed by religious individuals (the numbers prefixed by the letter J) and as secular individuals followed by burghs and a trade guild (the numbers prefixed by the letter K).

Many of these seals have appeared in the literature since the late 18th century and the following concordance gives the most frequent references which are not repeated in the separate catalogue entries.

Hutton I = Hutton, George Henry, *Sigilla*, National Archives of Scotland, ms GD.103/2/15, *c*1795.

Hutton II = Hutton, George Henry, *Seals*, National Archives of Scotland, ms GD.103/2/16, 1800.

Laing I = Laing, Henry, *Descriptive Catalogue of Impressions from Ancient Scottish Seals*, Edinburgh, 1850.

Laing II = Laing, Henry, *Supplemental Descriptive Catalogue of Impressions from Ancient Scottish Seals*, Edinburgh, 1866.

Birch = Birch, Walter de Gray, *Catalogue of Seals in the Department of Manuscripts in the British Museum*, vol IV, (Seals of Scotland and Ireland), London, 1895.

Stevenson and Wood = Stevenson, J H and Wood, M, *Scottish Heraldic Seals: Royal, Official, Ecclesiastical, Collegiate, Burghal, Personal*, vols I-III, Glasgow, 1940.

		Hutton	Laing	Birch	Stevenson & Wood
J1	Brechin		I, no 985, 174	no 15,018, 77-78	I, 133
J2	Kirkwall	I, 121	I, no 1092, 196	no 15,087, 98	I, 160
J3	Dunkeld	I, 153	I, no 1016, 181	no 15,054, 88	I, 145
J4	Coupar Angus	I, 149; II, 139v-140	I, no 1001, 177	no 15,251, 141-142	I, 175
J5	Kelso	I, 5, 83	I, no 1060, 190	no 15,348, 167	I, 188
J6	Kilwinning	I, 16	I, no 1063, 1064, 191	no 15,356, 168-169	I, 189-190
J7	Whithorn				
J8	Dominicans, Edinburgh			no 15,305, 155	I, 206
J9	Henry le Chen				
J10	John, archdeacon of Glasgow		II, no 1145, 201	no 15,167, 118	I, 119
J11	Prior of Perth		II, no 1174, 207	no 15,413, 183	I, 207
J12	W Mathei, Arbroath	I, 48, 185	I, no 981, 174	no 15,213, 131	I, 169
J13	Crossraguel monk				
J14	Gattonside, monastic				
K1	Reawick, knight				
K2	Ralph of Coventry				
K3	Joan Beaufort		I, no 44, 11	no 14,895, 38	
K4	Burgh of Arbroath	I, 139	I, no 1149, 208	no 15,487, 206	I, 53
K5	Burgh of Crail		II, no 1206, 214		I, 56
K6	Hammermen of Dundee	I, 11, 85	II, no 1196, 212	no 15,511, 213-214	I, 60

In the following descriptions the words 'right and 'left' denote the positions features would have occupied on the impressions, *not as shown in the illustrations of the matrices*. This is to denote the intentions of the artist and to avoid confusion, particularly between the right and left hands of the figures.

BRECHIN CATHEDRAL CHAPTER
[H.NM 11]

Scotland, mid-13th century
Copper alloy; engraved and punched
H 56, W 38, D 4

CONDITION
Excellent, slightly worn on back.

INSCRIPTION

S'.CAPITULI:SANCTE*TR/INITATIS*D'.BRECHIN:✚ PATER FI/L Š'SPS.
(Lombardic) [for SIGILLUM CAPITULI SANCTE TRINITATIS DE BRECHIN
and PATER FILIUS SANCTUS SPIRITUS, 'The seal of the chapter of the
Holy Trinity of Brechin. Father. Son. Holy Spirit.']

PROVENANCE
Presented to the Society of Antiquaries of Scotland in 1853
by Patrick Chalmers on behalf of William Anderson, a
lawyer in Brechin, along with J11 and two 17th-century
matrices.[1] It had probably been in the possession of the
Spence family who were town clerks of the burgh for five
generations down to 1815.[2]

✚ ✚ ✚ ✚ ✚ ✚ ✚ ✚ ✚ ✚ ✚ ✚ ✚ ✚ ✚ ✚

The shape is a pointed oval. The Holy Trinity is represented as God the Father enthroned, with the Holy Ghost
as a dove swooping across his chest. God holds Christ on
the cross in both hands.

Within a cruciform nimbus God the Father has a
well-modelled face with large oval eyes, neat straight
hair and a short beard; his pose is symmetrical and
frontal, his feet and ankles appearing from under the
deep tubular folds of his robes, which form shallow swags
under the arms of the crucifix and cover God's right
hand.

The tau-shaped cross is rusticated, Christ is held in
a swaying pose, with crossed feet; within a small halo his
head, with long hair spreading over his shoulders, bears
the crown of thorns; the musculature of his arms and
torso is clearly shown as are the nails in his palms. The
Crucifixion projects in high relief, the foot of the cross
suspended in front of the throne base.

The throne has a seat with a reeded edge, over a
deep concave moulding, resting on short columns with
plain round capitals and bases; the whole on a moulded
corbel tapering into the lower point of the seal. Above
the figure group is a rounded trilobate arch on slender
shafts with crocket capitals, under an architectural
canopy consisting of a central gable with transept roofs
either side and a tower with two pinnacles and a spire;
a slender finial rises from each cusp of the main arch.
Within the arch are a sun at God's right shoulder, a crescent moon and star to his left and four further stars
scattered below.

The whole is metalwork of a very high order, with
deep modelling, fine detail and monumental figures
remarkable on this tiny scale. The engraving is very
precise and the punch was only used for the fine beaded
lines framing the inscription, under the trefoil arch and
inside the nimbus of God the Father. The lettering,
including the very small inscriptions under the arch, on

J1
front

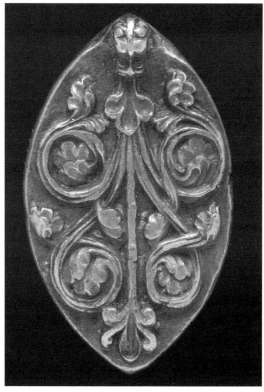

J1
back

God's left shoulder and on the cross, is clear, regular, precise and evenly spaced.

On the back of the matrix is an elaborate cast leaf ornament emerging from a leonine mask at the top and forming two spiral scrolls on either side of a central spine. The scrolls balance each other, but are not symmetrical, curling over and under in alternation on left and right. Fleshy leaf forms terminate the spine and tendrils and fill the centres of the scrolls.

✛ ✛ ✛ ✛ ✛ ✛ ✛ ✛ ✛ ✛ ✛ ✛ ✛ ✛ ✛

The earliest impression so far discovered is attached to a document of 1357,[3] but the style of the figures, architecture and leaf decoration on the back point to a date in the middle of the 13th century. There had been an earlier community of Culdees under a prior at Brechin. However, a papal bull of 1250 documents the emergence of a college of canons which replaced it.[4]

As the new arrangements were established, a chanter appears in 1246, a dean in 1248 and a chancellor in 1274. The office of treasurer had been established between 1219 and 1246. It was probably to celebrate the recognition of this more orthodox chapter that this very fine seal was commissioned.

Attempts to place the composition of the Trinity in the context of English 13th-century manuscript painting remain inconclusive and there are no Scottish examples surviving for comparison.[5] The depth and plasticity of the modelling on both sides of the matrix make sculpture in any case a more likely source of inspiration, but here virtually nothing remains in either country which would provide a parallel for the figures. The throne and the architectural setting, with the trilobate arch under a representation of the roof and spires of a church crossing, became an established convention in illumination by the mid-13th century. The rounded arch was more characteristic of English painting than French by the 1240s and 1250s, for example the Black Book of the Exchequer and a St Albans psalter illuminated after 1246.[6]

Unique to this matrix is the exuberant and highly decorative foliage on the back. Single trifid sprays of foliage form the handles of the earlier 13th-century matrices of the city of Exeter,[7] the burgesses of Burford[8] and Chichester Cathedral.[9] Gem matrices also sometimes had decorative handles as part of their metalwork settings.[10] However, none of them covered the entire surface of the matrix or were in such deep relief.

An object which shares many of the characteristics of the layout of the matrix handle is part of a mould for an openwork metalwork ornament in the Lindisfarne Priory Museum (fig 28). This was for making a mount about 18 cm square to decorate a coffer or cupboard door. It has a very similar symmetrical five-leaved motif at the top and circular scrolls with leafy terminals in a design

based on alternation, probably around a central spine. It is not known precisely where or when the mould was found at Lindisfarne, so there is no archaeological basis for dating it, but stylistic considerations point again to the mid-13th century.[11] The maker of the seal matrix elaborated on the format by doubling the leaf terminals giving the composition extra depth and richness.

It is unlikely that Brechin chapter commissioned their new matrix locally. Albin, bishop of Brechin (1246-69) continued the Scottish fashion of a profile standing figure established by Roger, bishop of St Andrews in 1198 on the obverse of his seal[12] and although it was finely engraved with much detail it lacks the originality and depth of J1.[13] The counterseal has an architectural framing which is very cursory in comparison. The seal of his successor William Comyn (1275-95), on the other

fig 28: MOULD FOR METALWORK
Stone, English, 1250-60 Lindisfarne Priory Museum, copyright English Heritage.
H 140, W 258 (approx)

hand, has very plastic high-relief modelling in the figure of Christ in Majesty on a throne under an architectural niche with pointed arches, tracery and canted piers.[14]

The chapter seal marks a transition by Brechin to employing artists from a more sophisticated milieu and the decoration on the back of J1 suggests Edinburgh, where in the second quarter of the 13th-century Holyrood Abbey had installed a west door to its chapel with rich 'stiff leaf' foliage similar in its exuberance and freedom of handling.[15] Although some stiff leaf carving had been introduced under the vault of the north west tower at Brechin Cathedral itself,[16] it is more conservative and the very high quality of the chapter matrix shows that its maker normally supplied the most discerning of patrons, in all probability the Scottish royal court.

This way of representing God, the crucified Christ and the Holy Spirit evolved in Europe in the 12th century, but seems to have been introduced to Scottish seal design with J1. Dunfermline Abbey, which like Brechin was dedicated to the Trinity, had a round chapter seal made in the first half of the 13th century which shows on the reverse a single enthroned figure with a cruciform nimbus, his right hand raised in blessing and a book in his right, with a bird-like form swooping by his elbow.[17] Abbot Ralph of Dunfermline, however, had adopted the Brechin iconography by the end of the 13th century.[18]

NOTES: [1] *PSAS*, vol I, 1853, 188-90. [2] Jervise 1861, 113-4. [3] Public Record Office, Kew, ms E39/6, an indenture against persons infringing the treaty for the ransom of David II, where a small oval counterseal, possibly a gem, was used. [4] Cowan and Easson 1976, 46, 203. [5] Henderson 1983, 404-13. [6] Morgan 1982, illus 277, cat no 83, 130, illus 291, cat no 86, 133-4. [7] Kingsford 1940, pl I, facing 176. [7] Hope 1895, 437-8. [9] Heslop 1986, pl XXII, 52. [10] Nelson 1936, no 28 pl II, 6 and 11 and no 30, pl II, 12 and 13. [11] I am grateful to Glyn Coppack and Martin Allfrey of English Heritage for information on this unpublished item. [12] Glenn 1999, 146-8. [13] Hunter Blair 1919, no 3599, 157-8. [14] Ibid, no 3600, 158. [15] Wilson 1984, 138. [16] Fawcett 1990, 160. [17] Birch 1907, no 101, 213; Gordon 1868, 408-9 both describe the swooping form as an 'estoile'. [18] Birch 1895, no 15282, 149.

ST MAGNUS CATHEDRAL, ORKNEY
[H.NM 114]

Norway, *c*1300-20
Copper alloy; engraved and punched
DIAM 75, D 10

CONDITION
Excellent, complete, very little wear.

INSCRIPTION
+SIGILLUM_CAPITULI_ORKADENSIS_ECCLESIEX
SANCTI+MAGNI‡ (Lombardic) ['Seal of the chapter of the church of Saint Magnus of Orkney']

PROVENANCE
One of eight lots purchased for the Society of Antiquaries of Scotland from the Gibson Craig sale, March 1887.[1]

✛ ✛ ✛ ✛ ✛ ✛ ✛ ✛ ✛ ✛ ✛ ✛ ✛ ✛

The round matrix shows the stoning of a standing figure and two kneeling praying monks, under a three-bay architectural canopy.

The standing central figure has a large balding head with a curly beard and no halo. Over a robe with vertical folds gathering on his feet, his mantle sweeps across his body to fall in a heavy chute covering his left hand; in his right hand he holds upright a large broad-bladed sword. A missile strikes him on the right forehead. At each side a small tonsured monk with hooded habit is being struck on the head by a stone with another in the air above. All three are on plain faceted tapering corbels.

The canopy consists of three pointed gables with rich leafy crockets, over traceried depressed cusped trilobate arches; the side arches with pointed trefoils above, the centre with a cusped vertical oval. Above are four tall slender finials and three simple pitched roofs, the centre with tile pattern, battlements and a wall with a vertical grid pattern below; those flanking plain. The four square supporting shafts are undecorated, except for a single step to the inner two, and finish without bases or indication of a ground plane.

The design is crisply and neatly carried out, effectively making use of a few decorative elements. The same three-petalled flower punch is used for the gable crockets and to punctuate the inscription, another for the roof tiles and a third for the beaded borders. The distinctive tall spiky lettering is even and competent, except for the S, which is smaller and upside down.

The handle is a fixed shaped ridge with a rectangular loop with an oval hole towards the top, a small moulding and a notch at the bottom end.

✛ ✛ ✛ ✛ ✛ ✛ ✛ ✛ ✛ ✛ ✛ ✛ ✛ ✛

fig 29: TRONDHEIM CHAPTER SEAL
Ink on paper, drawing composed from fragmentary impressions, matrix engraved before 1280, Norwegian, Riksarkivet, Oslo.
DIAM 80 (seal approx)

The design of this matrix is quite unlike other late 13th- or early 14th-century Scottish chapter seals. However, the architectural setting with its tall plain piers, rich scrolling crockets and emphatically patterned tiled roofs bears a general resemblance to the seal of Trondheim Cathedral in use by 1280.[2] A feature peculiar to both is the lack of any bases to the architectural clements, which simply fade out, and the arrangement of the figures on little individual corbels (fig 29). Orkney was in the diocese of Trondheim (then called Nidaros) until 1472 when control over it was transferred to St Andrews. The bishops and clergy of Kirkwall Cathedral from its foundation about 1137 until the 15th century were frequently from Norwegian families, sometimes settled in Orkney or Shetland, who participated in the affairs of the church and the politics of Norway itself.[3] It would have been natural for the chapter to have gone there for their matrix, which is rather too elaborate and refined a piece of craftsmanship to have been produced locally. The cathedral chapters of Bergen,[4] Oslo[5] and Stavanger all had handsome round seals with architectural framing at this period.[6]

James Thomson Gibson Craig (1799-1886) was a Writer to the Signet and, from his twenties onwards, an avid collector of books,[7] paintings, prints and *objets d'art*. He was a founding member of the Bannatyne Club and acquainted with all the leading antiquarians and artists of his day in Scotland and further afield.[8] After his death there were four sales of his effects and Scottish manuscripts at Dowells of Edinburgh, three of works of art at Christie's in London and finally that of his library by Sotheby, Wilkinson and Hodge.[9] The latter raised £15,509.4s.6d. and consisted of 9,404 lots including the Murthly Hours now in the National Library of Scotland.[10]

Writing of J2 in 1850, Henry Laing says 'From the original brass matrix in the Advocates' Library, Edinburgh'. It was apparently not known to Hutton who included a pencil, pen and wash drawing of a damaged impression in *Sigilla*, although he had studied other Advocates' matrices. Stevenson and Wood noted that it was still in use in Kirkwall in 1680. How it came into the hands of Gibson Craig is not known.

At first sight the iconography of this seal is rather puzzling. The tall central figure has been identified by at least one writer as St Magnus,[11] but in all later representations he is shown as a handsome young man in contemporary medieval dress including the garland headdress denoting his status as jarl.[12] The description of St Magnus as he appeared in a warning dream to Alexander II in Kerrera Sound was 'tall and slender and youthful; the fairest of men and nobly dressed'.[13] On the seal a balding man wearing something approximating to a toga is shown, holding aloft a broad-bladed sword,[14] in fact the usual iconography for St Paul, well known to 13th- and 14th-century Norwegian panel painters.[15]

Devising a figure that would be instantly recognised as Magnus posed some difficulties for the medieval artist. His violent murder, struck with a sword at the command of his cousin Haakon, was for entirely political motives, but he was to be seen as a Christian martyr. The author of the special prayers for use on April 16 (the anniversary of his death) and December 13 (the anniversary of the translation of his relics into the new cathedral in Kirkwall), writing in the second half of the 12th century,[16] overcame this difficulty by comparing Magnus with St Paul. This was an established tradition, particularly in relation to the life of Christ, where the sacrifice of Isaac by his father Abraham in the Old Testament was seen as an antetype to the Crucifixion in the New Testament and the escape of Jonah from the whale a symbolic precursor of the Resurrection.[17]

Magnus, who died in 1115 or 1116, was the son of Erlend, one of the two rulers of the Orkney islands. According to medieval tradition, after an early career as a pirate, he converted to Christianity and thereafter refused to fight or take part in raids on the British coast. Instead, he escaped to the Scottish court and lived there as a religious penitent. When the earl of Orkney died, Magnus inherited rulership jointly with his cousin Haakon, who ambushed and killed him on the island of Egilsay.[18] (Modern writers point out that Magnus' family were already fully converted to Christianity and that his only substantiated refusal to fight was in 1098 when he was forced to accompany an expedition led by Magnus Barelegs.[19]) Paul was also high born, persecuted Christians in his early life, then converted and the instrument of his martyrdom too was a sword. The hymns for St Magnus contain the lines '*ut paulus domino magnus convertitur*' (like Paul, Magnus converted to the Lord) and goes on to compare their lives and martyrdoms.[20] A major feature of Paul's creed was personal chastity, and Magnus is also celebrated in the offices of both his feast days for his continence sustained throughout ten years of marriage.[21]

The kneeling figures are presumably the two companions who according to the Sagas were still with Magnus when Haakon's men captured him in hiding on the island. The version of events in the Latin Life describes the assassins breaking into the church where Magnus spent the night in prayer and desecrating the holy place.[22] This violence is possibly represented by the flying missiles, and the manner in which they are shown hitting the victims on the back of the head is very similar to the standard medieval iconography for the martyrdom of St Stephen. St Paul, of course, took a leading part in the stoning of Stephen and the seal maker may well have known the scene from a painted altar frontal cycle showing them both. Altogether, this is a subtle and allusive scheme devised by either the artist or his patron from well-known textual sources.[23]

NOTES: [1] Society of Antiquaries of Scotland Manuscripts *Minute Book 1880-87*, NMS Library. [2] Trætteberg 1953, 44-5, nos 27-8, 53-4. [3] Cant 1972, 5, 12-16. [4] Glenn 1999, 157-60. [5] Trætteberg 1977, no 29, 31-3, 123-4. [6] KLNM III 1958; Scheffer, 201-3; Trætteberg, 203-6. [7] Fletcher 1902, 395-9; Ricci 1930, 192. [8] DNB 1887, 445; Edinburgh University Library, ms La IV 17, letters to David Laing, 1827-77. [9] S C Christie sale catalogues: Ancient and Modern Pictures, April 23rd 1887; Valuable Collection of Objets d'Art, April 25th 1887; Prints and Drawings, April 27th 1887. Sotheby, Wilkinson and Hodge sale catalogue: The Gibson Craig Library, June 27th and nine following days. [10] Higgitt 2000, 38, 39, 40, 285. [11] Birch 1895, no 15087, 98. [12] Blindheim 1988, 165-82. [13] Anderson 1990 vol II, 556-7. [14] David Caldwell points out that the lobated pommel of the sword is a particularly Scandinavian style of design. [15] Morgan 1995, pls 22, 25; Achen 1996, 36-9, 84-6. [16] Blindheim 1988, 165. [17] Mâle 1961, 141, 144-5. [18] Anderson 1990, vol II, 160-2; Palsson and Edwards 1978, ch 50, 87-8. [19] I am indebted to Barbara Crawford, Department of History, University of St Andrews, for her comments on these points and for providing me with a copy of her text on St Magnus for the forthcoming edition of DNB. [20] Breviarium Aberdonense 1854, fol lxxxvii *et verso*. [21] Mooney 1935, 287, 289 gives a fanciful verse translation of the relevant passages by Sir David O Hunter Blair; the chastity of Magnus is further emphasised in 15th-century additions to the liturgy, Eggen 1968, 142 '*Spreto virgo seculo annorum curricolo decem est cum virgine*'. [22] Metcalfe 1889, 239. [23] Foote, 1988, discusses in detail the accretion of motifs to the St Magnus legend, from the 12th-century *Vita S. Magni comitis*, through the *Orkneyinga Saga* to later liturgical sources.

Dunkeld Cathedral Chapter

[H.NM 17]

Scotland, *c*1320.[1]
Copper alloy; engraved and punched
DIAM 53, D 28

CONDITION
Good, crack from saint's left shoulder to lower edge, very
little wear, minor dents at rim.

INSCRIPTION
+S.'CAPITVLI·DVNKELD'.AD:CAVSAS:&:CEⁿTA·NEGOCIA (in centre)
s'.COLV/MBA· (Lombardic) [for *SIGILLUM CAPITULI DUNKELDENSIS
AD CAUSAS ET CETERA NEGOCIA* (in centre) *SANCTUS COLUMBA*, 'Seal
of the chapter of Dunkeld for (legal) proceedings and other
negotiations'(in centre) 'St Columba'].

PROVENANCE
Purchased by the Society of Antiquaries of Scotland in
1874 from the Faculty of Advocates,[2] who had bought it
from James Sutherland in 1705.[3]

+ + + + + + + + + + + + + + + +

On the round matrix St Columba is shown as a bishop
enthroned, flanked by two censing angels.

The beardless saint with a plain halo wears a mitre,
a chasuble over an alb with embroidered apparels at neck
and hem and gloves. An embroidered maniple flows
from his right arm. He raises his left hand in blessing and
holds a spiral-headed crozier in his right. His throne has
a decorated cushion and frontal, a convex incised edge
and a short column at each side with a moulded spherical
capital. It rests on a simple curved ledge.

The half-length angels emerge from formalised
clouds with their wings spreading above and below
inside the beaded border of the inscription. Their censers,
on waving beaded chains, fly up to the shoulders of St
Columba.

The principal figure is strongly modelled in high
relief and has a handsome monumental presence. The
lettering is clear, regular and well formed except for the
letters 'S' in CAVSAS which are reversed.

The handle is a plain tapering central spine with a
tall loop at the top.

+ + + + + + + + + + + + + + +

The negotiations leading up to the sale of a cabinet containing 'Coins and Medals relating to Scotland ; including
also a small collection (in a separate drawer) of some Rings
or Seals with Runes, a few gold ornaments, and Matrixes of
some ecclesiastical Seals' are chronicled in the printed
*Report of the Curators of the Library as to the Faculty's Collection
of Coins*, with an appendix by David Laing dated 7 June
1872. The museum also acquired a small archive that
included manuscript catalogues of the coin collection,
which sadly do not mention the seal matrices. There is also
a handwritten report of 1832 by James Spence to the
Advocates Committee 'to Examine and Arrange their

fig 30: DUNKELD CHAPTER SEAL (REVERSE)
Plaster, 19th-century impression from the (lost)
1295 French matrix, NMS cast collection.
DIAM 74 Dunkeld Chapter seal.

J3

Collection of Coins and Medals' which lists on page three '5 seal stamps'. These are identified in another manuscript catalogue volume dated 1856 by George Sim as being of the monasteries of St Mary of Melrose, St Anthony, Leith and St Andrews, of the abbey of Kinloss, Moray, of Robert III, of the chapter of Dunkeld and another unspecified (presumably K6).

James Sutherland (c1638-1719) was an eminent self-taught botanist, bibliophile and numismatist who corresponded widely with other antiquarians including Sir Hans Sloane. His collection seems to have been formed by exchange with other enthusiasts and by purchase, often from local people who had made chance finds.[4]

By tradition, the relics of St Columba, the Irish missionary who founded Iona Abbey, were brought to Dunkeld by King Kenneth macAlpin before 849. The cathedral was consequently dedicated to Columba.[5] Water in which his bones had been submerged was still being drunk as a protection against plague in the early 16th century.[6]

The matrices made for the bishops of Dunkeld in the second half of the 13th century were notably fine. An impression of the seal of Richard of Inverkeithing (1251-72) is very sculptural and has an elaborate canopy;[7] that of William (c1283-87) is elegantly modelled in high relief and has finely hatched decoration;[8] while Matthew Crambeth (1288-1309) based his on the episcopal seal of William Fraser, his powerful contemporary as bishop of St Andrews.[9]

The chapter replaced their late 12th-century seal with a spectacular double matrix showing the reliquary of St Columba on the obverse and the saint in an architectural framework flanked by censing angels and with five clerics in the arcade below on the reverse (fig 30). There is strong documentary evidence that the double matrix was obtained in Paris in 1295,[10] and the composition of the *ad causas* seal is obviously copied from the figure of Columba and the two angels on it. However, there is no surrounding architecture and the fashionable French X-framed throne with animal-head finials has been replaced by a more sober Scottish bench.

No instances of this seal appearing attached to a document have so far been discovered.

NOTES: [1] Seals *ad causas* for business use by religious communities make their appearance in Scotland after about 1310, their shape being more usually a pointed oval, Harvey and McGuinness 1996, 72-3. [2] NMAS 1892, 369; Brown 1989, 156, 158-9. [3] Pinkerton 1976, vol I, 248 [4] British Library MS Sloane 4038. [5] Duncan 1992, 104. [6] Myln 1823, 43. [7] Hunter Blair 1919, no 3607, 160. [8] Ibid, no 3606, 160. [9] Glenn 1999, 149-51, illus 3,4. [10] Glenn 2003, forthcoming.

COUPAR ANGUS ABBEY
[H.NM 160]

Probably Scotland, before 1449
Silver; engraved and punched
H 60, W 41, D 3

CONDITION
Excellent on seal face, back mutilated.

INSCRIPTION
+S'.COMVNE:CAP/LI::MON/*DE*CVPRO** (Lombardic)
[for SIGILLUM COMMUNE CAPITULI MONASTERII DE CUPRO, 'Common seal of the chapter of Coupar']

PROVENANCE
Purchased by the museum with two later matrices from the 1913 London sale of the Dinsdale Collection.[1] It was in the possession of a London silversmith by the 18th century and by 1792 had been bought at auction by Joseph Dinsdale of Upton in Essex.[2]

+ + + + + + + + + + + + + + +

Within the pointed oval shape the composition is in two registers, the Virgin and Child enthroned in an elaborate architectural structure above; a kneeling cleric facing forward in a round-headed niche below, flanked by the armorial shields of Scotland (on the left) and the family of Hay (on the right).

The Virgin and Child have no halos. She has a veil draped over her head which falls to cover her right arm and breast and a shallow crown with a cross; he is bareheaded. The Virgin's mantle hangs in chutes of folds over her knees and scoops between them and to the side. The

J4

standing Child wears a simple shift straight from shoulders to feet. She holds a flower spray in her right hand and he gestures towards it with his. They are on a bench with moulded edge and finely hatched front.

The structure consists of a central canopy jutting out over the figures in five bays each with a sharply pointed gable containing cusped blind tracery and tall spiky pinnacles between; in the centre is a squat three-sided tower. At each side is a traceried wing, the bottom edge sloping upwards to give an impression of perspective; each wing has its own gable and pinnacles and a two-light composition with trefoil heads under a lozenge framing a quatrefoil.

The tonsured figure below wears a monastic habit and holds a crozier in his right arm; the sides of his niche are coursed masonry. The arms are a lion rampant within a tressure and three hatched escutcheons. The small lettering, within a pronounced beaded border, is neat, regular and well formed, punctuated by five-petalled flower heads, miniature 'x' forms and trefoils. The matrix is a very skilled and finely executed piece of silver-smithing. A six-pointed star punched on the edge of the matrix at the top left of the point may be a silversmith's mark, rather than the more usual indication of the right way up to impress the seal.

On the back are the remains of a hinged (?) ridged handle and traces of solder, where the surface has been carved flush at a later date, probably so that it could be displayed on a flat surface.[3]

✝ ✝ ✝ ✝ ✝ ✝ ✝ ✝ ✝ ✝ ✝ ✝ ✝ ✝ ✝ ✝

By the 16th century Coupar Angus was the richest of the eleven or twelve Cistercian abbeys in Scotland, surpassing even its mother house at Melrose, and like all the others was dedicated to the Blessed Virgin Mary.[4] An impression from this matrix is attached to a Grandtully charter of 10 July 1449.[5] The tabernacle work is typical of English church woodwork of the period and presumably of that of Scotland also, but so little of the latter survives that efforts at comparison are futile. Such compositions were fairly common in European International Gothic art of the 15th century. It is the only silver medieval matrix in this collection, but others survived from Scotland at least until the early 19th century.[6]

The heraldry points not only to Coupar Angus' position as a royal foundation, but to the Hay family who had been associated with the abbey since the reign of William the Lion.[7] William de Hay was a witness to the royal charter confirming its rights,[8] and also to two grants of lands to the abbey.[9] He himself granted it land in the late 12th century.[10] The family connection with Coupar Angus Abbey is also evident in 13th-century documents.[11] In 1436 another William succeeded as eleventh lord of Erroll, was created earl in 1452 and served as Constable of Scotland under James II.[12] It seems likely that William Hay of Erroll either gave the matrix to the abbey, or that it celebrates some further benefaction from his family.

In the mid-15th century another influential figure associated with Coupar Angus Abbey was Thomas Livingstone, formerly abbot of Dundrennan.[13] In 1433 he was one of the eight representatives sent by James I to the Council of Basle,[14] where he made powerful and influential friends.[15] Soon after 1441 Livingston was nominated 'commendator' of Coupar Angus, an arrangement which lasted until his death in 1460.[16] He would certainly have been ambitious and sophisticated enough to appreciate a fine silver seal, but it is doubtful if he ever had much direct personal contact with the abbey.

NOTES: [1] NMAS manuscript register. [2] Hutton c1795, 149. [3] Hutton 1800, 140 has a pencil sketch of the face, back and top edge of the matrix showing it in its present condition and giving a detail of the stamped star mark. [4] Cowan and Easson 1976, 72-4. [5] National Archives of Scotland ms GD 121/1/4/10/14. Stevenson and Wood 1940, vol I, 175, mis-date it to 29 July. The text of the charter was published in Fraser 1868, vol I, item 11, 14-16 without any mention of its seals. [6] National Archives of Scotland, ms GD.103/2/17, item 10, letter to Hutton from David Deuchar, 17 July 1804, about the dispersal of the McGown collection in London. [7] Easson 1947, vol I, 94, 97, 98, 109. [8] Barrow 1971, no 69, 172, between 1165 and 1171. [9] Ibid, no 275, 302, between 1177 and 1190; no 420, 399, between 1198 and 1202. [10] Ibid, no 322, 331-2, between 1187 and 1195. [11] Rogers 1879, x-xix. [12] Easson 1947, 97. [13] Burns 1962, 12. [14] Rogers 1879, 51-2. [15] Ibid, 76, 79, these included Aeneas Silvius Piccolomini, later to become pope Pius II (1458-64), who had famously visited Scotland as a young man. [16] Rogers 1879, xlix; Easson 1947, 273.

KELSO ABBEY
[H.NM 16]

Scotland, mid-16th century or later
Copper alloy; engraved and punched
DIAM 60, W 76 (with lugs), D 2

CONDITION
Good, small chip to lower edge; one pin from counterseal
broken off in lower right-hand lug.

INSCRIPTION
/S'GILLVM+CONMVNE+STE+MARIE+DE+KEL/CO (at sides) C
(reversed)/G (Lombardic) [for SIGILLUM COMMUNE SANCTE MARIE
DE KELCHO, 'Common seal of Saint Mary of Kelso']

PROVENANCE
Presented to the Society of Antiquaries of Scotland by Dr
David Spence in 1781.[1]

✛ ✛ ✛ ✛ ✛ ✛ ✛ ✛ ✛ ✛ ✛ ✛ ✛ ✛ ✛ ✛

The round matrix with four circular lugs shows the Virgin
standing under an architectural canopy, with the naked
Child on her left arm, his feet held in her right hand; he
reaches up to clasp her neck. The Virgin has a rayed
nimbus, the Child a simple halo. She wears a cloak draped
over her head and a long mantle billowing around her
figure and falling in cushions of folds at her feet.

The canopy consists of an openwork tracery gable
with five crocket finials and two triangular crestings,
each topped with a knop of three berries. Underneath is
a cusped cinquefoil arch over the figures and two groups
of shafts forming side bays to the structure. It stands on a

J5

forward sloping platform; the figures are indicated on a
projecting plane, balanced on the line border of the
inscription. The background of the central bay is scattered with stars. The inscription combines features of
Lombardic and Roman with some markedly Italianate
letter forms.

The back is completely plain, with an engraved ✛
marking the top.

✛ ✛ ✛ ✛ ✛ ✛ ✛ ✛ ✛ ✛ ✛ ✛ ✛ ✛ ✛ ✛

Kelso was a Tironensian abbey, founded in the 1120s
under royal patronage, which flourished until the later
16th century in spite of centuries of raids and border
skirmishes with the English. In 1517 it still claimed to
house 36-40 monks, plus the abbot and prior, in times
of peace.[2] The massive remains of its 12th-century buildings still stand. The skill of the original scriptorium and
the riches of the library are demonstrated by a charter
decorated with a joint portrait of David I and Malcolm IV,[3]
and a finely illuminated manuscript of the writings of St
Augustine.[4]

This matrix comes at the end of a tradition of distinguished Kelso seals. The first abbey seal, which
appears on a document of 1171, is one of the most handsome 12th-century Scottish ecclesiastical seals known to
us.[5] J5 is a rather crude reworking of the 14th-century
double seal, which has a standing Virgin and Child with
foliage behind, under a delicate Gothic canopy on the
obverse. On the reverse is a standing figure of St John the
Evangelist, to whom the abbey is dedicated along with
the Virgin, under a similar canopy.[6] The lugs on J5 show
that it too was part of a double matrix (see J6 and K5)
and presumably the missing half again carried an image
of St John.

It has been suggested that the initials 'C' and 'G'
stand for Cardinal de Guise, nominated Commendator of
Kelso after 1542.[7] In spite of its Marian iconography
Stevenson and Wood record that it was still in use in
1571-72, more than a decade after the Reformation had
been authorised by the Scottish Parliament.

NOTES: [1] Hutton c1795, 5; Wilson 1849, no 23, 92, wrongly
identified as the seal of St Mary's Convent, Elcho; attributed in
error to the Advocates Library by Laing 1850, no 1060, 190; and
subsequently by Birch 1895, no 15348, 167. [2] Cowan and Easson
1976, 68-9. [3] Duke of Roxburghe muniments, on loan to the
National Library of Scotland. [4] Trinity College, Dublin, ms 226.
[5] Hunter Blair 1919, no 3665, 179; Laing 1850, no 1057, 189-90,
pl XXV, fig 2. [6] Birch 1907, nos 114 and 115, 239, 241. [7] Birch
1895, no 15348, 167.

J6
KILWINNING ABBEY
[H.277 A&B]

Scotland, obverse *c*1400, reverse 16th century
Copper alloy with silvered surface; engraved
DIAM 48, W 65 (with lugs), D 4 (reverse), D 16 (obverse plus pins)

CONDITION
Excellent, silvering more worn on reverse, quantities of wax embedded in obverse.

INSCRIPTION
(obverse)+S:CONMVNE:ABB'IS:&:CONVENTVS:MONASTERII·DE·KYLWYNYN (Lombardic) (reverse)+S·COMMVNE·CAPITVLI·MONASTERII· DE·KILVYNYNG (Roman) [for (obverse) *SIGILLUM COMMUNE ABBATIS ET CONVENTUS MONASTERII DE KILWYNYN*, 'Common seal of the abbot and convent of the monastery of Kilwinning' and (reverse) *SIGILLUM COMMUNE CAPITULI MONASTERII DE KILWYNYNG*, 'Common seal of the chapter of the monastery of Kilwinning'].

PROVENANCE
Still at Kilwinning in 1789,[1] it was bought by the museum from a London dealer in 1987.

✛ ✛ ✛ ✛ ✛ ✛ ✛ ✛ ✛ ✛ ✛ ✛ ✛ ✛ ✛ ✛

The matrices, for seal and counterseal, are round, each with four circular lugs, three of the lugs on the obverse holding thick cylindrical pins, the top pin scratched with an *.

OBVERSE
In the centre, a crowned Virgin and Child with plain haloes are enthroned under a five-bay Gothic architectural canopy. The Child stands on the Virgin's right knee and reaches up with his left hand to touch her veil. Her mantle is held by a girdle and falls in deep folds over her knees. The area behind them is decorated with four sprays of trefoil leaves. A line of six small crosses decorate the step of the throne.

The canopy above them consists of a five pointed shallow arch under five crocketted gables, with tall finials between each and a rectangular tower (?) in the centre. Similar gables and finials crown the two traceried bays on either side, each of which has a quatrefoil above a paired cusped lancet. The legend is between beaded and plain moulded borders.

REVERSE
An abbot with a crocketted crozier in his right hand and a book in his left stands under a canopy composed of the same elements as that on the obverse, against a background of scrolling tendrils with trefoil leaves between vertical borders of small crosses. The foreground is indicated by horizontal stripes.

The architecture differs from the obverse by having larger flanking bays, light cross-hatching in the tracery and by entirely filling the circular space at the top. The lettering, between plain moulded borders, is larger, clearer and less regular than on the obverse.

Although a perfect fit, and obviously designed as a pair, the matrices appear to have been made at different dates and by different hands. The backs of the matrices are plain and flat.

✛ ✛ ✛ ✛ ✛ ✛ ✛ ✛ ✛ ✛ ✛ ✛ ✛ ✛ ✛ ✛

The differences in legend, lettering and architecture were noticed in the mid-19th century,[2] and further commented on at a meeting of the Society of Antiquaries in 1853 when a detached impression from a previous reverse was also exhibited 'which precisely corresponds with the other on the obverse'.[3]

This slightly ambiguous account plus the fact that the face of J6 with the enthroned Virgin is more carefully executed makes it clear that the matrix with the standing abbot is the replacement.

Laing and Birch describe this figure as St Winnin. Also called Kinewin[4] and Vinin,[5] there is much confusion about his identity. One scholar equates him with Finnian of Moville, a teacher of Columba,[6] while others think he may be Finan of Clonard or even that the two saints may be the same person.[7] Either way, there are no details of his life, and no identifiable iconography. The figure, which has no halo, could as easily be the Tironensian abbot of Kilwinning. The other known Kilwinning seal, that of a 14th-century abbot, shows him kneeling below a representation of the Virgin and Child.[8]

NOTES: [1] Hutton *c* 1795, no 16, gives unfinished pencil sketches of J6 inscribed 'Drawn from impressions upon paper communicated by the Revd. Mr Pollock of Kilwinning 1789'. [2] Laing 1850, no 1063, 1064, 191. [3] Scott 1853, 71. [4] Anderson 1990, vol II, 700. [5] Cowan and Easson 1976, 69. [6] Watson 1926, 165, 187. [7] Sharpe 1995, 11, 317-18. [8] Birch 1895, no 15359, 169.

CONVENT OF WHITHORN

[H.NM 147]

Scotland, early 14th century
Copper alloy, with traces of gilding on the back; engraved
H 50, W 30, D 12

CONDITION

Very good, some scratches, no losses or serious damage.

INSCRIPTION

+s':CONVENTVS:CANDIDE:CASE (Lombardic) [for *SIGILLUM CON-VENTUS CANDIDE CASE*, 'Seal of the convent of Candida Casa'].

PROVENANCE

Found in the manse garden at Soulseat 1891,[1] presented to the museum by the Rev. James Aikman Paton, 1902.[2]

✛ ✛ ✛ ✛ ✛ ✛ ✛ ✛ ✛ ✛ ✛ ✛ ✛ ✛ ✛ ✛

Within the pointed oval shape the *Agnus Dei*, with a shaggy fleece, faces left and looks back over its shoulder at a tall slender cross with four thin flowing pennants; it bleeds from the breast into a large chalice on a ribbed conical foot. Above, there is a sun and a crescent moon, below, a lily with a three-leafed plant spray on either side. The inscription is framed by a single engraved line.

The fixed straight handle is a notched pointed loop with an oval hole.

✛ ✛ ✛ ✛ ✛ ✛ ✛ ✛ ✛ ✛ ✛ ✛ ✛ ✛ ✛ ✛

'Candida Casa' the 'Shining white house' was the early medieval name for Whithorn, the church which Bede tells us had been built by St Ninian 'a long time before [St Columba]'.[3] Bishops were recorded there in the 8th century, the see then lapsed and was revived about 1128. There was probably already a community associated with the cathedral, but this was superseded by Premonstratensian canons introduced by Bishop Christian in 1175-77.[4] Whithorn was a daughter house of Soulseat about 40 kilometres to the north-west, where J7 was found.[5]

The rather archaic form of the Lamb is taken from the counterseal of Gilbert, Bishop of Whithorn (1235-53).[6] This is known from an impression in Durham Cathedral archives (fig 31) and was a carved jasper gem, supposed by Birch to be Early Christian, but in fact more probably dating from the late 12th or early 13th century.[7]

NOTES: [1] Dalrymple 1894, 53. [2] *PSAS*, vol XXXVI, 1902, 590. [3] Anderson 1991, 7-8; for other Whithorn finds see A9 (page 17), B5-B6 (pages 24-6), C1 (pages 29-33), D1-D3 (pages 48-9). [4] Cowan and Easson 1976, 212. [5] Ibid, 102. [6] Birch 1907, no 83, 177; Hunter Blair 1919, no 3631, 170, pl II. [7] Birch 1895, no 17291, 679.

fig 31: GILBERT, BISHOP OF WHITHORN
Wax, impression of his counterseal – a gem of *c*1200, English, 1248, photo Durham Cathedral Chapter Archives (Ms misc 801; Hunter Blair 3631).
H 38, W 25 (seal approx)

J7

DOMINICAN FRIARY, EDINBURGH
[H.1992.1892]

Scotland, 1300-50
Copper alloy; cast and engraved
H 50, W 32, D 15

CONDITION
Complete except for chipped edges, but heavily corroded back and front.

INSCRIPTION
+S CONVENTUS FRM PDICATOR DE CASTRO PVELLAR (Lombardic) [for *SIGILLUM CONVENTUS FRATRUM PREDICATORUM*[1] *DE CASTRO PUELLARUM*, 'Seal of the convent of preaching brothers of the castle of maidens'].

PROVENANCE
Found at Topcliffe, near Thirsk, Yorkshire, purchased by the museum 1992.[2]

+ + + + + + + + + + + + + + +

The composition within the pointed oval is split horizontally, in the upper section Christ and the Virgin are seated on a bench, he places a crown on her bowed head with his right hand and holds a book in his left, while her hands are clasped in prayer.

In the lower part, under three plain gables is the facade of a castle with coursed masonry, three towers with battlements and a large round headed central portal. A human head appears on top of the central tower and half-figures on each flanking one.

The handle consists of a tapering central spine with large round loop at the top.

+ + + + + + + + + + + + + + + +

fig 32: EDINBURGH DOMINICANS
Wax, impression from J8 while still in good condition, Scottish, 1486, photo National Archives of Scotland.
H 50, W 32 (impression)

The large Dominican Friary stood between the Cowgate and Drummond Street, south of the Canongate, the main thoroughfare of medieval Edinburgh.[3] It was founded about 1230 on land given to the order by Alexander II and entertained numerous distinguished visitors, including Henry VI of England and his queen, before its destruction by the mob in 1559.[4]

The 14th-century seal of the prior of the Edinburgh Dominicans is also known, the design being a slightly different version of the Coronation of the Virgin above a kneeling figure of the prior in profile.[5] The earliest impression of J8 is attached to a charter of 12 December 1486.[6] In 1561 it had been replaced by a similar matrix, on which EDINBURGH replaced CASTRO PUELLARUM in the legend.[7]

The place name 'Maidens' Castle' was already used for Edinburgh by Geoffrey of Monmouth in the 1140s, and it appears again in documents of 1174 and 1175. Other sites with the same name were to be found in Fife, Stirling, Yorkshire, Westmorland, Cumberland and Dorset.[8] The exact significance is debatable, but it has been attached to the legend of St Monenna who came to Scotland with a group of maidens and founded seven churches one of them on the rock at Edinburgh.[9]

NOTES: [1] For 'PREDICATORUM', see also J11 (page 135). [2] Smith 1991, 331. [3] Moir Bryce 1911, plan facing 48. [4] RCAHMS 1951, 125. [5] Birch 1895, no 15304, 154. [6] National Archives of Scotland ms GD 172/76; Stevenson and Wood 1940, vol I, 206. [7] Smith, loc cit. [8] Wheeler 1943, 9. [9] Watson 1926, 150, 342.

J9
Henry le Chen, Bishop of Aberdeen
[H.NM 209]

Scotland, c 1300-28
Copper alloy, gilt; cast engraved, punched
H 65, W 42, D 3

CONDITION
Mostly quite good, lower point of oval broken off, gilding worn.

INSCRIPTION
os:hēriciod'iogᆞraooepioaberdoneň (Lombardic) [for *SIGILLUM HENRICI DEI GRATIA EPISCOPI ABERDONENSIS*, 'Seal of Henry by the grace of God bishop of Aberdeen']

PROVENANCE
Found in a field at Furtho Manor, near Stony Stratford, Northamptonshire. Given by Mr Jones, Furtho Manor.[1]

++++++++++++++++

Within a pointed oval the Virgin and Child are shown half-length, above a standing figure of a bishop, framed by a Gothic architectural canopy.

The Virgin has a shallow crown over a shoulder-length veil, the Child a cruciform nimbus. He leans on the Virgin's left shoulder and reaches across her breast towards an apple (?), which she holds in her right hand.

The bishop raises his right hand in blessing and holds a crozier with crocket decoration in his left. His mitre is low with a central vertical band of decoration, revealing a fringe of tight curls on his forehead. The features of his youthful beardless face and his ears are carefully engraved, his hands are unnaturally large but the episcopal ring on his right hand is clearly indicated. His elaborate formal vestments consist of an alb and dalmatic, with stiff embroidered apparels at neck, cuffs and hem held at the throat by a morse. Over this swathed in deep V-folds is an undecorated chasuble. Plain boots are visible below the vestments.

The architectural framing consists of a crocketted pointed arch on two piers, having an interior arch of the same profile, the space between filled by a central quatrefoil flanked by four rosettes. Underneath is a rounded cusped arch below a trefoil. The piers have three small spires with trifid finials. They are in four registers, the top three composed of trefoils under gables and paired lancets, the bottom a single keyhole-shaped arch. Within this canopy, the Virgin and Child appear above a moulded string course and the bishop framed by a moulded ogival arch with scrolls in the spandrels above. Two small rosettes ornament the inner moulded and beaded border of the legend half-way up. Punches have been used for these, the rosettes

fig 33: **Henry le Chen**
Wax, impression from his smaller seal, Scottish, 1292, photo The National Archives, Kew
(MS SC 13/D 14).
H 53, W 35

J9

under the main arch and the hem of the bishop's vestments.

The inscription is even and clear. The back is plain and flat.

✝ ✝ ✝ ✝ ✝ ✝ ✝ ✝ ✝ ✝ ✝ ✝ ✝ ✝ ✝ ✝

The medieval dedication of the cathedral of Aberdeen was to St Machar, an obscure saint with no known iconography, although there may have been a lost Latin *Vita*;[2] the Virgin represents an alternative dedication. It is unusual for the standing bishop normal on a seal of dignity to be combined as on J9 with a patron saint to whom he is not kneeling in prayer.[3]

Only two medieval bishops of Aberdeen bore the forename Henry and de Lychtone (1422-40) can be ruled out on stylistic grounds as the owner of this matrix. Henry le Chen (1282-1328) came of a prominent Scoto-Norman family based in north-east Aberdeenshire and Moray. In spite of supporting the English cause until at least 1308, he eventually came into the obedience of Robert Bruce. Surviving further political difficulties, he was finally remitted from all rancour in December 1318, and seems to have had an uneventful final ten years as bishop.[4] Another smaller seal of le Chen's (fig 33) is known from an impression of 1292 in the Public Record Office; while another is attached to a charter of 1310.[5] It shows him in prayer below the Virgin of the Assumption and is surrounded by the apparently private prayer PRESVLIS : ESTO ; PIA : ME/MOR : ASCENDO : MARIA. In spite of its use on the latter very public document, its size and design would have been much more usual on a personal or counterseal, while J9 was obviously intended as his formal seal of dignity as bishop.

Furtho Manor, where J9 was found near some foundations beside an old road, lies in the Honour of Huntingdon. This large tract of land came into the possession of the Scottish royal family with the marriage of David I and remained important throughout the 12th century.[6] William the Lion was still keenly interested in his Northamptonshire properties, himself visiting Silverstone and Brackley, respectively about ten and twenty-five kilometres away from Furtho, in 1194.[7] William was following one of the principal routes south on his way to Winchester, partly along Watling Street, and Henry le Chen's entourage was presumably on a similar journey when this matrix was lost. Although the Scottish presence in Huntingdon had declined by the early 14th century, some families like the Balliols and the Bruces still held land there and Alexander Comyn, earl of Buchan, inherited through his wife Elizabeth de Quincy lands around Eynesbury (St Neots) in 1275.[8] The le Chen and Comyn families were close political allies,[9] and at least one source states that Henry's mother was in fact the sister of John Comyn, lord of Badenoch.[10] The Comyns were not purely absentee landlords of their English estates and Alexander is recorded in the Midlands in 1281 protecting his interests.[11] Henry le Chen's travels very possibly included a visit to his Comyn connections at Eynesbury en route. The rare survival of the matrix is due to some mishap along the way, as bishops' seals of office were otherwise always ceremoniously destroyed at the time of their death.[12]

It is difficult to say at what stage in le Chen's long career J9 was made. Other bishops replaced their seals two or three times with grander or more elaborate versions. A design in which the prelate stands under an architectural canopy with supporting piers first appears in Scotland with the second seal of William Fraser, bishop of St Andrews, attached to a document of 1288,[13] and the piers, gable arch, layout of the legend and the rich beaded borders of J9 bear a close resemblance to it. Like Fraser's previous seal, this is also remarkable for including shields with his personal family heraldry, something which does not seem to occur on English bishop's seals until about a decade later,[14] or in France until the mid-14th century.[15] It is quite likely that le Chen's arms appeared on the missing lower point of the matrix, as they did on Fraser's second seal and perhaps on that of Matthew Crambeth, bishop of Dunkeld (1289-1309).[16]

The canopy on le Chen's matrix has rather more complex gables and piers than Fraser's and a second story has been added to the composition. If J9 was made for le Chen's appointment in 1282 it was more fashionable than the seals of the premier Scottish bishop at St Andrews. If it marks his joining the fold of Bruce's party or even his final exoneration in 1318 it shows him rather belatedly following the lead of Fraser, a frequent associate,[17] a major political force for many years and familiar with French courtly practices.[18]

NOTES: [1] *PSAS*, vol LXXXI, 1948, 194. [2] Horstmann 1881, 189-208. [3] Heslop 1986, fig 153, 274. [4] Duncan 1988, 416-17. [5] Public Record Office, Kew, loose seals SC13/D14; Birch 1907, no 67, 145; National Archives of Scotland ms GD SP 13/5. [6] Ferguson 1994, 18, 22. [7] Barrow 1971, 81, 156, 99. [8] Farrer 1923-5, vol II, 371. [9] Young 1997, 140, 167, 194. [10] Keith 1824, 109. [11] Young 1997, 80. [12] This was particularly well documented at Durham (Hope 1887, 271). [13] Birch 1907, no 59, 129; Hunter Blair 1919, no 3624, 166, pl I. [14] Hope 1887, 278. [15] Bedos-Rezak 1993, VII, 30. [16] Birch 1895, no 15040, 83, cast of an unknown impression; Laing 1866, no 1017, 171, pl X, fig 7, has a shield-shaped blob, the illustration based on 'Mr Doubleday's Collection of Casts', 'Paris'; the fine impression in the Archives Nationales now has the lower section broken off (Glenn 1999, illus 4, 151). [17] For example, they were probably both members of the Council of Twelve chosen in 1295 (Young 1997, 140). [18] Glenn 1999, 10. [19] I am grateful to Alan Young for reading the draft of this entry and giving me his comments.

John, Archdeacon of Glasgow
[H.102A]

Scotland, late 13th century to 1337
Copper alloy; cast, engraved and punched
H 40, W 23, D 10

CONDITION
Excellent.

INSCRIPTION
S' IOH'IS/ARCh ID' GLASCVEИS' (Lombardic) [for *SIGILLUM IOHANNIS ARCHIDIACONI GLASCUENSIS*, 'Seal of John archdeacon of Glasgow'].

PROVENANCE
At Trinity College, Glenalmond in 1866,[1] possibly taken to Edinburgh after a disastrous fire at the college in 1876.[2] Acquired by the museum before 1892 probably with 16 matrices and seals of Episcopal bishops of Scotland.[3]

+++++++++++++++++

Within a pointed oval St Kentigern as bishop stands blessing the kneeling, praying figure of the archdeacon, both figures in profile; a salmon with a ring in its mouth rises vertically between them.

The saint, on the left, wears a mitre and embroidered vestments and carries a large crozier with pronounced wavy crockets in his left hand, he has no halo. The priest is tonsured and wearing a simple habit with decorated collar. The figures are supported on a

J10

tapering base with a leaf motif, under a pointed trilobate arch with tall frondlike crockets above and a bird reguardant in the centre. Two spherical motifs on stems above the archdeacon's head appear to be part of the architectural ornament.

This is a fairly mechanically produced personal seal, the modelling of the figures is rather summary and the head of John, in particular, is disproportionately large. The inscription within beaded borders is a little uneven with one reversed 'N'. The handle is a fixed ridge with simple loop, with a round hole at the top.

+++++++++++++++++

Archdeacon John, who was elected bishop of Glasgow in 1337,[4] was a member of the powerful Wishart dynasty of clerics. Robert of the same family was bishop of Glasgow (1271-1316) with his kinsman Thomas as dean in the 1280s and 1290s, while William Wishart was archdeacon of Teviotdale and a canon of Dunkeld.[5]

The iconography is an abbreviated version of that worked out at Glasgow Cathedral for its patron saint Kentigern, popularly called Mungo. The bird represents the pet robin of his master St Serf, whom Kentigern as a boy restored to life.[6] The salmon is symbolic of another folkloric addition to the saint's life, written in the 12th century, borrowed from early Irish romances.[7] In this story Riderich, the Cumbrian king whose realm had been Christianised by Kentigern, gave his wife Langueth a ring which she passed on to her lover. The king retrieved it and flung it into the Clyde, then challenged the queen to produce it on pain of death. Kentigern saved the situation by dispatching a messenger to fish, who miraculously caught a salmon which had swallowed the ring.

The first reference to the saint on a Glasgow seal is on the slightly larger counterseal of bishop William de Bondington (1233-58). The design of J10 seems to be based on this except that Bondington naturally wears a mitre and the saint is identified only by the legend ORA PRO NOBIS BEATE KENTEGERNE [pray for us blessed Kentigern].[8] Bishop Robert Wishart had at least four seals made, each elaborating further on the theme of Kentigern. From the first the salmon and the bird were included, but by the time the fourth was created the counterseal also included a remarkable series of narrative scenes in three architectural tiers telling the story of Riderich and Langueth.[9] Archdeacon John simply added the two most frequent features from his illustrious kinsman's seal to his own more modest matrix.

NOTES: [1] Laing 1866, no 1145, 201. [2] Information kindly provided by Felicity Gibbon, archivist of Glenalmond College. [3] NMAS 1892, nos 89-106, 370. [4] Watt 1969, 171. [5] Barrow 1973, 241-2. [6] Anderson 1990, vol I, 130. [7] Ibid, 136. [8] Laing 1850, no 945, pl XV, fig 5, 164. [9] Ibid, no 947, pl XVI, fig 1, 164-5.

OFFICE OF THE DOMINICAN PRIOR, PERTH
[H.NM 47]

Scotland, late 15th century
Copper alloy; engraved
H 50, W 34, D 15

CONDITION
Excellent.

INSCRIPTION
S' officii:Poris:or/d':Pdicatū'de:Pth (black letter) [for *Sigillum officii Prioris ordinis Predicatorum de Perth*, 'Seal of office of the prior of the order of preachers of Perth']

PROVENANCE
Presented to the Society of Antiquaries of Scotland by William Anderson of Brechin, 1853.[1]

✦ ✦ ✦ ✦ ✦ ✦ ✦ ✦ ✦ ✦ ✦ ✦ ✦ ✦ ✦ ✦

The pointed oval shape contains, within a very schematised framework of vertical architectural elements, a half-length standing Virgin and Child adored by a left facing kneeling figure in a plain round-headed niche below.

Neither Virgin nor Child has a halo. The Virgin wears a tall leafy crown and cradles the Child on her left hip. The folds of her veil and robe are indicated by simply engraved lines, as are those of the cleric's cloak below. He also wears a close-fitting cap and a large collar. The architecture consists of groups of thin finials, three either side of the figures and five forming a canopy at the top, with very slight indications of crockets and knops. The lettering, within a plain inner and a beaded outer border, is poorly formed and irregular in size and spacing.

The handle is a ridge with double curved profile, pierced by a round hole.

✦ ✦ ✦ ✦ ✦ ✦ ✦ ✦ ✦ ✦ ✦ ✦ ✦ ✦ ✦ ✦

'Ordo Predicatorum' was the usual medieval term for the Dominicans (see also J8). Their priory in Perth was founded before 1240 and destroyed in 1559.[2] A late 13th-century seal matrix of the Carmelite friars of Perth excavated in the 1980s is similarly crude in execution.[3]

NOTES: [1] See J1. [2] Cowan and Easson 1976, 119. [3] Cherry 1989, 154.

J11

W MATHEW, MONK OF ARBROATH
[H.NM 29]

Scotland or England, *c*1300-50
Copper alloy; cast and engraved
H 30, W 22, D 25

CONDITION
Very good, small crack through inscription, dent in upper
left-hand side.

INSCRIPTION
s'/F·W·MATh'I·MONA/C'·DABIRBROThO/T ((Lombardic)
[for *SIGILLUM FRATRIS W MATHEI MONACHI DE ABIRBROTHOT*, 'Seal of
brother W (son of) Mathew monk of Arbroath'.]

PROVENANCE
Found in the ruins of Arbroath Abbey about 1770,
deposited with the Society of Antiquaries of Scotland in
1833 by St Vigean's Lodge of Freemasons, Arbroath.[1]

✣ ✣ ✣ ✣ ✣ ✣ ✣ ✣ ✣ ✣ ✣ ✣ ✣ ✣ ✣ ✣ ✣

In the oval shape without points St Thomas of Canterbury stands in a central frontal pose, his right hand raised
in blessing, his left holding a cross. He has no halo. An
angel, with long wings spreading up and behind the
saint, kneels on each side waving a censer which floats
above his shoulders. Under a triangular arch below, a
half-length praying monk with tonsure and hood faces
left. This figure and the rudimentary trefoil arch with
triangular centre above the composition break into the

plain line border of the inscription. The rounded lettering
is quite even and distinct.

The tall tapering hexagonal handle has a trefoil
knop with an irregular round hole.

✣ ✣ ✣ ✣ ✣ ✣ ✣ ✣ ✣ ✣ ✣ ✣ ✣ ✣ ✣ ✣

Attempts have been made to identify 'W Mathei', but
they are not convincing.[2] Medieval matrices with
handles of this type were among the commonest in use
from the 14th century onwards,[3] pointing to a date after
1300, which is much later than any of the individuals
suggested from the quoted documentary sources.
Additionally, the letter before the name is undoubtedly
'F' as read by Laing[4] and Birch[5] and not 'P' for 'Prioris' as
Gilruth tentatively claimed. Nor do any firm candidates
emerge in the early 14th century.[6] Similar oval examples
without points on tall hexagonal handles with trefoil
loops, celebrating various single saints, occur in England.
A matrix close in design to J12, with a figure of St
Margaret, was excavated in Lincolnshire and there are
others in Cambridge and Birmingham.[7]

The Tironensian abbey of Arbroath was founded
by William the Lion in 1178 in honour of St Thomas
Becket.[8] Presumably the seal shows the owner praying to
St Thomas, but it includes none of the features of the
Becket iconography established in the first half of the
13th century (see K4, page 141).

NOTES: [1] *Archaeologia Scotica* 1890, 21; Hutton *c*1795, 48 is a
paper impression of J12 captioned in ink 'From the matrix, found
some years ago among the ruins at Arbroath, now in my possession, 1796', 185 is a careful pen and wash drawing also of J12,
with the additional pencil inscription 'It was used for some time by
the Lodge of St Thomas at Arbroath'; Wilson 1849, no 22, 92.
[2] Gilruth 1937, 64-7. [3] Harvey and McGuinness 1996, 8-9, fig 8.
[4] Laing 1850, no 981, 174. [5] Birch 1895, no 15213, 131.
[6] Arbroath Liber 1848, *passim*. [7] Rigold 1977, no 11, 327, fig 3,
328. [8] Cowan and Easson 1976, 66-7.

J12

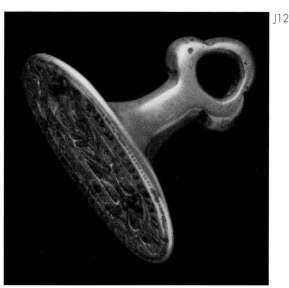

J12

MONK OF CROSSRAGUEL ABBEY
[H.NM 201]

Scotland, 1300-50
Copper alloy; cast and punched
H 34, W 21, D 8

CONDITION
Good, two small chips on back, possibly casting faults.

INSCRIPTION
S·H·MONACHi·DECARREC· (Lombardic) [for SIGILLUM H. MONACHI DE CARREC., 'Seal of H monk of Carrick']

PROVENANCE
Found by HM Office of Works, during excavations at Crossraguel in 1919.[1]

✚ ✚ ✚ ✚ ✚ ✚ ✚ ✚ ✚ ✚ ✚ ✚ ✚ ✚ ✚ ✚

Within the pointed oval the composition is divided horizontally, half-length figures of the Virgin *lactans* and Child, without halos, in the upper register and a kneeling praying monk, also half-length, facing left in the lower. The architectural framing consists of a simple pointed trilobate arch at the top, a triangular gable with a trefoil arch over the figure of the monk and plain blind arcading in the space between the two registers. The modelling of the figures is cursory and the lettering, within beaded borders, is uneven in size and irregular in form.

The handle is a pointed ridge, stepped to a curved loop with a round hole.

✚ ✚ ✚ ✚ ✚ ✚ ✚ ✚ ✚ ✚ ✚ ✚ ✚ ✚ ✚ ✚

Crossraguel was a Cluniac house, the foundation date of which is unclear. There was an oratory on the site in the early 13th century, but the first abbots mentioned in the chronicles do not appear until the 1270s, although building work may have been in progress in the previous decade.[2]

J13

The design of the matrix is one found frequently on seals of minor ecclesiastical figures in northern Europe. Crossraguel stands in the district of Carrick, but 'H. de Carrec' was probably actually the monk's own family name. The Carricks were a prominent Ayrshire family by the 13th century, kinsmen of the holders of the earldom of the same name, which passed in her own right to Marjorie, mother of King Robert Bruce.[3] Seals for other clerics of the family were inscribed 'GILBERTI DE KERIK' (archdeacon of Glasgow c 1476) and 'IOHANNIS DE CARRIG' (chancellor of Glasgow 1371).[4]

NOTES: [1] MacDonald 1919, 24. [2] Cowan and Easson 1976, 63-4. [3] Barrow 1988, 25. [4] Birch 1895, no 15169, 118 and no 15177, 120.

J14

ELIAS, A MONK OR LAY BROTHER FROM GATTONSIDE
[H.NM 116]

Scotland, 13th century
Copper alloy; engraved
H 35, W 22, D 10

CONDITION
Good.

INSCRIPTION
+CVLPIS HELIE PARCITO X_PE_S (Lombardic) [for *CULPIS HELIE PARCITO CHRISTE* (?) *SIGILLUM*, 'Christ have mercy upon Elias for his sins. (?)Seal'].

PROVENANCE
Exhibited at the Society of Antiquaries of Scotland in 1887 by James Tait of Gattonside, Melrose,[1] purchased that year.[2]

+ + + + + + + + + + + + + + + +

The pointed oval seal matrix shows a half-length Virgin wearing a crown holding the Child in her left arm. Underneath is the head and shoulders of a praying monk (?) in profile facing left, below a trilobate arch. The inscription, between beaded borders, is crudely engraved, as are the figures.

The handle is a central shallow spine, having an oval loop with a round hole at the top.

+ + + + + + + + + + + + + + + +

J14

Gattonside was a grange of the immensely wealthy abbey of Melrose sited just across the river Tweed from the main buildings. Elias, from the quality of his matrix and the absence of a letter 'F' for *frater* (cf J12) or the word *monachi* (cf J13), was probably a lay brother with some official function such as cellarer, which required him to have a seal in order to transact abbey business.

NOTES: [1] *PSAS*, vol XXI, 1887, 202. [2] NMAS 1892, 370.

K1   B44, 28

REAWICK KNIGHT
[H.NM 42]

Shetland or Scandinavia, *c*1200[1]
Copper alloy; engraved and stamped
DIAM 84, D 8

CONDITION
Excellent.

INSCRIPTION
+ SIGILL BEИE DICAMUS DCI AИИV F:IV(?).[2] (Lombardic)

PROVENANCE
Found at Reawick, Shetland, purchased after 1849, before 1892.[3]

+ + + + + + + + + + + + + + + +

On a round seal a knight on a stallion galloping from left to right wears a mail hauberk and chausses with rowel spurs. He has a mail coif surmounted by a round helmet with an ornamented rim and a ball finial. He carries a large sword in his right hand stretched out behind him and a triangular shield with a pointed boss held close to his chest. The prancing horse has a flowing mane, shaggy legs and a long wavy tail. The horse trappings consist of reins, bit and bridle, stirrups, chest piece, saddle and flowing horse cloth.

The inscription, between beaded borders, is uneven, both letters 'S' and all the 'N's are reversed and part of the legend is upside down. Horse and rider, by contrast, are vigorously and realistically portrayed in careful detail.

The back of the matrix is flat, but has engraved motifs apparently unrelated to the front and to each other, consisting of an obelisk filled with scroll ornament, with two small scrolls projecting from the top; a large scrolling ornament placed sideways to the left and an indistinguishable D-shape containing a head (?) to the right.

This object is either unfinished or an experiment. The edge has not been finished off and the round design is placed asymmetrically on the metal plate. The intention was clearly to produce a seal matrix, but the artist was unsure how to arrange the lettering so that it was the right way round on the impression or radiated from the centre in the usual way.

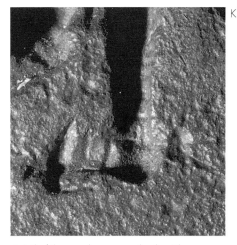

✛ ✛ ✛ ✛ ✛ ✛ ✛ ✛ ✛ ✛ ✛ ✛ ✛ ✛ ✛

The motif of a rider on a prancing horse is one of the earliest to be used on royal seals in Scotland, England and Scandinavia.[4] It quickly passed to the aristocracy,[5] but did not generally filter further down through medieval society. The type of shield and sword, the energetically galloping horse, its wavy tail, luxuriant mane and elaborately detailed trappings point to a date well after 1150.[6] Although the figure and the animal are skilfully observed and engraved, compared with most contemporary examples, it has an informal, almost folkloric quality which suggests that the artist was probably working in a fairly local ambience.

Detail of the rowel spur worn by the rider

NOTES: [1] Ellis 1995, 128. In personal communications, Blanche Ellis confirms that a rowel spur is unlikely to appear in any image before this date; Claud Blair agrees with a date in the second half of the 12th century for the armour and lettering, while finding this type of spur well before the earliest French example recorded (1211) very remarkable. [2] The meaning is unclear; the engraver seems to have been illiterate, at least in Latin. The legend starts off quite properly with SIGILL [for *SIGILLUM*, 'seal'] but then reads *BENEDICAMUS* ['we bless']; the remaining part is unintelligible. John Blair, The Queen's College Oxford, kindly contributed his comments on this inscription. [3] Wilson 1849, *passim*; NMAS 1892, no 42, 369; the find site has also been spelt Raewick in some publications. [4] Harvey and McGuinness 1996, pl 5, 6, pl 23, 28, Duncan II of Scotland (1094), William I of England (1066-87); KLNM, vol IX, 49-50, Knut den Helliges of Denmark (1080-86). [5] Clanchy 1993, pl I, charter of Ilbert de Lacy, *c* 1090. [6] London 1984, no 376, no 377, 419; Heslop 1986, pl XXVa and b; Bedos-Rezak 1993, VI, fig I, 25, fig III, 26, fig V, 27, fig VI, 28.

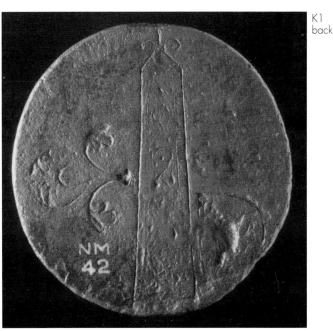

K2
RALPH OF COVENTRY
[H.NM 43]

C60, 49

Scotland, 13th century
Copper alloy; engraved
H 20, W 38, D 8

CONDITION
Very good.

INSCRIPTION
+s'·RADVLFI·DECOVITR· (Lombardic) [for *SIGILLUM RADULFI DE COVINTRE*, 'seal of Ralph of Coventry']

PROVENANCE
Donated to the museum by Daniel Wilson in 1851, along with two other matrices found at Culross Abbey.[1]

✛ ✛ ✛ ✛ ✛ ✛ ✛ ✛ ✛ ✛ ✛ ✛ ✛ ✛ ✛ ✛

In a horizontal design on a pointed oval seal, a bird with a long curved beak stands in the centre, its head turned back to look to the left. Three sprigs of foliage surround it. The engraving is fairly sketchy and the lettering, within two beaded lines, is uneven.

The handle is a plain tapering ridge with a roughly circular loop at one end.

✛ ✛ ✛ ✛ ✛ ✛ ✛ ✛ ✛ ✛ ✛ ✛ ✛ ✛ ✛ ✛

This is a very typical design for a non-heraldic personal seal of the later 13th century. Coventry, now called Coven Trees, is a hamlet in Forgandenny parish, about five kilometres south of the centre of Perth. The Cistercian abbey of Culross on the Fife coast of the Firth of Forth was founded about 1217.[2]

NOTES: [1] *Archaeologia Scotica*, vol V, 1890, 78; NMAS 1892, no 43, 369. [2] Cowan and Easson 1976, 74.

K3
QUEEN JOAN BEAUFORT
[H.NM 163]

E95, 97

Scotland, after 1424
Gold; cast and engraved
DIAM 20, D 5

CONDITION
Good, the engraving a little worn.

PROVENANCE
Found by labourers digging the foundations for a house in Kinross in 1829,[1] purchased by the museum in 1919.[2]

✛ ✛ ✛ ✛ ✛ ✛ ✛ ✛ ✛ ✛ ✛ ✛ ✛ ✛ ✛ ✛

The round matrix has a plain line border and a shield showing the impaled arms of Scotland alongside France and England quarterly. The spaces around the shield are

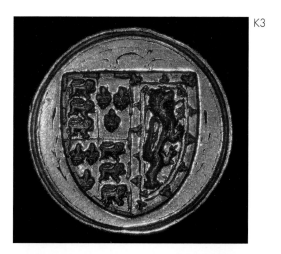
K3

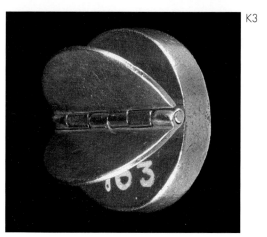
K3

140

delicately engraved with a leaf spray either side and a cusped trefoil above, framed by two fine circles. On the reverse is a handle consisting of two hinged semicircles the full size of the matrix.

+++++++++++++++++

Joan Beaufort, daughter of the earl of Somerset, married James I in 1424, remaining in Scotland after his death and becoming the wife of James Stewart, 'The Black Knight of Lorne'.[3] This is clearly a small personal seal made for the queen. In England gold and silver matrices were made for royal, aristocratic and senior ecclesiastical dignitaries particularly in the 15th century.[4] The Scottish monarchs had privy seals in precious metals from at least the reign of Robert Bruce.[5]

Kinross is on the shore of Loch Leven close to the small island where the Douglases had built one of the first fortified Scottish tower houses after the Wars of Independence.[6] It lies on the route from the royal palace at Stirling to the important burgh and port of Perth.

The matrix was deemed Treasure Trove, but Mr Williamson, the owner of the land where it was found, contested this and finally obtained a judgement in his favour in 1846.

NOTES: [1] Drysdale 1857, 420. [2] *PSAS*, vol LIV, 1919, 14-15. [3] Donaldson and Morpeth 1988, 109. [4] Harvey and McGuinness 1996, 13. [5] Duncan 1988, 188. [6] Tabraham 1986, 48-9.

K4   C59, 48-49
BURGH OF ARBROATH
H.NM 33

Scotland, early 14th century
Lead; engraved
DIAM 69, D 18

CONDITION
Handle slightly bent, small cracks behind figure of saint, back dirty.

INSCRIPTION
*s' COɅVnItATIS:BVRGI:DEABIRBROt hot: SANCTVS:Thos (inverted below the figures)(Lombardic) [for *SIGILLUM COMUNITATIS BURGI DE ABERBROTHOC* and *SANCTUS THOMAS*, 'seal of the community of the burgh of Arbroath' and 'Saint Thomas']

PROVENANCE
In 1789 this matrix was in the possession of George Lyell of Kinneff,[1] by 1850 it had been acquired by George Sim,[2] who as curator of coins donated it to the museum in 1864.[3]

+ + + + + + + + + + + + + + + +

The scene depicted on this round matrix is the murder of St Thomas of Canterbury, with the saint fallen to the ground facing right, before the priest Grim in a pulpit holding a tall processional cross in his right hand; four knights stand behind Thomas with swords, the foremost holding that which had struck the fatal blow.

The knights wear surcoats over their mail and large cylindrical helms with horizontal ridges across the face; the knight at the rear also has a sword held upright in his right hand. St Thomas wears a long hooded robe and a round cap. Grim's dress is indistinct, but he appears to have a hat. He has a chrism (?) in his left hand. Above the figures is a sun and a crescent moon, beneath them the flagged floor of the cathedral is indicated by rough irregular hatching.

The matrix is crudely engraved with a thick blunt tool, the faces are indicated caricature fashion. The plain borders to the inscription are accurate circles, the compass point from which they were inscribed is clearly visible in the centre of the composition. The lettering is badly drawn and spaced and irregular in size, for example one 'N' is reversed, two different kinds of 'T' are used and the final 's' of THOMAS is squeezed in face downwards.

The handle is a central spine tapering at each end, with an irregular cylindrical knop in the centre.

+ + + + + + + + + + + + + + +

Arbroath Abbey was founded by William the Lion, who had known Thomas Becket, soon after the death of the saint in 1170 (see also J12). Representations of the martyrdom appeared on the seals of the bishops of Canterbury (where he was murdered in his own cathedral) in 1193 and 1207.[4] By 1233, on the third seal of Canterbury Cathedral Priory, it had been elaborated and refined into a tableau, which was in turn adopted by Arbroath Abbey, probably before 1250.[5] The burgh matrix is a very crude copy of that design.

NOTES: [1] Hutton *c*1795, 139, a good pen and wash drawing captioned 'Drawn from an impression communicated by the Rev'd Mr Gleig of Arbroath'. [2] Laing 1850, no 1149, 208. [3] *PSAS*, vol V, 1864, 342. [4] Borenius 1929, figs 1, 2, and 10, 42-5. [5] Harvey and McGuinness 1996, pl 109, 110-11.

K4

BURGH OF CRAIL

[H. QL.1961.124]

Scotland or Flanders, 1500-50
Matrices: copper alloy; engraved
DIAM 73, W 100 (with lugs), D 4
Press: oak and iron; carved, cast
H 154, W 160, D 160

CONDITION
Images good, crack in back of obverse shows slightly on
front at top right hand and bottom left; all four lugs broken
off the reverse matrix.

INSCRIPTION
Obverse and reverse: +:SIGILLVM:COMMVNE:BVRGI:DE:KARALE:
Reverse: +:SIGILLVM:COMMVNE: BVRGI:DE:KARALE: (transitional
Lombardic/ Roman) ['common seal of the burgh of Crail']

PROVENANCE
Held in the burgh offices until 1961 when it passed to the
museum.

+ + + + + + + + + + + + + + + +

The round matrices, for seal and counterseal, each originally had four circular lugs to fit on to the pins of the press.

OBVERSE
A ship with furled sails on a single mast, a streaming
pennant bearing a saltire, dragon-head prow and high
scroll-ended stern, sails from left to right on a choppy sea.
The plump heads of seven passengers appear over the
side of the deck. In the sky above are a crescent moon
and eight five-pointed stars.

REVERSE
The Virgin and Child, with plain halos, are enthroned
between two three-quarter-length censing angels. The

Virgin has a shallow crown with cruciform cresting, over
long wavy hair which cascades down her shoulders.
Her robe, which is embroidered at the neck and front
fastening, is voluminous, billowing out below her elbows
on both sides and enclosing the naked child who rests on
her left knee supported by her left arm. At her feet, the
folds are shown as horizontal swathes with a wavy edge
concealing much of the throne. He strains with his right
arm to reach an apple which his mother holds in her
right hand.

The throne incorporates motifs in the Renaissance
style such as the two vase-shaped ornaments either side
of the Virgin and the decorative plant forms on the front
of the seat. Behind her is a round arched niche with an
urn-shaped finial, framed by scrolled cresting. The angels
have long wavy hair, their wings fall closely behind them
and their very large censers are footed bowl forms with
relief decoration.

The inscriptions, between plain borders, are clear
and regular, combining some Roman elements with
basically Lombardic letter forms.

The backs of the matrices are plain and flat, with
two roughly engraved crosses to indicate the top of each.

This seal survives complete with its press, which
consists of a square oak base with moulded edges and a
round iron baseplate with four lugs holding tall pins (one
missing) let into the centre, under a diagonal iron bridge
with a central downwards screw.

+ + + + + + + + + + + + + + + +

The royal burgh of Crail, which was given its charter in
the 12th century, already had two harbours by 1371.[1] Its
exports and trade across the North Sea were generally
smaller than those of other Fife and Tayside ports such
as Inverkeithing, Perth, Dundee, Pittenweem and St
Andrews from the 14th to the 16th centuries.[2] However,
Crail's close links with Flanders and neighbouring areas

K5
obverse

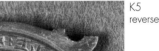

K5
reverse

are demonstrated by some of the architecture of the town and by the fine bell made for St Mary's Church in 1520, bearing the arms of Mechelen and probably made by Willem van den Ghein.[3] The drapery style and the broad flat face of the Virgin and her flowing hair are strongly influenced by Flemish art of the period.[4]

Although the figure style and the lettering point to a date into the 16th century the ship is an archaic type for that date. Sometimes described as a 'lymphad', the heraldic term for a West Highland or Irish galley,[5] it does not in fact seem to be being rowed but is closer to the vessel known as a hulk.[6] Other seals and matrices for Crail are recorded all featuring ships.[7] This was the most common motif for the seals of coastal towns in Britain and Europe.[8] It is quite likely that the old fashioned vessel on the Crail matrix was copied from an earlier seal, possibly even by an engraver in Flanders.

The press which is probably original, is a very rare survival.

NOTES: [1] Ewan 1990, 6. [2] McNeill and MacQueen 1996, 248-55. [3] RCAHMS 1996, 57-8. [4] Bruges 1998, no 23, 101, no 28, 106, no 33, 118. [5] Stevenson and Wood 1940, vol I, 56. [6] Hutchinson 1997, figs 1.4-1.6, 11-14, fig 3.2, 51. [7] Laing 1866, nos 1204, 1205, 1206, 214; Birch 1895, no 15498, 210, no 17299, 683. [8] Hutchinson 1997, fig 1.4, 11, fig 3.1, 48, fig 4.8, 80, fig 9.4, 154; Pedrick 1904, *passim*, Bedos 1980, *passim*.

K5
with press

HAMMERMEN OF DUNDEE
[H.NM 41]

Scotland, 15th century
Copper alloy; engraved and punched
DIAM 39, D 5

CONDITION
Very good, dent in bottom edge.

INSCRIPTION
S+[c]+artis+malliat/ou̲ +scī+elegi+d'dūd' (black letter) [for *Sigillum commune artis malliatorum sancti elegi de Dunde*, 'seal of the community of hammermen of Saint Eloi of Dundee'].

PROVENANCE
Acquired from the Faculty of Advocates in 1874.[1]

++++++++++++++++

On a round matrix, St Eloi as bishop with a tall mitre and flowing chasuble stands in the centre, a hammer in his right hand a long crook-headed crozier in his left, under a low Gothic canopy and between two slender reeded shafts. On either side is a baluster vase containing a spray of flowers and at his feet an armorial shield bearing a goldsmith's hammer.

The inscription between plain borders is in competent black letter.

On the back, the handle has been broken off, leaving the remains of the hinge. Two fleur-de-lis are stamped either side of the handle to mark the top.

++++++++++++++++

The hammermen of Dundee are documented in their own Locked Book of Statutes, Acts and Ordinances which was begun in 1587.[2] By that date the guild was already long established and referring to their rules as being of 'use and wont' in their 'old foundation'. The hammermen, of whom there were thirty-five brethren in 1587, followed a number of different trades, making among other things locks, armour, harness, guns and knives. Ranging from goldsmiths to blacksmiths they jealously guarded their own skills and ruled that a member could only practise in the distinct craft into which they had first been admitted.[3]

St Eloi, or Eligius (*c*588-660) was the patron saint of goldsmiths, and is also sometimes depicted shoeing a horse.[4] The flowers in the vases are presumably intended for the lilies which were the emblem of the medieval burgh of Dundee.

NOTES: [1] See J3, page 124. [2] Warden 1872, 471-502. [3] Ibid, 472-3. [4] Farmer 1992, 156-7.

IVORY CARVINGS

The ivory carvings in the Museum of Scotland are all in one respect or another distinctively Scottish or Scandinavian, except the Kirkton of Craig crucifix figure (L8). Pieces in a more mainstream European style were probably also imported from England and France or influenced local artists in the 12th to the 15th centuries, but very little evidence for this survives and none of it in this collection. The carving of the Jedburgh comb (fig 34, page 146) found in the 1984 excavations of the abbey's monastic buildings,[1] although elusive when it comes to relating it closely to sculp-

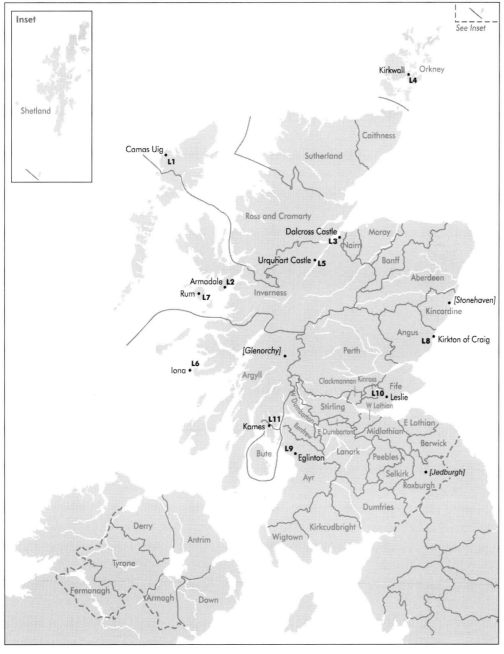

Place names in brackets denote comparative material.

fig 34: COMB
Walrus ivory, Scottish (?), first half of the
12th century, NMS, on loan to Historic Scotland
at Jedburgh Abbey.
H 50, w 44

ture and manuscript illumination, does seem to draw on the same sources as art from Canterbury and possibly the Low Countries.[2] It can be tentatively dated to the early 12th century and may well have arrived with some of the Norman incomers of the period.[3] However, a contemporary account of a miracle supposed to have taken place near Melrose, about eighteen kilometres away, in 1165 tells of a craftsman collecting the antlers and harder bones of a stag to make combs, tablets, chess sets and other items, suggesting that a local industry was plausible.[4]

In the later period, Gothic ivories decorated in a manner derived basically from French art must also have occurred in Scotland, as we know they did in England[5] and Scandinavia.[6] These were usually intricately carved and therefore fragile, most frequently with obvious religious imagery and consequently prime targets for post-Reformation destruction. No doubt future excavation and chance finds will bring objects of this class with a Scottish medieval provenance to light.

The chesspieces are indicative of a courtly way of life, in which the importance of the game and its accessories is borne out by medieval Scottish and Irish literature. A poem of about 1250 addressed to Aenghus Mór Mac Domhnaill, King of the Isles, lists among the lands, horses, hounds, herds, armour and treasure he has inherited from his father 'his brown ivory chessmen'.[7] Clearly, a legacy worthy of mention. 'Brown' may be a description of walrus as opposed to the whiter elephant ivory or merely poetic licence. Flattering his patron, the poet addresses Aenghus as 'lord of Coll', 'king of Lewis' and 'Ireland's king', neatly defining the area over which chessmen in the style of the Lewis pieces (L1a-L1k) were distributed.

Chess references also occur in the Irish *leabhar na g-ceart* or Book of Rights, showing that the game was a favourite pastime of princes and chieftains.[8] For example, at a great gathering, along with the wine and the drinking horns, sets of chessmen with their boards are to be laid out for honoured guests;[9] while a chess-board and 'white' chessmen are among the entitlements of a fortunate individual along with drinking horns, cups, greyhounds, steeds and lances.[10] The use of the term 'white' here presumably applies to ivory carvings and walrus would have been the only type available in a sufficiently large quantity.

If the speculations about its heraldry and provenance put forward in this cat-alogue are accepted, the later chesspiece given to the museum in 1782 (L2) shows that Scandinavian taste was also prevalent on the west coast in the areas further south largely colonised by Norman families who had arrived in the 12th century. In the West Highlands, it is still apparent in the late 15th- or early 16th-century king discovered in Dunstaffnage Castle and first published by Pennant in 1772.[11]

Other ivory carvings elsewhere may come from the west and the Hebrides, but their medieval provenance has been lost or forgotten. For instance, some con-fusion has arisen over finds from Skye. About 1860 a visitor to Armadale Castle was told by the then Lord MacDonald that 'several chessmen, carved in ivory, were found in [the] loch at Monkstadt during the process of draining and are now in the possession of Lord Londesborough'.[12] By the 18th century the lands of the MacDonald kin stretched from Armadale in the south of Skye to their mansion at Monkstadt, completed in 1741 north of the village of Uig.[13] This house was partly built using stone taken from the medieval Duntulm Castle, and necessitated the partial draining of the adjacent loch.

Lord Londesborough bought the eleven Lewis Chessmen now in the Museum of Scotland after the sale of Charles Kirkpatrick Sharpe in 1852, when they were catalogued as 'found in 1831, in the Parish of Uig, in the Island of Skye'.[14] 'Uig' is a fairly common Gaelic place name, meaning simply a bay, and there were parishes of that name in the north of both Lewis and Skye, accounting for the error of the Edinburgh auctioneers. Lord MacDonald, of all people, would surely have been acutely aware of the difference, but he may have been depending on infor-mation given at second hand.

The Skye chesspiece (L2) given to the museum by one of Lord MacDonald's forebears was known to the visitor of 1860, and he illustrates it without associating it with the statement about the loch. In any case, its condition precludes it having spent any length of time in water and it never belonged to Lord Londesborough.[15]

The latter, however, had another single ivory chessman, an enthroned bishop with three small attendant figures, now in the British Museum.[16] This is in the same tradition as the Lewis Chessmen, although the more flowing and naturalistic drapery, the addition of the smaller figures and the leafier foliage on the throne back point to a date into the 13th century, but before the Vatican bishop which is here compared with L2. Neither the British Museum nor Londesborough attrib-uted any provenance to his single bishop and it is just possible that Lord MacDonald was aware of local information that had not been passed on.

The ivories in this section of the collection which are most characteristi-cally Scottish are the two caskets (L9 and L10). They have entirely West Highland decoration of plaited interlace and strapwork and they are objects with a significance very specific to the locality. Along with certain features of the Guthrie Bell Shrine (H1) and the Quigrich (H6), the crosses and carved grave stones of the area,[17] and the two splendid harps in the Museum of Scotland,[18] they represent elements of both survival and conscious revival of earlier Celtic and Insular artistic ideals.

Although elephant ivory was always more prized than any other type for its whiteness and fine texture, by the 12th century it was so scarce in northern Europe that walrus was almost always used instead. In Scotland walrus and whales stranded on the beaches probably provided a small supply, although the Basques in northern Spain already had a thriving whaling industry.[19] Archaeological and literary evidence suggests that extensive hunting of whales also took place off Scandinavian shores from the late Iron Age.[20]

NOTES: [1] Entrusted to NMS under Treasure Trove arrangements and on long-term loan to Historic Scotland at Jedburgh Abbey. [2] Higgitt 1995, 83-4. [3] Higgitt 1987, 122-4. [4] Raine 1835, 180-88. [5] London 1987, 107-13. [6] Liebgott 1985, 53-76. [7] Clancy 1998, 288-9. I am indebted to David Sellar for this reference. [8] O'Donovan 1847, lxi-ii. [9] Ibid, 241-2. [10] Ibid, 247-8. [11] Laing 1857, 366-8. [12] Smith 1862, 104. [13] Miket and Roberts 1990, 60. [14] Tait and Nisbet 1851, lot 531, 21. [15] Miket and Roberts 1990, do not mention the chesspiece in their text, but illustrate it twice, 12 and 57, saying in the first caption that it was 'discovered in Loch St Columba, Kilmuir, during an attempt to drain the loch in 1763'. Kilmuir is a hamlet just north of Uig and St Columba a more modern name for the loch. [16] Fairholt and Wright 1857, pl XXVIII; Dalton 1909, cat no 160, 73-4, pl XXXIV. [17] Steer and Bannerman 1977, *passim*. [18] Edinburgh 1982, cat nos 22-3, 60-61. [19] Williamson 1982, 15. [20] Szabo 2001, 137-50.

ELEVEN LEWIS CHESSMEN
[H.NS 19-29]

Scandinavia, late 12th century

PROVENANCE
Found at Camas Uig, Isle of Lewis, 1831.

+ + + + + + + + + + + + + + + +

In the catalogue entries the Lewis chessmen in the British Museum are referred to by the numbers given to them by Dalton in his *Catalogue of the Ivory Carvings of the Christian Era in the British Museum* (London 1909), which still has the most convenient set of illustrations for easy reference.

+ + + + + + + + + + + + + + + +

Apart from L1(a-k), there are another 82 ivory pieces from the same Lewis hoard in the British Museum, including kings, queens, bishops, knights, warders, pawns, plain tablemen and a belt buckle.[1] Since their discovery, numerous more or less fanciful tales have grown up around it.[2]

In April 1831 they were exhibited to the Society of Antiquaries of Scotland by one Roderick Ririe of Stornoway,[3] but while the Society debated how best to acquire them they passed to an Edinburgh dealer named Forrest, who showed them to journalists from *The Scotsman* resulting in a report in that newspaper on June 29th 1831.[4] By October of the same year he had offered to sell the majority to the British Museum.[5]

The Antiquaries were told at their meeting that the pieces 'were lately found buried fifteen feet under a bank of sand in the Island of Lewis'. A similar account appeared in *The Scotsman*: 'a peasant of the place [the parish of Uig] while digging a sand bank, found upward of 70 pieces of bone, most of them representing Kings, Bishops and Knights, dismounted or on horseback.' Sir Frederic Madden, Assistant Keeper of Manuscripts at the British Museum, accepted this version of events.[6]

However, it emerged that Forrest had, possibly unwittingly, misled Madden on at least one other point and perhaps about the circumstances of the discovery as well. Joseph Stevenson, who was also in the Department of Manuscripts, writing to David Laing in Edinburgh in February 1832, mentioned the chessmen saying 'they excite great admiration here'.[7] Evidently Laing's reply contained unwelcome news, because the following August Stevenson wrote, 'The fact that you mentioned regarding the chess-men, namely that there are some in the possession of gentlemen in Edinburgh, seems very curious as the individual by whom they were sold to the museum stated that these were the whole which had been found'.[8]

The gentleman in question was Charles Kirkpatrick Sharpe, an Edinburgh genealogist, writer and collector of antiquities including manuscripts,[9] sculpture[10] and prints,[11] who had managed to buy ten of the chesspieces, apparently from Ririe, and subsequently added another bishop obtained 'from a person residing in Lewis'.[12] These eleven were sold in 1851, after the death of Sharpe, and passed into the Londesborough Collection,[13] which was auctioned in 1888, when they were finally acquired by the Society of Antiquaries of Scotland for the museum.[14]

Sharpe's description of the find site was read by Laing to the Society of Antiquaries of Scotland in March 1833. It said 'These chess-men discovered in the Isle of Lewis had never been under water; they were found in a vaulted room (as it was described to me), about six feet long; they were slightly covered with sand, and there was a quantity of ashes on the floor. I could not learn whether there was anything like a chimney.'[15] This comes from the text of an undated note in Sharpe's handwriting apparently made for his own records and attached to a list of the ten pieces bought in Edinburgh.[16] It reads like information gleaned from someone on Lewis, possibly when Sharpe was negotiating for the extra piece. Daniel Wilson, repeating the same information, gives the impression that he had discussed the matter with Sharpe in person.[17]

Laing himself was suspicious: 'To serve some purpose, contradictory statements were circulated by the persons who discovered or who afterwards obtained possession of these Chess-men.' One likely aim would have been to avoid any question of ownership, which might have arisen if they were found deliberately stored or hidden in a structure on an identifiable landholding, as opposed to merely lost on the common foreshore.

To this uncertainty have been added numerous speculations redolent of the West Highlands at their most Celtic and romantic, involving nuns whiling away their seclusion with chess games, a peasant who fled in terror thinking the figures were elves and a sensational story of a 17th-century shipwreck followed by murder, rape and a hanging.

None of this suggests a likely explanation for the presence of such a large collection of sophisticated and elaborate objects carved from an expensive and prized material in somewhere as remote as Camas Uig. Recent scholarship, discussed below, concludes that the chessmen are Scandinavian and date from the second half of the 12th century. Certainly nothing survives on or near Lewis with which they can be associated. The finders produced no tools, raw materials or partly carved pieces so it was presumably not the remains of an ivory carver's workshop. In any case, although the island was strategically important in the period, there is no evidence of a prosperous settled community to provide a local market for such luxury goods. Indeed it is said that when Reginald (Ragnvald), King of Man, gave his brother Olave (Olaf) the isle of Lodhus (Lewis), it was thinly populated, 'mountainous and stony and unfit for tillage in all parts', to such an extent that he insisted he was unable to maintain himself and his army there; although *Eirspennill's Hakon Hakon's son's Saga* for 1230-31 has the Norwegians driving Thormod, Thorkel's son, out of the island and looting 'great treasure that he had'.[18]

The most plausible theory, however, is that the hoard represents the stock in trade of a peripatetic salesman who somehow abandoned it on his travels. If he was taking shelter during a voyage, Uig is on a very obvious route from any Scandinavian port to the west of Scotland, Man and the Irish Sea.

Chess, introduced from Arabic culture, is documented as a mainly upper class European activity well before AD 1000.[19] It is mentioned in wills, romances and manuscripts which explain the rules and lay out chess problems and their solutions. Indeed, it became such a craze that the church made futile attempts to ban it (and the associated gambling), particularly for those in holy orders.[20] There is much argument about its dissemination into northern Europe, but it seems to have been well established from England to Iceland in the 12th century.[21] Although a number of other realistically carved figurative chessmen survive from the earlier middle ages, probably preserved because of their richness and complexity, the more usual set seems to have been of much plainer abstract or semi-abstract pieces.[22]

Our putative merchant, therefore, was aiming for a wealthy market with considerable pretensions to grandeur. The existence of another ivory queen (fig 35), from the same workshop tradition as the Lewis chessmen, found at the beginning of the 19th century in a bog in county Meath and now in the National Museum of Ireland, has been largely ignored in the modern literature, but seems to hint at his targets.[23] Meath itself was the stronghold of the powerful Irish Ua Máel Sechlainn kings of Mide and was granted to Hugh de Lacy by Henry II of England in a charter of 1172 after the Anglo-Norman invasion.[24] Either group could have aspired to the necessary lifestyle. Murchad, King of Meath was rich and cosmopolitan enough to found Bective Abbey in 1147, one of the first Cistercian houses in Ireland, while de Lacy is credited with church building at Cannistown, the founding of the Augustinian priory at Duleek, the construction of a system of defensive mottes throughout Meath and even with suspected royal aspirations after his marriage to an Irish princess.[25]

On the way south the salesman could have visited the courts of Somerled and his descendants, of Fergus of Galloway and his, or of the king of Man. The Lewis chessmen and the Irish queen testify to the cultural ambitions of these magnates of Ireland and the Isles.[26]

Two pieces of evidence which more or less clinch the Scandinavian origin of the chessmen have been published fairly recently. An illustration of fragments of an ivory carving, engraved when it was found in the late 19th century, was rediscovered in an album recording excavations in the ruins of the 12th-century church of St Olaf in Trondheim.[27] It shows a female head with a short veil, held in place by a circlet with beaded ornament, apparently the base of a crown (fig 36). Her right hand is raised to her cheek in exactly the same idiosyncratic pose as all the Lewis queens and the figure from county Meath. The shoulder-length veil is folded in a very similar manner to that on L1(e) and some of the British Museum queens, particularly Dalton 86 and 88, the former of which also has a decorative border of dots like the Trondheim queen.[28]

It has been calculated that when complete the Trondheim piece would have been about 9 centimetres high. This compares with a range of 7 to 9.6 centimetres for the London queens,[29] 7.5 centimetres for the Dublin example[30] and 7.1 to 9.6 for the three in Edinburgh. There seems little doubt that they all belonged to very similar sets. The object itself is sadly lost and the description which accompanied it is extremely brief, although it does tell us that the figure was 'beautifully carved in ivory'.[31]

Trondheim was established before AD 1000, and by the 12th century was a busy port handling luxury goods like walrus tusks, mainly from

fig 35: **QUEEN FROM A CHESS SET**
Walrus ivory, Scandinavian, first half of the 13th century. National Museum of Ireland – Ard Mhúsaem na hÉireann.
H 73, DIAM 33

fig 36: **QUEEN FROM A CHESS SET**
Detail of pl III, *Undersøgelser i Trondhiem*, by Otto Krefting, Kristiania, 1890, Supplement I, *Kunst og Haandverk fra Norges Fortid.*

fig 37: MUNKHOLM FRAGMENT
Walrus ivory, Trondheim Fjord, second half of the
12th century, Nationalmuseet, photo Antikvarisk
Topografisk Arkiv, Copenhagen.
H 94, L 125

Greenland, furs, falcons and other hawks and also large quantities of the more mundane stockfish – cod caught in northern waters and dried on the islands of Lofoten above the Arctic Circle.[32] These trades gave the town widespread cosmopolitan links in spite of its comparatively remote geographical position. This period also saw the beginning of work on Trondheim's great cathedral and produced craftsmen practising a number of well-established skills.[33] In 1153 it was pronounced an archbishopric, furthering its status and influence in Norway and beyond.

The second discovery was a fragment of carved walrus ivory found in the debris of a workshop which specialised in producing bone and antler combs in Lund, in south-west Sweden. When placed alongside a Lewis knight it is quite self-evidently the front legs of the horse and the rider's feet in stirrups from an almost identical piece.[34] The chessmen do not resemble what we know of 12th-century carving in Lund, notably on the cathedral,[35] and there are few other signs of walrus ivory being worked in the town, so Scandinavian scholars conclude that this piece too was more likely to have been imported from a Norwegian workshop.[36]

For comparative material which might link the style of the Lewis chessmen with Trondheim we can look at stone carving, wood carving and a group of carved ivory artefacts, most of which unfortunately have no early provenance. A carved walrus ivory panel decorated on both sides and now in the Nationalmuseet in Copenhagen is perhaps part of a crozier and was found on the island of Munkholm in Trondheim Fjord in 1715.[37] Its decoration consists of biting quadrupeds entwined in leafy scrolls, which interlace very much in the manner of some of the panels on the throne backs of the Lewis kings, queens and bishops.[38] However, the Munkholm fragment (fig 37) is much more delicately and elaborately carved, with whole animals playing a prominent part, whereas on the chessmen out of 23 throne backs, only three have whole creatures and six simply biting heads. This difference in intricacy and quality of execution would be easily explained by the different functions of the objects.

Other ivories which have been convincingly linked to the Munkholm panel are a reliquary in the British Museum with no recorded medieval history and two fittings on a sword which has been in the Danish Royal Collections since 1824.[39] The 14th-century copper gilt mounts added to the reliquary appear to be Norwegian or Danish. Again there is similar scroll decoration and the less elaborate areas of the reliquary relate particularly closely to several of the chessmen.[40]

These items can only be linked with Trondheim by association. More positive proof that the town was the source of the Lewis hoard should be provided by the wood carving of the stave churches there and in the surrounding area of Trøndelag, but this has an element of folk art and a tendency towards the archaic which makes it different in character from the more sophisticated ivory carvings.[41] The scrolls and beasts on bench ends from Værnes and Sakshaug, however, strongly echo the Lewis ornament. Sakshaug particularly has a crouching dragon with a convoluted tail generically very similar to one on a British Museum king.[42] The chair from Tyldal just south of the boundary of Trøndelag has panels of strapwork interlace on the back rest which compare with many of the throne sides of the chessmen.[43] The capitals of the south doorway of Hopperstad stave church in Sogn, further south towards Bergen, have addorsed leafy scrolls with central vertical foliage gathered together halfway down by rings, a motif used on six of the chessmen,[44] while the resemblance between the biting serpent heads over the north door to the choir and those on the throne backs has been noted by others.[45] The depiction of secular dress and armour, with the lively observation of human expressions characteristic of the chessmen is paralleled in some of the later 12th-century stave church carving.[46] The facial type of at least one king is very close to a head from the North Trøndelag church of Mære, itself strongly influenced by 8th- and 9th-century art.[47]

The stone carvings relevant to the chessmen from 12th-century Trondheim are now detached. They were removed from smaller disused structures as building materials for works at the cathedral after its many fires, particularly that of 1531, and were rediscovered during 19th-century excavations.[48] They show signs of influence from Canterbury and Normandy, but also a certain disregard of classic Norman practices probably attributable to the carvers' less rigidly conventional training in their traditional medium of wood. One particular fragmentary capital has a large palmette among interlacing leafy scrolls which turned upside down has many of the elements of the 'cone and pouch motif' that one writer regarded as a diagnostic feature of the chessmen.[49]

On the other hand, many of the scroll and animal motifs were the stock in trade of northern European Romanesque art where influences spread from France to England, thence to Scandinavia and possibly back again. The heads can only be compared with a few of the grotesque column masks in late 12th-century stave churches, but resemble corbels all over England and France.[50] The probability of a Nordic, or specifically northern Norwegian origin seems pressing, but ultimately cannot be proved. Assertions by O'Donovan that the chessmen might be Irish, by Daniel Wilson that they were arguably Scottish and by Dalton that they could be English were fuelled by an understandable patriotism, but in the end seem less likely than Madden's original argument that the details of the costume, especially the armour, the known skill of the carvers of the area and the numerous mentions of chess in the Sagas all 'point towards the North as their birth-place'.[51] In the absence of sufficient comparative material, however, his conclusion that they were made in Iceland must be seen as impossible to prove one way or the other.

If the country of origin is open to question, there has also been some disagreement about their date, which Madden put about the middle of the 12th century. This line was still being taken by the British Museum in the 1970s[52] and by Lasko in 1984,[53] but by 1992 Stratford was cataloguing them as 'Third quarter of 12th cent'.[54] My own comparisons with stave church carvings indicate a date towards the end of the century, although the dating of the churches themselves is open to debate.[55] Using some of the same comparisons, and calling on the evidence of ecclesiastical costume depicted on 12th-century seals, Heslop also maintains that 'the third quarter of the 12th century is too early a date for these ivories'.[56]

Until the modern awareness of the implications for nature conservancy, ivory had been highly prized as a material for fine carved decoration since the earliest civilisations. The best ivory for the purpose, with the densest texture and generally available in the largest workable pieces came from the elephant. Supplies of elephant ivory were increasingly difficult to obtain in the earlier Middle Ages and by the 11th century parts of France, in addition to Britain, Scandinavia and most of the rest of northern Europe was obliged to fall back on walrus ivory, whalebone and, for lesser articles, antler and mammal bones.[57] The principal differences are that walrus ivory only comes in smaller pieces, it has a thinner solid outer covering (dentine) and a rough, crumbly inner structure (osteodentine) and the surface is not so white.[58] The carver, therefore, has to try as far as possible to avoid revealing the unsatisfactory surface provided by the core of the tusk, which usually means working in fairly low relief. In the case of elephant ivory, the pulpy matter in the central cavity was always removed before work began, leaving a homogeneous block or panel.

The considerable expertise of the artist of the Lewis chessmen as both carver and designer is shown by the fact that he carved his figures in the round and in considerable detail, only in a few places piercing the outer shell of the walrus tusk. In addition, although each piece is highly individual in pose and shape, they all remain sufficiently solid blocks to withstand the wear and tear of use as playing pieces.

The condition of the Edinburgh pieces is on the whole good, although, as has been pointed out, their surface is greyer than that of their London counterparts. There is no trace of the red pigment Madden saw on some of those in the British Museum. The channelling of the surface may have been made by tiny insects, but it has also been suggested that it is the effect of exposure to the very acid stems of grasses growing in the sands of Uig.[59]

Charles Kirkpatrick Sharpe was a considerable connoisseur of both the fine and applied arts.[60] According to Daniel Wilson, 'Ten of these [chessmen] he selected from the whole, previous to their possessor, Mr Roderick Ririe, offering them to the Trustees'. There was no attempt to assemble a matching set, but rather to choose examples of different types, some with unusual characteristics. Consequently, we have large and small kings and queens, bishops standing and enthroned and one of each type of warder. Sharpe also picked out the only two queens with elaborate hairstyles, the larger of the two geometric throne backs and the most wonderfully naturalistic and ferocious of the berserkers.

NOTES: [1] Madden 1832, 203-91; Dalton 1909, nos 78-145, 63-73, pls XXXVIII-XLVIII. [2] Stratford 1997, 50-53. [3] Laing 1857, 367. [4] 'We have been favoured with a sight of these ancient relics, by Mr J. A. Forrest, opposite the Tron church, who has lately purchased them.' [5] Stratford 1997, 4-5. [6] Ibid, 212. [7] Edinburgh University Library, ms La IV 17, 8979. [8] Edinburgh University Library, ms La IV 17, 8980. [9] Scone Liber 1843, xix, 'the original charters of Scone Abbey partly belong to the earl of Mansfield, partly to the Bannatyne Club and partly to Mr K Sharpe'. [10] Edinburgh University Library, ms La IV 6, 12, letter from Sharpe to David Laing: 'I have got Cardinal Beaton's arms from his palace in Blackfriars wynd ... the stone is large but thin as a wafer.' This panel is now in the collections of NMS. [11] Ibid, *passim*; Laing was helping him to add to his collection from at least 1828 to 1839. [12] Wilson 1863, 342, note 1: 'Ten of these he selected from the whole, previous to their possessor, Mr Roderick Ririe, offering them to the Trustees.' [13] Fairholt and Wright 1857, 10, pl 8 and text following. [14] *PSAS* 1888, 9-14. [15] Laing 1857, 368. [16] Edinburgh University Library, ms La IV 6, 114. [17] Ibid, 'Charles Kirkpatrick Sharpe, Esq., from whom I derived these particulars ... '; Wilson speculates (353) that the structure was a 'Scottish Weem', an Iron Age underground storehouse. [18] MacLeod 1833, 153, mentions 'the ruins of religious houses' in the parish of Uig; these are not noted in RCAHMS 1928 or Burgess and Church 1995; Mackenzie 1903, 31-2, quotes the passage on Olaf from Camden; Anderson 1990, vol II, 473-8 [19] Murray 1913, 402, 405-7. [20] Ibid, 410; Gamer 1954, 739-40. [21] Fiske 1905, 7-9; Murray 1913, 443-6. [22] Kluge-Pinsker 1991, 50-54, cat nos A5-A6, A8-A34, A36-A38, A41-A44, A46-A53, A55-A56, 106-154. [23] O'Donovan 1847, lxii-iv (this is the only evidence about its provenance); Westwood 1876, 289; Murray 1913, 759; Liddell 1938, 133 (then in the Petrie collection); Dublin 1983, no 91, 189; now National Museum of Ireland, registration number T 1041. [24] Graham and Proudfoot 1993, 66-7. [25] Graham 1975, 224, 226; Duffy 1997, 93-4; Harbison 1992, 225, 258-9, 271-3. [26] Duffy 1992, 125-33 for the military and political links within the area, 1150-70; Duncan and Brown 1956, 196, note that significantly Fergus was styled prince of Galloway and Somerled kinglet (regulus) of Argyll. Fergus was also styled 'King of the Gallovidians' (rex Galvitensium), see Barrow 1960, 98. [27] McLees and Ekroll 1990, 152, fig 3. [28] Dalton 1909, 66-7, pl XLI. [29] Stratford 1997, 54. [30] Information kindly provided by Raghnall Ó Floinn. [31] McLees and Ekroll 1990, 151. [32] Sawyer and Sawyer 1993, 42, 152-3, 157. [33] Blindheim 1965, 7-21. [34] Stratford 1997, fig 55, 45, for an excellent illustration demonstrating the similarity. [35] Karlsson, *et al* 1995, 62-79, pls 63-80. [36] Paris, Berlin, Copenhagen 1992-93, no 613, 390. [37] Liebgott 1985, 30, figs 21-2. [38] Dalton 1909, nos 80, 81, pl XXXIX, no 84, pl XLI, nos 89, 90, 91, pl XLIII; L1(a), L1(e), L1(f), L1(h). [39] Stratford 1997, fig 51, 43. [40] Ibid, fig 50, 42; compare with Dalton 90, pl XLIII; L1(a), L1(e), L1(f), L1(h). [41] Blindheim 1965, 15-17, pls 33-47. [42] Ibid, fig 61; Bergendahl Hohler 1999, I, 72, 74, fig 126; compare with Dalton 78, pl XXXIX. [43] Paris, Berlin, Copenhagen 1992-93, no 457, 347; Andersen 1997, 24-7, figs 12-13, pl facing 32; Bergendahl Hohler 1999, I, 72-3, fig 122; compare with Madden 1832, no 1, pl XLVI, no 5, 219. [44] Bergendahl Hohler, I, 1999, I, 170, II, pl 211, 204, pl 210, 205. [45] Taylor 1978, fig 10, 13. [46] Blindheim 1965, pls 197-9. [47] Ibid, pls 47-8; compare with Dalton 82, pl XXXVIII; Madden, 215, describes this figure as 'of ruder appearance and workmanship' and suggests the ornament 'would also indicate an earlier period of art than most of the other pieces'. [48] Blindheim 1965, 7-21. [49] Ibid, pl 17; Taylor 1978, 11-13. [50] Bergendahl Hohler 1999, II, pl 240, 217; Stone 1972, pl 46B, 69, 244, note 14, likens the 'striated cloaks and mournful stare' of the chessmen to figures on the chancel arch at Kilpeck, Herefordshire. The same could be said of the four pairs of embracing figures on the font at Tryde near the southernmost coast of Sweden, where one of the kings also shares the long plaited hair of the Lewis kings (Karlsson *et al* 1995, 166-77, pls 189-93). [51] Madden 1832, 291; Goldschmidt 1926, 49-51, terms the chessmen 'Um 1200. Norwegisch'. [52] Taylor 1978 14-15. [53] London 1984, no 212, 212. [54] Paris, Berlin, Copenhagen 1992-1993, no 615, 390-91. [55] Due to the frequent fires, the ability to dismantle and re-erect the wooden buildings and the conservatism of the carvers, dating of the stave churches themselves is fraught with difficulty. [56] Heslop 1980, 108-9. [57] Gaborit-Chopin 1992, 204-5. [58] Gaborit-Chopin 1978, 12. [59] Stratford 1997, 54-5, 'Appendix B, Technical observations', gives detailed notes on the condition of the British Muscum picccs by their Department of Scientific Research. [60] Tait and Nisbet, 1851, lots 1-1269; Cadell, D N B (forthcoming).

L1(a)
KING
[H.NS 19]

Walrus ivory; carved, incised, punched
H 95, W 55, D 40

CONDITION
Good, the piece is solid bone and has no cracks or losses, some discolour-ation, a red stain on the front of the crown, extensive fine channelling on the robes, particularly the lower front.

INSCRIPTION
Londesborough (printed paper label stuck to the base)

✦ ✦ ✦ ✦ ✦ ✦ ✦ ✦ ✦ ✦ ✦ ✦ ✦ ✦ ✦

The figure holds a wide sword in a scabbard across his knees and is seated on an elaborately carved throne. His crown has four wide fleurons with flattened tops, each incised with two curving vertical lines. He has bulging oval eyes under heavy brows and a long flattened nose, his mouth and beard indicated by a large down-turned curve. His hair falls on his shoul-ders at the back in four spiral ringlets. He wears a simple cloak covering his left arm, open down the right-hand side with a border, plain above and chevron from knee-level down. It is held by a round brooch on his right shoulder. Under it is a long-sleeved mantle with an edging of dots below a single line at the cuffs and of continuous adjoined discs at the hem. Two small feet protrude at each side. The garments are gathered into four flat folds falling vertically from his knees.

The long fingers of each hand, more naturalistically carved than the schematised face, tightly grasp the hilt of the sword and the tip of the scabbard. The sword has a plain semicircular pommel and a guard decorated with a row of dots. The scabbard is ornamented with three diagonal bands, behind which another runs down the centre.

The back of the throne, which reaches half-way up the king's shoulders, has a plain band running along the bottom and sides, terminating at the top on each side in a grotesque biting animal head with small ears and large staring eyes. An upcurving stretcher carved with two horizontal lines joins the heads and a similar straight stretcher marks the level of the seat. Tendrils of large fleshy leaves curl asymmetrically round them both, covering the entire back of the throne; from a central spiral, two C-shapes are wrapped over the top stretcher, a further spiral fills the bottom left hand corner and a curling blossom the bottom right. The low sides have different geometrical motifs within plain framing. Below the king's right elbow a saltire, a lozenge and a circle are interwoven concentrically; on the other side there is a large central cross with squared interlace in the corner spaces.

✛ ✛ ✛ ✛ ✛ ✛ ✛ ✛ ✛ ✛ ✛ ✛ ✛ ✛ ✛ ✛

The height, facial features and robes are so close to Dalton 79 that they are surely opposite numbers from the same set. There are also strong similarities between the throne backs. L1(e) and Dalton 84 are probably the queens which go with them.

L1(b)
KING
[H.NS 20]

Walrus ivory; carved, engraved, punched
H 74, W 38, D 32

CONDITION
Fair, the central core of osteodentine is granular and detached from the solid outer dentine; there are two large vertical cracks in the throne to the figure's left; the face and torso are very worn and discoloured; there is extensive random channelling on the drapery below the knees.

✛ ✛ ✛ ✛ ✛ ✛ ✛ ✛ ✛ ✛ ✛ ✛ ✛ ✛ ✛ ✛ ✛

The figure holds a wide sword in a scabbard across his knees and is seated on an elaborately carved throne. His crown has four small fleurons and carved line borders. He has large mournful eyes and a snub nose with pronounced nostrils, bulging cheeks, a long upper lip and a straight pursed mouth over a short beard. His hair falls on the back of his shoulders in four spiral ringlets. The king wears a plain cloak falling over his left shoulder and arm, the hems marked by double incised lines. It falls in two parallel tubular folds over his left forearm and in four vertical pleats from his knees, the lower edge rising diagonally from his right foot. The sleeve of the plain mantle beneath is visible on his right arm, with a deep turned back cuff edged with two incised lines. The mantle covers his right leg with V-shaped drapery and emerges from under the cloak on the other side in a sweeping triangular fold.

The long bony fingers of each hand tightly grasp the sword by the hilt and the tip. The sword has a semicircular pommel and a guard with a

straight upper and an up-curved lower edge, fitting against the top of the scabbard. The scabbard is decorated with two bands of engraved lines with dots between running from side to side and a pair of incised lines down the centre to the tip.

The back of the throne, which reaches half-way up the king's shoulders, is framed by two vertical grooves on either side and a single curving plain moulding along the slightly splayed top edge. It is decorated with two horizontal bands of carving; above addorsed C-scrolls banded together in the centre, terminating in large fleshy leaves; below, lattice diaper consisting of one central lozenge surrounded by six triangles, the lattice being of raised tubular mouldings with a central groove, interlaced at the intersections. The lozenge is filled with a quatrefoil, the triangles with trefoils.

The low sides have panels of geometric interlace differing slightly from each other, both based on a central cross. Below the king's right elbow, this consists of four squares locked together by a larger central square which alternately passes over and under their outlines. This is carried out in mouldings with a central engraved line.

On the other side the mouldings are plain, the central square omitted and the four squares interlocked with each other, curving over and under in the centre.

✣ ✣ ✣ ✣ ✣ ✣ ✣ ✣ ✣ ✣ ✣ ✣ ✣ ✣ ✣

The fold patterns and the decoration of the scabbard pair with Dalton 83, which also matches the smaller size. The London piece is in better condition and may give an impression of the original facial features of L1(b). Both throne backs are divided horizontally between panels of geometric motifs and panels of leafy scrolls.

L1(b)

L1(b)

L1(c)
QUEEN
[H.NS 21]

Walrus ivory; carved, engraved, punched
H 95, W 52, D 38

CONDITION
Good, the central osteodentine is firmly integrated with the outer dentine,
the front of the figure is discoloured and extensively channelled, there are
fine vertical cracks in the back.

✦ ✦ ✦ ✦ ✦ ✦ ✦ ✦ ✦ ✦ ✦ ✦ ✦ ✦ ✦ ✦

The figure is seated on a carved throne in a symmetrical frontal pose, her
head is thrust slightly forward, her right hand raised to her right cheek,
her left forearm resting horizontally across her knees to cup her right
elbow in her left hand. Her tall crown has a deckled upper edge, larger and
smaller curves alternating, a round hole pierced below each of the larger.
She has strongly emphasised oval bulging eyes, the pupils indicated by
punched dots, the eyelids, eyebrows and nose shown as clearly chiselled
planes. The drooping, slightly crooked mouth is more naturalistically
carved and gives the face a faintly ironic expression. Her head-dress is
drawn back in a loop at either side and gathered up at the centre back,
where it is held just below the crown by a horizontal band engraved with
two lines, which draws it together into a central pleat.

The queen wears a long plain cloak covering both arms down to the
elbows and falling over her knees to the ground. An under dress is visible

in the centre front decorated with engraved Vs; its lower sleeves end in cuffs outlined by four lines. The cloak also has two lines at the hem. The schematised hands are broad and flat, with large thumbs and short thin fingers.

The square, slightly bowed, throne back, which reaches to just below the queen's shoulders, has a single line border and a central lozenge, the points extending to the centre of each side. The lozenge is carved with a pattern of geometrically interlaced bands, the centre of each marked with a single line. The symmetrical composition forms four other lozenges, each with four subsidiary lozenges, the whole connected and passing alternately over and under at the intersections.

The low sides of the throne have square panels of carved ornament quite different from each other. At the queen's right side a saltire cross is imposed on a lozenge, within interwoven strapwork. At her left, a saltire is interlaced with a Greek cross with round terminals, a lozenge and four semicircles.

✛ ✛ ✛ ✛ ✛ ✛ ✛ ✛ ✛ ✛ ✛ ✛ ✛ ✛ ✛ ✛

The front view of this queen, her crown and robe resemble Dalton 86, but she is 16 millimetres higher and so presumably not from the same set. The geometric interlace on the throne back relates to some of the panels on the sides of other pieces, but is otherwise unique in the Lewis hoard. The nearest comparison is a bishop, Dalton 93, where fretwork fills the whole surface of the throne back and has a curved scallop edged frieze above. Among the Lewis queens, only L1(c) and (d) have the elaborate looped head-dress at the back. The rest have short pleated veils like L1(e).

L1(c)

L1(c)

L1(d)
QUEEN
[H.NS 22]

Walrus ivory; engraved, carved, punched
H 71, W 37, D 34

CONDITION
Poor, the central osteodentine is crumbling and fragmented and coming away from the solid dentine, the figure's right hand side is badly eroded and part of the right hand is missing; extensive channelling to the left hand side of the cloak. It was pointed out to Sharpe that the right hand side of the throne is a separate piece of ivory attached during the carving.[1]

INSCRIPTION
Lord Londesborough (printed paper label stuck to the base)

✠ ✠ ✠ ✠ ✠ ✠ ✠ ✠ ✠ ✠ ✠ ✠ ✠ ✠ ✠ ✠

The figure is seated on a carved throne in a symmetrical frontal pose, her shoulders hunched and head thrust forward, her right hand raised to her right cheek, her left forearm resting horizontally across her lap to support her right arm at the elbow. Her shallow crown has four broad flat fleurons and is decorated with engraved lines, two forming a circular band with a row of dots between and two vertically in the centre of each fleuron. She has oval eyes, only slightly bulging, a broad prominent nose and small down-curved mouth. One hand is badly damaged, the other mostly concealed by a cloak.

Her plain cloak covers both arms to the elbows and falls in three folds on each side, the edges marked by double lines, that on her right folded back in one pleat. Over her knees, the mantle beneath forms a pair of deep symmetrical folds with a zig-zag hem dropping to a central point.

A further garment below is indicated by fine vertical tubular folds. On her forearms plain sleeves reach half-way to the wrists, revealing the cuffs with fine circular ribbing.

The queen's elaborate head-dress consists of looped bands passing from above the ears in front down the shoulders and up to the crown at the centre back, drawn together at the nape of the neck by a horizontal band engraved with two lines. The long hair is in two heavy spiral plaits echoing the loops of the head-dress.

The rectangular throne back, which comes half-way up the figure's shoulders, has carved decoration in two tiers, and canted corners with vertical bands of circles. The upper part has a large symmetrical blossom in an inverted heart shape in the centre, with exuberant fleshy leaves curling upwards and inwards at each side of the top. Below are two fluted panels, with a saltire-shaped knot surrounded by four tiny circles in the square between.

The low sides of the throne have curved upper edges, rising to a flat arm-rest at the front, above quite dissimilar square panels of carved decoration. Below her right elbow is a very worn design of saltire on lozenge interlace. On the other side is a simple square cross, the bands which outline it having a central line and passing alternately over and under. There are small concentric circles in each spandrel.

✝ ✝ ✝ ✝ ✝ ✝ ✝ ✝ ✝ ✝ ✝ ✝ ✝ ✝ ✝ ✝

The drapery patterns and face are very similar to Dalton 87, which also has a throne back in two tiers, scrolls above and semicircles below. Both pieces are smaller than all the other queens and they may have faced each other in the same set.

NOTE: [1] Wilson 1863, fig 181, 343, 344 n.1.

L1(d)

L1(d)

QUEEN

[H.NS 23]

Walrus ivory; carved, incised, punched
H 95, W 54, D 38

CONDITION
Good, the osteodentine core is coming away from the outer dentine, but the latter is very solid; the whole surface is discoloured, particularly the right hand side of the head and the right shoulder, with widespread channelling.

✠ ✠ ✠ ✠ ✠ ✠ ✠ ✠ ✠ ✠ ✠ ✠ ✠ ✠ ✠ ✠

The figure is seated on a carved throne, in a symmetrical frontal pose, her head tilted slightly forward, her right hand raised to her right cheek, her left hand resting on her left knee and holding a plain curved drinking horn. Her tall crown has a deckled upper edge, larger and smaller arcs alternating and a round hole pierced under each of the larger. She has oval eyes in deep round sockets set close to her long flat nose. The down-turned mouth has a long upper lip above and deep jutting chin below.

The queen's cloak, bordered with double lines at the front and a single line at the hem, covers the shoulders and upper arms and is drawn back in a single zig-zag fold to show the mantle beneath, which falls in a flattened chute of semicircular folds between her knees. Her cuff is marked by four engraved lines. The head-dress is a plain veil with a single line border at the bottom. It crosses her forehead under the crown and falls over her ears to shoulder level, forming seven flat, curving, vertical pleats across the back.

The rectangular throne back, which comes to just below the veil, has richly carved decoration of fleshy scrolls and leaves, centralised, but not symmetrical. There are two tiers of addorsed scrolls, held together in the centre by horizontal bands, the upper engraved with two lines, the lower with three. The two upper scrolls spiral upwards from the centre, the left hand passing over and in front of the curved top of the throne and terminating towards the centre in a three-petalled blossom pointing upwards; the right hand passing behind and over the throne top, terminating half-way down the right-hand side in a scrolled frond pointing downwards. The two larger lower spiral scrolls curl inwards from the sides to the wider central horizontal band and terminate in sprays of leaves in the two bottom corners. Within them two smaller concentric scrolls with symmetrical large fleshy, frilly blossoms spread upwards, the left hand in front of the larger scroll, the right hand behind (there is a change of mind by the carver at this point), to join at the upper, narrower central band.

The low sides of the throne are vertical rectangles, with plain frames, which at the front edge project upwards to form square finials. Under the queen's right shoulder the pattern of plaited strapwork is based on a saltire and a lozenge. On the other side, four vertical and four horizontal straps are interwoven at right angles to form a single rectangular design.

✠ ✠ ✠ ✠ ✠ ✠ ✠ ✠ ✠ ✠ ✠ ✠ ✠ ✠ ✠

One of the London queens (Dalton 84) also carries a horn and has a throne back with asymmetrical foliage scrolls and a curved top. It is the same height as L1(e) and presumably from the same set.

L1 (f)
BISHOP
[H.NS 24]

Walrus ivory; carved, incised, punched
H 92, W 41, D 36

CONDITION
Very good, slight discolouration, some channelling, particularly on the cope.

INSCRIPTION
Lord Londesborough (printed paper label stuck to the base)

✛ ✛ ✛ ✛ ✛ ✛ ✛ ✛ ✛ ✛ ✛ ✛ ✛ ✛ ✛ ✛

The figure appears almost to be standing from the front, but seen from the rear is seated on a carved throne facing straight ahead. He holds a crozier in both hands, the right above the left at a slight angle in front of him, the crook touching his right cheek, the shaft slightly to his right. Between the hands and the head, the staff of the crozier, a plain stout cylinder tapering slightly into the round knop, is carved *à jour*. It has a simple spiral crook.

The beardless bishop has small, almost round, protruding eyes with a dot for the pupil and engraved arched eyebrows, a large triangular nose with prominent nostrils and a single line for his down-turned mouth. His hair is straight, shown by vertical carved lines, cut level at neck length, covering his ears. His shallow mitre, which rises to a point at the centre front and back, has a line bordering the lower edge and two running up the centre of each point. It has two lappets at the centre back, falling to

below his shoulders, tapering towards the top where they converge at the centre of the mitre. The ends are engraved with saltire crosses below a single line. A cruciform orphrey is engraved at the centre of his back.

The throne back, carved with spiral scrolls, is an irregular rectangle, within a plain border, coming to the middle of the bishop's back. The scrolls are in two tiers around a central lozenge just over half-way up. The upper scrolls spiral upwards and outwards, behind the top of the throne, returning over it to curl back towards the centre, with S-shaped tendrils curving back into the top corners and sides. The two larger, lower scrolls are joined by a plain horizontal band in the centre below the lozenge. They spiral in from the sides about three-quarters of the way down the throne back, bifurcating into stems which merge into the scrolls above and tendrils which also divide, giving a tight curl in the centre on either side and a fleshy serrated blossom in each bottom corner.

The low sides of the throne are rectangular with plain frames rising at the front to form square finials. At the bishop's right side is carved a saltire cross formed of lines interwoven at the centre. On the other side an interwoven saltire criss-crosses a circle within a lozenge.

+ + + + + + + + + + + + + + + +

The front of L1(f) is not very close to any of the other bishops, but the rear view is a match for Dalton 89, which has the same cope decoration and a similar throne back with spiralling scrolls. Both pieces are probably from the same set as L1(e) and Dalton 84.

L1 (f)

L1 (f)

L1(g)
BISHOP
[H.NS 25]

Walrus ivory; carved, incised, punched
H 95, W 49, D 32

CONDITION
Very good, solid dentine, slightly crazed, some discolouration at each side of head and centre front behind the crozier.

✛ ✛ ✛ ✛ ✛ ✛ ✛ ✛ ✛ ✛ ✛ ✛ ✛ ✛ ✛ ✛

The figure is standing, truncated at the bottom, with no feet and the lower part of the vestments trimmed. The pose is frontal and symmetrical, the large square right hand raised in blessing palm outwards, the left forearm passing horizontally across the body, the left hand grasping a crozier, the crook of which rests against the left cheek. The crozier is carved *à jour* between hand and chin.

The beardless bishop has a broad face with a heavy jawline, a low forehead, oval bulging eyes with dots for the pupils under jutting eyebrows, a long broad nose and down turned mouth. His straight hair is shown as vertical engraved lines and is cut in a slant from below the mitre over each eye, half covering the ears to a straight neck-length fringe at the back.

His shallow mitre rises to a point at front and back and is undecorated. It has two lappets at the back, falling to below his shoulders, tapering towards the top where they converge at the centre of the mitre hem. The ends are engraved with saltire crosses below a single line.

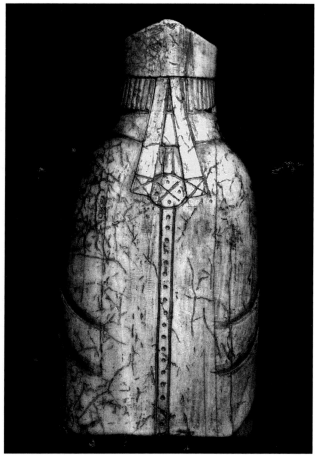

The bishop's chasuble, with an amice at the neck, is entirely smooth apart from two flattened schematised folds flowing from the sides over the forearms and into a point where it falls in the centre front. In the centre back, two vertical lines with a row of dots between and a circle containing a saltire with four dots at shoulder level indicate an orphrey. The cuffs are decorated with two single lines with a row of dots between. Under the chasuble in front is the stiff dalmatic with a plain line border and appearing below it and to the sides are the vertical folds of the alb.

+ + + + + + + + + + + + + + + +

Of the thirteen London bishops, five are enthroned and eight simply standing like L1(g). The plainer standing pieces are not easily sorted into sets.

L1(g)   L1(g)

BISHOP

[H.NS 26]
Walrus ivory; carved, incised, punched
H 75, W 40, D 25

CONDITION
Very good, discolouration in a band across the top of the head and down over the figure's right ear and on the chest, general crazing on vestments, mostly solid dentine, small grainy area of osteodentine firmly attached.

✣ ✣ ✣ ✣ ✣ ✣ ✣ ✣ ✣ ✣ ✣ ✣ ✣ ✣ ✣ ✣

The figure is seated on a carved throne facing straight ahead, a crozier held vertically in front of him in both hands, the right above the left, the crook touching his left cheek, the shaft slightly towards his left knee. The crozier has a plain cylindrical shaft, bulging gently in the middle, a ring knop and a spiral crook. The section between hands and chin is carved *à jour*.

The face has a wide jaw and narrow forehead, prominent bulging eyes with dots for the pupils, surrounded by engraved lines, a small short nose, long upper lip, narrow down-turned mouth and deep chin. The fringe of straight hair, carved in vertical lines, slants from each side of the forehead to cover the ears and meet the collar at the back. The shallow mitre has a point at front and back and is undecorated. Two lappets at the centre back fall below his shoulders, tapering towards the top where they converge at the centre of the mitre hem. The ends are engraved with a saltire below a single line.

The bishop's chasuble, with the amice showing as a deep flat band at the neck, covers his shoulders and upper arms and is drawn back in two folds to reveal the dalmatic and alb. Two concentric circles containing a

saltire and three vertical lines below indicate an orphrey in the centre back. The cope is fastened under the chin with a wide rectangular morse and has two engraved lines down the centre front, the lower part of which falls in three deep V-shaped folds between the figure's knees. The dalmatic beneath has a border of a row of dots within a single line. The fine vertical folds of the alb and horizontal lines on the ends of the stole are visible below.

The throne back has two vertical side posts with biting animal head terminals at the top. Between is a panel of leafy scrollwork, forming two addorsed C-shapes in the upper part each containing a curling palmette and giving a curved top edge to the throne. Two large single petals, projecting horizontally to the sides, separate this from an inverted heart shape in the lower part which frames a spray of three leaves between two in-turned spirals.

The low rectangular sides of the throne are carved with four diagonally placed oval petals with a central circle, imposed on an irregular oval. Below the bishop's left elbow this has four additional arcs incised on the oval between the petals.

✠ ✠ ✠ ✠ ✠ ✠ ✠ ✠ ✠ ✠ ✠ ✠ ✠ ✠ ✠ ✠

The pose, facial expression and the arrangement of the vestments are closest to Dalton 93, also a smaller piece than most of the bishops. The throne backs of the two figures share the plain borders and have the same type of biting animal head, but Dalton 93 has a geometric fret for decoration (see L1[c]) instead of scrolls.

L1(i)
KNIGHT
[H.NS 27]

Walrus ivory; carved, incised, punched
H 91, W 26, L 46

CONDITION
Poor, stained, cracked, the face very worn and damaged, thin outer dentine on a large crumbling osteodentine core; the surface extensively channelled. The more complicated shape has made greater demands on the material than the simpler pieces.

✣ ✣ ✣ ✣ ✣ ✣ ✣ ✣ ✣ ✣ ✣ ✣ ✣ ✣ ✣ ✣

The knight with spear and shield is mounted on a horse standing four square and facing forwards. The knight wears a pointed helmet, the edge bordered with a single line, with pendant round flaps, each incised with a saltire, one over each ear and one centre back, and possibly a nasal. He has a plain belt and baldrick for the shield diagonally across his back. His long surcoat splits back and front falling in three zig-zag folds on each side of the horse and his boots are plain with long pointed toes.

The spear has a stout cylindrical shaft and a pointed, bevelled head. The long kite-shaped shield has a single line border. The harness consists of reins, a bridle with cheek pieces, stirrups on long leathers and a horse cloth, falling nearly to the ground, with line and dot borders. The ground is indicated by thick wavy carved lines.

The horse is stocky, its cropped mane shown by a series of transverse lines, its long straight forelock falling down its nose and covering its

eyes. It has small round nostrils and a single straight line for its mouth. Its forelegs are very schematised with slight indication of hocks, its plump hindquarters are naturalistic and it has a long straight tail falling to the ground.

+ + + + + + + + + + + + + + +

Fifteen figures of knights on horseback are known from the Lewis hoard. The fourteen in London and L1(i) are mounted on similar stout little horses with short manes and long forelocks, all having long horse cloths and standing on a wavy ground line. All the knights have shoulder-length straight hair showing below their helmets. The latter are round with a brim in four cases, but otherwise conical, seven (Dalton 109-15) with pendant flaps like L1(i). The Edinburgh piece does not share the proto-heraldic devices which decorate the long kite-shaped shields of the British Museum knights. Most of the 15 are too similar to be convincingly assigned to separate sets.

L1(i)

L1(i)

L1(j)
WARDER
[H.NS 28]

Whale tooth; carved, incised, punched
H 96, W 44, D 34

CONDITION
Good, chips to the sword blade, general discolouration, channelling and linear corrosion of the surface; mostly solid dentine, small cracks in lower back.

INSCRIPTION
Lord Londesborough (printed paper label)

✢ ✢ ✢ ✢ ✢ ✢ ✢ ✢ ✢ ✢ ✢ ✢ ✢ ✢ ✢ ✢

The standing figure of a warrior wears a plain conical helmet and a long plain surcoat with a flowing box-pleat front and back and a split revealing an undergarment with an upturned incised arc at the hem below his right arm. The cuff is marked by a single line. His bulbous oval eyes ringed by carved lines peer out from under the rim of his helmet and he has a long hooked nose with flaring nostrils above a wide down-turned incision representing mouth and moustache over a large spreading beard. His straight hair, shown as carved lines, falls on each side of his face covering his ears and forming a long regular shoulder-length bob at the back.

He carries a long broad sword with a rounded pommel, held vertically in his right hand, reaching from waist height to the brim of his

helmet and a shield concealing his right arm and side from shoulder to hem. The shield is an elongated triangle with slightly curved sides and top. It is decorated with an incised cross made up of a wavy line framed by straight lines, with a square motif at the centre.

+ + + + + + + + + + + + + + + +

This is the tallest by four millimetres of the dozen Lewis warders. It is very similar to Dalton 116, including the devices on their shields which are very alike. As with the knights, it is impossible to categorise the warders into related groups.

The material is dense and regular, without the spongy texture of the osteodentine which is present in the core of the other Edinburgh pieces. This suggests that it is not carved from walrus ivory but from a tooth, probably of a sperm whale, as are, for example, gaming pieces in the Musée de Cluny in Paris.[1] A neat round hole in the base represents the central pulpy cavity of the tooth, perhaps enlarged to hold a spindle while the figure was being carved.[2]

NOTES: [1] Goret and Poplin 1998, 502-4. [2] Ibid, fig 7, 503.

L1 (j)   L1 (j)

WARDER

[H.NS 29]

Walrus ivory; carved, incised, punched
H 83, W 40, D 23

CONDITION
Fair, the surface with iridescent discolouration and channelling on all
surfaces; solid dentine, small area only of osteodentine at the base.

＋＋＋＋＋＋＋＋＋＋＋＋＋＋＋

The standing figure of a warrior wears a plain conical helmet and a long
surcoat with a central pleat in the back, marked by three carved con-
verging lines, the bottom of a similar pleat showing below the shield at
centre front. The cuff is marked by a line of dots within a single line. His
bulbous close-set eyes peer out from under the rim of his helmet above a
large triangular nose and his protruding teeth bite the top of the shield
which conceals his chin. His straight hair, shown as carved vertical lines,
falls either side of his face, covering his ears and forming a regular bob to
the bottom of his neck at the back.

He holds the kite-shaped shield against the front of his body with
his crooked left arm, the hand hidden. In his right hand, this arm also
crooked, he holds a broad sword with a channelled blade, round pommel
and dotted guard, vertically at a slight angle to touch his right cheek.
There is a central motif on the shield, partly hidden by the sword, consisting of a lozenge containing a cross.

＋＋＋＋＋＋＋＋＋＋＋＋＋＋＋

Of the ten warders in the British Museum, three also bite the top of their shields (Dalton 123-5), a gesture described in Scandinavian literature from the 12th century.[1] Dalton points out that the three 'berserkers' in London differ in costume and in the shape of their shields from the other warders, but L1(k) bears a strong resemblance to L1(j) facially and in the very simple treatment of his garments.

NOTE: [1] Madden 1832, 271-2, it was part of the frenzy into which warriors worked themselves before and during battle, known as 'Berserksgangr'.

L1(k)   L1(k)

SKYE CHESS PIECE

[H.NS 15]

Scotland, mid-13th century
Walrus ivory; carved, incised, drilled
H 94, W 42, L 68

CONDITION
Fairly good, portion of the top frieze broken off, leaf chipped off above figure
with demi fleur-de-lis shield, large split below on base, split at lower edge on
other side, splits in frieze, some discolouration; a plug apparently of resin and
wood shavings has been inserted into the base to consolidate the piece.

PROVENANCE
Presented to the Society of Antiquaries of Scotland in November 1782 by
Lord MacDonald of Skye.[1]

✢ ✢ ✢ ✢ ✢ ✢ ✢ ✢ ✢ ✢ ✢ ✢ ✢ ✢ ✢ ✢ ✢

The large handsome chesspiece is carved in very high relief with extensive
use of openwork. The osteodentine core has been hollowed out of the top
part and cut right through between the legs of the figures. A shallow hole
has been drilled in the top of the core, probably to take a spindle to hold
the piece in place while it was being carved.

  The sculpture consists of two male figures in mail coifs, hauberks
and chausses sitting back to back, their legs apart, holding broad swords in

their right hands, the points over their right shoulders and small shields strapped to their left forearms. They have naturalistic conventionally ugly faces, similar but not the same.

The shields are emblazoned with heraldry. One has an overall field of diagonal lattice, each lozenge with a central dot, and a fleur-de-lis dimidiated. The other carries a bendy of three plain raised bars alternating with lines of drilled holes. Both swords have round pommels, rectangular guards and channelled blades, the mail is indicated by repeated horizontal lines with widely spaced dots between.

The bearer of the bendy shield has a flat rubbery face with two heavy vertical furrows in the brow, large deep-set elongated oval eyes, a broken nose, a twisted up-curving mouth and a long straight beard under his bulging cheeks. The other has a larger head and face, the features also rubbery, but somewhat sunken around the mouth. Again he has a brow with two deep furrows, large rather sunken eyes and a small hooked nose. His mouth is slightly open under a long upper lip and his big cleft chin juts forward under fat bulging cheeks.

The figures are seated on the formalised stump of a tree. Its flattened branches are bordered by single lines and entwined in a figure of eight formation on each side of the chesspiece. At the top they sprout into scrolling leaves, originally forming a continuous frieze along both sides and above the heads of the figures. At ground level they divide into large roots coiling over the figures' feet among leaf scrolls and podded fruits.

✛ ✛ ✛ ✛ ✛ ✛ ✛ ✛ ✛ ✛ ✛ ✛ ✛ ✛ ✛ ✛

L2

When it was acquired in 1782 the piece was described as 'The handle of an ancient Gaelic durk', but Daniel Wilson in his catalogue recognised it as a 'Chessman'.[2] A visitor to the MacDonalds at Armadale in the 1850s refers to the gift and combines the two theories, speculating that it had been made as a chesspiece and reused as a dirk handle.[3] The most exhaustive and erudite scholar of the game in the 20th century dismissed it, along with the pieces in the Ashmolean and Bargello discussed below, as 'probably not chessmen at all'. However, Murray's great expertise was in history, literature and philology. The visual arts were of little interest to him and he was quite prepared to suggest that the Lewis chessmen were not as old as the 13th century, but 'may be 17th century Icelandic only'.[4]

In fact, the rectangular form with the indent at the centre top of each long side clearly echoes plain abstract rooks or castles of the 11th and 12th centuries,[5] not to mention an elaborate piece in the Louvre which is carved on one side with two knights in armour in mounted combat.[6] To clinch matters, the foliage forms are so similar to those on the throne of an indisputable bishop in the Vatican that they are quite probably from the same set.[7]

The nationality and date of the piece are more difficult to establish. Some of its characteristics are reminiscent of 13th-century Scandinavian work. The curling leaf ends and the beaded lines running up the centre of some of the tendrils have parallels on a carved ivory casket now in Stockholm and attributed to a Trondheim workshop.[8] The related bishop in the Vatican is in the tradition going back to the Lewis chessmen, with the addition of little figures in attendance which is a notable feature of kings, queens and bishops from succeeding periods in the Nationalmuseet in Copenhagen.

Three broadly comparable chesspieces are attributed to one English workshop of about 1240-50.[9] Each shows a knight in combat, two on horseback and one fighting hand-to-hand with a dragon. They are also surrounded by stylised plant forms, but of a lighter, more elegantly Gothic type than on the Skye chesspiece. The knights are dashing idealised figures with intimidating helmets and flying surcoats. The more homely characters on L2 do, however, relate to other English art forms. Warriors in very similar armour appear in English manuscript illumination from at least the period of the Winchester Bible in the third quarter of the 12th century,[10] and are still in abundant evidence in the Maciejowski Bible almost a century later,[11] but the combination of the armour, the chunky proportions, informal poses and particularly the grotesque faces are strikingly similar to the illustrations of Matthew Paris.[12] A monk of St Albans known as an illuminator, painter, scribe and historian, there is evidence that he died in 1259.[13]

Paris famously visited Bergen in 1246 at the behest of Haakon IV and the Fåberg panel in Oldsaksamlingen in Oslo[14] has even been attributed to him, one Scandinavian writer going so far as to describe him as 'the father of medieval art in Norway'.[15] Certainly he was influential there and the figures on L2 may reflect his style transmitted through the same Norwegian source as the foliage carving.

The features that point to an earliest possible date for the Skye chesspiece are the shields and their heraldry. Their small size and 'heater' shape are in strong contrast to the long kite-shaped shields of the Lewis chessmen and the Winchester Bible. Instead they share the proportions of the examples shown by Paris and in the Maciejowski Bible. One authority on arms and armour firmly dates this change to about 1250.[16]

The heraldry equally indicates a date around the middle of the 13th century at the earliest. The fleur-de-lis is of a very decorative and evolved form, with exuberantly curling but fine and elegant petals. The practice of dimidiation of a heraldic device was unusual in 13th-century Scotland, even to indicate very rich and powerful family alliances. Without any clues as to what colours may have originally been indicated on the shields, either with paint or by the application of metal foils, it is difficult to say precisely whether a specific personal armorial identification was intended, but some deductions can be made.

On the evidence of seal impressions, both devices were rare in early Scottish heraldry. This form of bendy was originally associated with the dukes of Burgundy and their circle and is recorded by Matthew Paris as in use by only two Norman families in England in the reign of Henry III.[17] The fleur-de-lis is a very ancient decorative device which came to be used as the symbol of the French royal house as early as the 10th century.[18] It appears in late 12th- and 13th-century Scotland in two clearly marked clusters. The larger is around Coldingham in Berwickshire and seems to be associated with the priory,[19] the smaller is in the west and linked to the Montgomery family.

Robert of Montgomery arrived with the wave of immigrants from England and Normandy introduced into Scotland under William the Lion, establishing himself as lord of Eaglesham, about twelve kilometres south of Glasgow, soon after 1157.[20] From the outset he was closely associated with the powerful Stewart family and it is almost certain that Walter Stewart granted Robert the fief of his lands. The Montgomery family muniments were lost in a fire at Eglinton Castle in the early 16th century, leaving us with a scanty record of some of his immediate descendants and their marriages.[21] However, we do know that John de Montgomery, third lord of

Eaglesham, married Helen, the daughter of Robert de Kent of Innerwick near the East Lothian coast and further consolidated the family fortunes by acquiring a third of her father's estates. John's seal, known from a Melrose charter of between 1208 and 1224 granting the abbey lands in Innerwick, is a handsome fleur-de-lis, with well-shaped fat curling petals.[22]

A similar badge was adopted by Richard Falconer of Hawkerston, also from Innerwick,[23] and Nicholas of Merns[24] for their seals on the same charter. They may have been either Montgomery kinsmen or beholden to them in some way. Camden tells us that 'many Gentlemen begin to bear arms by borrowing from their Lords Arms of whom they held in Fee, or to whom they were most devoted'.[25]

Later Montgomeries expanded the heraldry to three fleur-de-lis with various embellishments, particularly after they became earls of Eglinton in the 16th century. Lord MacDonald, who presented this chesspiece to the Society of Antiquaries, was the son of Sir Alexander MacDonald and Lady Margaret Montgomery, who married in 1739, much to the satisfaction of her brother the earl.[26] His letter of approval survives as does another making generous financial arrangements and providing for her trousseau. It is quite possible that L2 was a family keepsake which she passed on to her son. This would mean that the heraldry was not purely decorative, but related to some Montgomery marriage or other event. The bendy blazon remains a mystery. One of the two such shields described by Matthew Paris is that of Piers de Montfort of Beaudesert, Warwickshire.[27] Parts of the de Montfort family came to Scotland in the same movement as the Montgomeries,[28] but the devices on their known seals were entirely different.[29]

If one accepts stylistic arguments for dating and the Montgomery connection, here again is evidence of the taste and pursuits of Scottish high-ranking noble families in the 13th century. The chesspiece takes features from the art of Scandinavia and England, but combines them in a manner indicating an accomplished and original artist working at some remove in Scotland.

NOTES: [1] Smellie 1782, 71-2. [2] Wilson 1849, 99. [3] Smith 1862, 104-5. [4] Murray 1913, 762, n 9, 759. [5] Kluge-Pinsker 1991, pl 2,12, nos A19, 118-19, A21, 120-1, A23, 122-3, A24, 123-4, A29, 128. [6] Beckwith 1972, no 165, 158, pls 259 and 260, 159. [7] Goldschmidt 1926, no 246, pl LXX, 52. [8] Goldschmidt 1918, no 144, pl XLIX, 39; Andersen 1997, pl 35, 51-2. [9] London 1987, nos 146-8, 253-4. [10] Oakeshott 1981, fig 11, 23, pl VIII, between 58 and 59. [11] Cockerell and Plummer c 1970, eg no 87, 74, no 150, 116, no 207, 158, no 210, 160. [12] James 1926, pl III, p 263, p 279, pl VIII, f 37. [13] Vaughan 1958, 7-9. [14] Horgen 2000, no 31, 37. [15] Vaughan 1958, 205-7. [16] Blair 1958, 181. [17] Wagner 1967, 211. [18] Wagner 1956, 13; Pastoureau 1995, 66-8. [19] Hunter Blair 1915, no 2745, 290, nos 2748 and 2750, 291, no 2774, 295, no 2782,

296, nos 2786, 2788 and 2789, 297, nos 2970 and 2971, 326, nos 2975, 2978, 2979 and 2983, 327. [20] Barrow 1973, 331, 344. [21] Fraser 1859, 7-12. [22] Melrose Liber 1837, vol I, no 61, 50-51; Fraser 1859, 10, with engraved illustration; Laing 1850, no 590, 100, misdates the charter to c AD 1176, an error perpetuated by Stevenson and Wood. [23] Stevenson and Wood 1940, vol II, 352, Richard adds two falcons reguardant perched on the flower; he was married to Helen de Montgomery's sister (Kelso Liber 1846, vol I, no 251, 209-10). [24] Laing 1850, no 587, 100. 'Merns' equates with the modern Newton Mearns and Mearnskirk about four kilometres from Eaglesham. About 1240 John of Stevenston, bordering the Montgomery lands at Ardrossan, also had a fleur-de-lis (Hunter Blair 1915, no 2994, 329). [25] Wagner 1956, 19. [26] Fraser 1859, 106, 119, 333, 334. [27] Wagner 1967, 211. [28] Barrow 1973, 332. [29] Laing 1866, no 735, 123, an eagle preying on a bird, 20 July 1295.

L3   B40, 27
DALCROSS PLAYING PIECE
[K.2001.504]

Scotland, 12th century
Bone; carved
DIAM 38, D 7

CONDITION
Good, small area of damage on the rim, discoloured.

PROVENANCE
Found under the stone flooring of the hall, Dalcross Castle, Inverness-shire, exhibited to the Society of Antiquaries of Scotland in January 1897, deposited in the museum that year by W L Carruthers.[1]

✛ ✛ ✛ ✛ ✛ ✛ ✛ ✛ ✛ ✛ ✛ ✛ ✛ ✛ ✛ ✛

L3

fig 38: TABLE GAME BOARD
Bone, English, 11th century, copyright,
Gloucester City Museum and Art Gallery.
L 600, W 450 (as reconstructed)

grotesque figures. A playing piece found in Vordingborg in southern Sjælland can be presumed to be Danish or at least Scandinavian.[6] It is decorated with a male figure holding a scaly dragon in each hand with large claws, flecked bodies and prominent round eyes very like the beast on L3. Another example without an early provenance, now in the Victoria and Albert Museum is comparable to L3; carved with a double-headed monster, it has also been seen as 'more Scandinavian than French in origin'.[7]

As this and the two following Museum of Scotland pieces came from coastal north-east Scotland, and a fourth where the monster has a human head was found in Stonehaven,[8] it could be argued that they were all imports. However, such minor products not requiring major technical skills are just as likely to have been produced locally under Scandinavian influence.

NOTES: [1] *PSAS*, vol XXXI, 1897, 80; National Museum of Antiquities of Scotland manuscript register 1892-1914, 97. The present Dalcross Castle was built in the 17th century. [2] Murray 1941, 57-63, the original game was already popular in the later Roman empire. [3] Stewart and Watkins 1984, 185-90. [4] Kluge-Pinsker 1991, 58-61, figs 33-5. [5] Dalton 1909, 74-6; Goldschmidt 1918, nos 169-300, pls LIII-LIX, 42-52; Goldschmidt 1926, nos 278-80, pl LXXIII, 56. [6] Paris, Berlin, Copenhagen 1992-1993, no 605a, 388. [7] Beckwith 1972, no 110, 145, illus 214, 154. [8] *PSAS*, vol XXIX, 1895, 65; Goldschmidt 1918, fig 9, 8; Goldschmidt 1926, 56 describes L3 as French and gives no attribution for L4 or L5.

The circular playing piece is undecorated on one face and has plain vertical edges. The carved side has a grotesque beast in profile in low relief. It has a bird-like head with a long jagged crest behind, a large round eye with a central dot and a curved beak. The flecked S-shaped body ends in a large claw foot and an arm reaches up to hold the long bushy feathered tail, which sweeps across the playing piece at the beast's shoulder level.

+ + + + + + + + + + + + + + +

Comparatively large numbers of round bone playing pieces are extant from 12th-century Europe. They were used with dice to play a number of 'table' games on a board similar to that used for modern backgammon.[2] On the whole the boards did not survive, but there are two bone mounted examples, one from the 11th century found at Gloucester with associated playing pieces (fig 38),[3] and a similar 12th-century example from Saint-Denis.[4]

The playing pieces fall broadly into two categories, the majority have wider decorated borders framing more or less complicated scenes from Classical literature and the Old Testament, or monsters, animals or signs of the zodiac.[5] The less frequent type, to which L3, L4 and L5 belong, have plain borders and fairly roughly carved

L4
KIRKWALL PLAYING PIECE
[H.NS 4]

Scotland, 12th century
Bone; carved
DIAM 33, D 5

CONDITION
Discoloured, chips and wear to the edges.

PROVENANCE
Said to have been found in the ruins of the Bishop's Palace, Kirkwall, presented to the museum by the executors of Professor Stewart Traill in 1870 as part of a collection of antiquities from Orkney.[1]

+ + + + + + + + + + + + + + +

The round flat playing piece is carved with a grotesque hare, with a large head and long claws, within a plain border. The reverse is completely plain.[2]

+ + + + + + + + + + + + + + +

Thomas Stewart Traill, born in Kirkwall in 1781, became professor of medical jurisprudence in the University of

Edinburgh and was very proud of his Orcadian origins.[3] His bequest to the museum also included Egyptian and Roman antiquities. Two notebooks by Thomas Stewart Traill in the museum archive[4] contain detailed notes, measurements and drawings of Kirkwall Cathedral with its monuments, bells and collection plate.[5]

When the cathedral was moved from Birsay to Kirkwall and work on the new church began in 1137, a suitable dwelling for the bishop was also provided. By 1320 it was recorded as being for the most part in ruins and it was largely reconstructed by bishop Robert Reid (1541-58).[6] However, the masonry of the lower parts of the 12th-century hall, which is over twenty-seven metres long, show quite clearly that the original structure was part of the same building programme as the cathedral itself.[7]

NOTES: [1] *PSAS*, vol VIII, 1871, 389-91, names the bequest as that of Professor William Stewart Traill, but this is an error. The Society of Antiquaries manuscript minute book for 1868-80 gives him no forename, but in the 1892 NMAS printed catalogue the bequest is ascribed to Professor T S Traill. His cousin was named William and was probably one of his executors, leading to this confusion. There was no professor of the latter name in the University of Edinburgh in the 19th century and the two Williams registered as doctors were in Arbroath and Dunfermline, with no apparent Orkney connections (*The Medical Register*, London 1860, 1873, 1878). [2] See notes to L3. [3] Grant 1884, vol II, 449-50; DNB, vol LVII, 1899, 151; Traill 1883, 52. [4] NMS mss 555 and 556, deposited in 1890 by Joseph Anderson. [5] His father was the minister of Kirkwall. [6] Simpson 1965, 7-9. [7] Ibid, 11-12.

URQUHART CASTLE PLAYING PIECE
[H.HY 22]

Scotland, 12th century
Bone; carved
DIAM 30, D 6

CONDITION
Very worn, the texture of the bone very apparent back and front, part of the rim and both surfaces missing at top right.

PROVENANCE
Part of a collection of relics found at Urquhart Castle, Inverness-shire, during excavations by HM Office of Works, exhibited to the Society of Antiquaries of Scotland in 1924[1] and on loan to the museum until 1955 when it was donated by the trustees of the Countess of Seafield.

+ + + + + + + + + + + + + + +

The reverse and vertical edges are undecorated. The face has a plain rim and a man on horseback crudely carved filling the central space, riding from left to right, with a rabbit (?) in the background.[2]

+ + + + + + + + + + + + + + +

By the reign of William the Lion (1165-1214) Urquhart Castle was probably already in existence, its 12th-century timber structure standing on a natural vantage point on the shore of Loch Ness.[3]

NOTES: [1] *PSAS*, vol LVIII, 1924, 140. [2] See notes to L3. [3] Tabraham 1986, 31, 40.

L4

L5

Iona Playing Piece

L6   D21, 60

Iona Playing Piece
[H.NS 99]

Scotland, late 15th century
Whale(?)bone; carved
DIAM 38, D 6

CONDITION
Fair, chips to rim, chipping and a hole bored into the back.

PROVENANCE
Found when clearing the floor of the room north of the chapter house, Iona Abbey in 1951; presented by the Iona Trustees in 1952.[1]

+ + + + + + + + + + + + + + +

The reverse and vertical edges are undecorated. The face has a plain rim framing a carving of a mermaid wearing a crown, holding a fish by its tail in her right hand and her own tail in her left. The carving is fairly crude.

+ + + + + + + + + + + + + + +

Mermaids were favourite motifs for medieval manuscript border decoration, for wood carvings such as misericords and for stone sculpture. This particular example bears a striking similarity to an initial in the late 15th-century portion of the Glenorchy Psalter (fig 39)[2]. This illuminated book has a calendar of saints which very specifically link it with Argyll, including Iona, and by the

early 16th century belonged to Colin Campbell of Glenorchy, probably the 3rd laird, who died in 1523.[3] The psalter appears to have been a local product and the mermaid is even less elegant than her sister on the playing piece. A third such figure is carved on a stone cross at Campbeltown, but does not wear a crown.[4]

NOTES: [1] *PSAS*, vol LXXXVII, 1952-53, 203. [2] British Library, Egerton ms 2899. [3] British Museum 1925, 411-13. [4] Steer and Bannerman 1977, no 104, 159-60, pl 11, state that various dates between 1350 and 1500 are possible for the cross.

L6

fig 39: GLENORCHY PSALTER
Vellum, Egerton MS 2899, fol 121, recto, Scottish, late 15th century, reproduced by permission of the British Library.
241 x 172

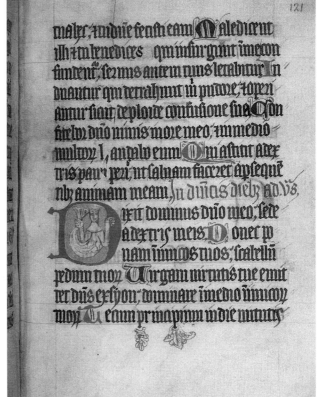

184

RUM TABLEMAN
[H.NS 92]

Scotland, c1500
Whalebone; carved, incised
DIAM 46, D 5

CONDITION
Good, some chips to the rim, discoloured.

PROVENANCE
Said to have been found in a cave on the east side of the island of Rum, Inverness-shire. Presented by Lady Monica Bullough in 1943.[1]

✦ ✦ ✦ ✦ ✦ ✦ ✦ ✦ ✦ ✦ ✦ ✦ ✦ ✦ ✦ ✦

The disc-shaped playing piece, which is plain on the sides and reverse, has a carved and incised ornament of inter-laced bands. The concentric and symmetrical motif, which covers the entire surface within a narrow plain vertical rim, is interwoven from ten semicircular curves at the circumference, through three tiers to the centre. each band is outlined by a single line incised along its edge.

✦ ✦ ✦ ✦ ✦ ✦ ✦ ✦ ✦ ✦ ✦ ✦ ✦ ✦ ✦ ✦

The decoration is very similar to that on West Highland carved gravestones and to the caskets L9 and L10.

NOTE: [1] *PSAS*, lxxviii (1943-44), 139.

KIRKTON OF CRAIG CRUCIFIX FIGURE
[H.KE 13]

Scotland, late 14th or early 15th century
Bone; carved
H 100, W 40, D 20

CONDITION
Discoloured, the arms and legs mostly broken off.

PROVENANCE
Dug up by Robert Gourlay, in his garden at Kirkton of Craig, Montrose, Angus about 1890, presented to the museum by his daughter Miss K D Gourlay in 1928.[1]

✦ ✦ ✦ ✦ ✦ ✦ ✦ ✦ ✦ ✦ ✦ ✦ ✦ ✦ ✦ ✦

The fragment of a corpus from an altar cross now consists only of the head, body and stumps of the arms and left leg. Christ's head wearing a schematised crown of thorns, indicated by rough horizontal carved dashes and parallel

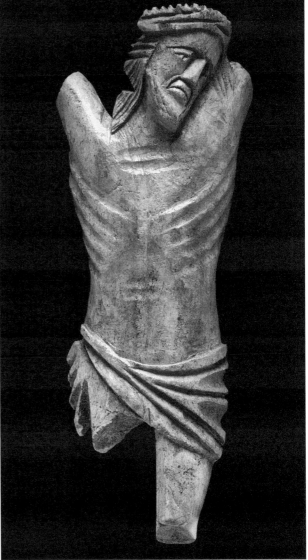

notching on the top edge, leans to rest on his left shoulder and arm. The expression of suffering and sorrow is conveyed in abstracted angular planes, the eyes open, the down-turned mouth in a deep grimace. His short beard is marked by a few short dashes on each side, the long hair on his right-hand side by three horizontals, above radiating lines reaching to his shoulder, with a deep V-shaped notch half-way down. A few cursory lines represent the hair against the left arm.

The arms were dragged upwards at a sharp angle, drawing the torso tight against the upper ribs, which along with the breastbone are naturalistically carved in low relief. Below the flat stomach, the perizoma fans in scooped folds from the right hip to cover the left, a small chute of drapery falling vertically behind the right leg. The upper left leg was either unusually uncovered, or more probably the remaining fragment represents tightly pulled drapery.

+ + + + + + + + + + + + + + + +

This type of Christ, forming a Y-shape and the drooping head with its agonized face appears in northern Europe, notably around Cologne, in the early 14th century.[2] The features and flat crown are very reminiscent of a magnificent large wooden crucifix from Westphalia dated on stylistic grounds to *c*1340[3] and is probably a copy of something similar, crudely made in Scotland a little later.

NOTE: [1] *PSAS* 1928, vol LXII, 83. [2] Francovich 1938, 183-95, fig 99, 131-49. [3] Paris 1968, no 160, 94, pl 56.

EGLINTON CASKET
[H.UD 10]

Scotland, *c*1500
Whalebone, copper alloy; carved, engraved, cast
H 118, D 105, L 262

CONDITION
Studs are missing from the metal straps above three of the hinges, two have been crudely repaired with metal patches; two studs are missing from the bottom of the straps on the back; the bottom two fleurons are broken off the lock and the end is missing from one of the hasps; a metal strip is lost from underneath the casket; there are long cracks in the whalebone half-way across the lid and from side to side of the front. There is a small blob of brown paint (?) on the lid.

PROVENANCE
Purchased at the Eglinton Castle sale, 4 December 1925.[1]

+ + + + + + + + + + + + + + + +

The rectangular casket with its hinged slightly convex lid is made from six panels of whalebone, held together by metal straps. The four right-angled corner pieces have decorative deckled edges marked by engraved V-shaped strokes. The base has a long projecting tab with oblique slanting ends in the centre front and back. These fit into slots cut into the front and rear panels. Each end of the lid is protected by a right-angled piece of metal, the vertical plane having a smaller deckle along the top edge and the horizontal a larger deckle notched on the apices and pierced with round holes, a horizontal line between

L9

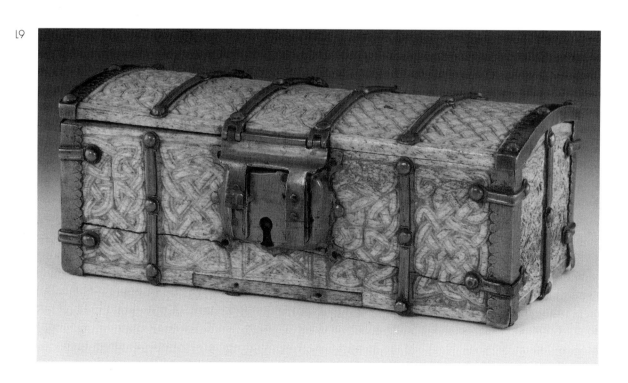

each. The casket is also bound with metal straps, each with two raised ribs and held by large round studs. Four run from back to front across the lid, four vertically down the back, one down the centre of each end and on either side of the lock on the front. Two short horizontal straps hold each corner piece in place. They are connected by flat metal straps on the bottom, originally four running from back to front and one from side to side at the centre of each end.

The lock, with two holes for the hasps and a large keyhole is encased in a rectangular decorative metal casing with a simple diagonally placed fleuron projecting from each corner with a round hole for a stud in the centre and a further round stud placed in the middle of each side. The square loops of the hasps are on plain flat straps descending from a concave crossbar with curved ends. The two hinges of the hasp and the four at the back of the lid are plain cylinders on shield-shaped plates held by larger round studs.

All the whalebone panels are carved in low relief with patterns of interlace and knotwork, emphasised by finely cut outlines. On the top there are five separate rectangular designs between the metal straps. From left to right these are; three tiers of curved knotwork; two tiers of right-angled strapwork with curved ends at the rear and a small central round bead; a repeat of the first design; and two rectangular integrated panels of right-angled woven strapwork bordered by prominent round beads.

On the front are four rectangular designs of curved knotwork, all slightly different, the two on the left of the lock having symmetrical patterns, the two on the right being more random. Below the lock is a small rectangle containing interwoven saltire crosses. There are two further curved knotwork designs on each end and five on the back, all in vertical rectangles and all slightly different.[2]

The underneath of the base is almost filled by two large square designs based on saltire crosses with a rectangular pattern of symmetrical strapwork between them. The interior is undecorated. There are traces of red colouring on the bottom of the casket and on all the interior surfaces.

+ + + + + + + + + + + + + + +

The workmanship of the Eglinton and Fife (L10) caskets is so similar that they may have come from the same workshop and the following comments apply to both. Ivory caskets of very similar size bound with metal straps including large square locks were produced in France in the second quarter of the 14th century, decorated with scenes from medieval romances carved in an elegant Gothic style. Fine examples survive in many collections including the Victoria and Albert Museum, the British Museum and the Louvre.[3] It is entirely likely that others were imported for patrons in Scotland. The Eglinton and Fife caskets are reinterpretations of the form, carved with decoration characteristic of the west of Scotland and Ireland. The very secular iconography of the French examples and the lack of any Christian symbolism on the Scottish argues that neither were intended for any religious purpose.

The scale of all these miniature coffers, the expensive material from which they were made, the elaborate ornamentation and their prominent locks suggests that they were intended to hold something very precious. Jewels or coinage are an obvious possibility, but doc-

L9

uments, apart from small personal letters (particularly if they had seals attached) would have had to have been too minutely folded to fit in.

The fact that in western Scotland, however, the caskets held some quite particular significance is demonstrated by their inclusion amongst the domestic objects shown on carved grave slabs. These could be seen as images of the standard ironbound strongbox, except that at least two seem to be views from above with carrying handles on the lids, hardly feasible on a heavy wooden chest and most have deckled decoration on the end straps very like L9 and L10.[4] The swords, galleys, bows and daggers which also feature on the slabs presumably indicated the status of the deceased; hatchets, hammers, tongs, anvils and shears their trades or in the later period their family names.[5] Three inscribed slabs with caskets commemorate men[6] and most have a sword as their main motif, but others may be female memorials. They seem to symbolise notable wealth in some form, whether earned, inherited, acquired through marriage or as one authority has speculated, donated to the burial church.[7]

The dating is again an area of uncertainty. The metalwork and locks on both L9 and L10 appear to be original and their simple decoration of fleurons and debased egg and dart belong to the late Gothic era. The shape with the convex lid is derived from full-sized wooden luggage chests where the lid was created from the natural curve of the timber and it is suggested was a practical design to drain off rain in transit.[8] English examples are extant with sufficient historical evidence to place them in the second half of the 15th century.[9]

The strapwork of the carved bone panels ultimately derives from Celtic ornament of the early medieval period,[10] but the closed up strands with little ground between, the chunky regular geometric layouts and the repetition of the same patterns are the marks of a much later period. Simple interwoven panels like those on the lids of both caskets are close to motifs used by 15th-century sculptors grouped as the 'Kintyre School',[11] and also to the Irish leather satchel traditionally made for the Book of Armagh. The latter must be of very late 15th-century date as it has a clumsy inscription in black letter.[12] The extra little motifs filling the fields where there is a small space, round beads on some panels of L9 and tiny flowerlets on the front of the Fife casket also indicate a late date, the former corresponding to work on the Kilfinan Cross,[13] the latter being entirely Gothic motifs.

Although it is, of course, possible that the owners of Eglinton Castle could have acquired their casket at any later date, the Montgomeries had close ties with Argyll and the Hebrides in the 15th and 16th centuries. At some date shortly before 1413, Sir John de Montgomerie, 10th lord of Eaglesham, also of Eglinton and Ardrossan, married Agnes of the Isles as his first wife and she was mother of his two eldest sons.[14] By 1499, his descendant Hugh, 1st earl of Eglinton was married to Helen Campbell, daughter of the first earl of Argyll and two of their fourteen children also made West Highland alliances.[15] The slightly tenuous comparisons with the stone carving of Kintyre and Kilfinan on Loch Fyne might suggest any of these brides as the source, but the probable date makes Helen and the Argyll Campbells the most likely.[16] If so, the elegant lady represented by the effigy on page 45 would have been her mother or step-mother, illustrating how the long standing traditions of Celtic Scotland co-existed in the same families with the tastes of an internationally connected court circle.

NOTES: [1] National Museum of Antiquities of Scotland manuscript register. [2] Graham Callander 1926, analyses the patterns in detail and illustrates all six surfaces of the casket. [3] Longhurst 1929, 53, pls XLVI-XLVII; Dalton 1909, no 368, 125-7, pls LXXXIV-LXXXVI; Paris 1981, nos 127-8, 172-5; Gibson 1994, nos 41, 42, 96-9. [4] Steer and Bannerman 1977, 175-7, fig 23, pls 4B, 4C, 6B, 18B, 18D, 23B, 23C. [5] Ibid, 85. [6] Ibid, no 78, 146, pl 23C, no 84, 151, pl 4B, no 90, 154, pl 18D. [7] Trenholme 1909, 143. [8] Eames 1977, 108. [9] Ibid, nos 45-7, 174-7, pls 50-52. [10] London, Edinburgh, Dublin 1989, 76, no 132, 139, no 131, 164. [11] Steer and Bannerman 1977, fig 10, 49. [12] Mahr and Raftery 1976, pls 84, 85, 155-6. [13] Steer and Bannerman 1977, fig 13, 56. [14] Fraser 1859, vol I, 22. [15] Ibid, 28-34. [16] See L2 for the 18th-century links between the Montgomeries and Skye.

L10

D18, 59-60

FIFE CASKET

[Q.L 1949.2]

Scotland, c1500
Whalebone, copper alloy; carved, engraved, cast
L 145, D 108, L 223

CONDITION

One metal strap missing below the lock, one endpiece to the lid a plain replacement, studs missing from just above the base on one end and three of the back straps, one corner piece is lost, two are broken; part of the whalebone is broken away at the back of the lid and there is a crack across one corner of the back.

PROVENANCE

Exhibited to the Society of Antiquaries of Scotland in 1886, when it belonged to Miss Drysdale, Kilrie House, near Kirkcaldy;[1] deposited in the museum, March 1949, by G S Tullis, Strathenry, Leslie, Fife.[2]

✠ ✠ ✠ ✠ ✠ ✠ ✠ ✠ ✠ ✠ ✠ ✠ ✠ ✠ ✠ ✠

The rectangular casket with its hinged slightly convex lid is made from six panels of whalebone, held together by metal straps. The bone panels are connected by a system of dovetails at the corners and on the edges of the base.

L10

The four metal right-angled corner pieces (one missing, two broken) have on each plane a vertical band between two engraved lines and a simplified egg and dart edging with three engraved lines marking each 'dart' and a round hole piercing each 'egg'. A similar decoration is used for the flat endpiece applied to the lid (one is an undecorated replacement), but the 'darts' have cross-hatching engraved within an outline.

The casket is also bound with metal straps which are oval in section, widening to flat discs through which they are studded to the bone panels. Four run from back to front of the lid, each with four studs and shield-shaped terminals, four forming the upper part of the hinges at the back and two attached to the hasps of the lock at the front. These terminals are roughly engraved with double lines down each side and in the centre.

Eight similar straps with only three studs run vertically up the casket, four on the back below the hinges, one in the centre of each end and one either side of the lock on the front. Two further vertical straps with only one stud run from the lock to the base. Two short straps of the same type with a stud at each end are applied horizontally to hold the corner pieces.

The lock, with a projecting rounded loop for the hasp and a large keyhole, is encased in a rectangular metal raised plate with a curving shaped edge. Two elongated oval hinged hasps descend direct from the straps on the lid to fit over the lock. They are roughly engraved with double outlines.

All the whalebone panels are carved in low relief with patterns of interlace and knotwork, emphasised by finely cut outlines. On the top there are five rectangular designs; three of knotwork based on three circles in each case with squared ends; alternating with two of angular strapwork in a regular woven pattern.

On the front there is an asymmetrical strapwork rectangle to the left of the lock with four small flowerlets in the centre; to the right two octagonal strapwork motifs one above the other, with Greek crosses in the centres. Around the lock is right-angled woven criss-cross to the left, rather random curvilinear strapwork to the right and a horizontal saltire motif below.

The back has three angular strapwork designs similar to those on the top and two loosely interlaced designs each based on eight circular

L10

motifs against a cross-hatched ground. One end has two panels of curving pointed knotwork; the other fluid curving plaited interlace on a ground of round bosses.[3] The underneath of the casket has two later wide shallow strips of wood running from front to back and covered with dark green woollen textile. Originally four flat strips of metal joined the vertical straps on the front and back panels.

The interior of the casket is stained red, but otherwise unadorned.

✢ ✢ ✢ ✢ ✢ ✢ ✢ ✢ ✢ ✢ ✢ ✢ ✢ ✢

In 1843 John Drysdale, Esq., was the land owner for Kilrie and North Piteadie in Fife.[4] It is not known if the family had any west Highland connections.

For comments on the style and dating of the Fife casket, see L9.[5]

NOTES: [1] Anderson 1886, 390. [2] NMS ms records in the department of History and Applied Art. [3] Anderson 1886, analyses and illustrates all the carved surfaces. [4] Jardine 1843, 808. [5] Graham Callander 1926, 110-12, makes a detailed comparison of the two objects.

L11   E22, 75-76
COVER OF THE BUTE MAZER
[QL.1979.11]

Scotland, early 16th century
Silver, gilt, whalebone; cast, saw pierced, carved
DIAM 241, D 5

CONDITION
Very good, small chip to the rim, two fine cracks following the natural grain of the bone.

PROVENANCE
See C2, page 34.

✢ ✢ ✢ ✢ ✢ ✢ ✢ ✢ ✢ ✢ ✢ ✢ ✢ ✢

The thin circular disc has a central metalwork knop consisting of a cinquefoil with a stud through each petal and a central sphere. This is riveted through the bone to a second cinquefoil on the underside.

The upper surface is covered with intricate carving. Five spokes radiate from the petals of the cinquefoil knop crossing two concentric pentagons in the centre of each side. The spokes and the outer pentagon, whose angles reach the rim of the circle, are emphasised by pronounced continuous beading. The inner pentagon is marked only by a band with a central line which meanders off at the angles into entwined leafy foliage. At each intersection of spoke and pentagon there is a large prominent round flowerhead resembling a stylised marguerite. The foliage mostly consists of deeply cut kite-shaped leaves sprouting four, or occasionally three, to a stem. The stems form five overlapping semicircles outside the smaller pentagon and centred on its sides, the overlap giving three plaited loops in each case. The leaves in the five central diamond shapes are elongated and those in the smaller sections near the rim are reduced in size and complexity.

The underside is plain, apart from the cinquefoil fixing for the knop. There are traces of small pins near the rim, suggesting that the cover originally had a small band of silver covering its outer edge.

✢ ✢ ✢ ✢ ✢ ✢ ✢ ✢ ✢ ✢ ✢ ✢ ✢ ✢

It is known that around 1500 Ninian Bannatyne, probably the man whose name appears on the rim of the Bute Mazer, employed a silversmith in Glasgow.[1] It is likely that the bone cover was made at the same time. Certainly it was carefully designed to echo the cinquefoils of the 14th-century enamelled heraldry and engraved on the print.[2]

The complicated geometrical layout is reminiscent of late English Perpendicular architecture, particularly vault patterns, but virtually nothing of this kind survives in Scotland. However, there may well have been tombs and chantries in Glasgow Cathedral itself which would have inspired such decoration. No comparable ivories are known, but the wood carvers' skill at designing and carving intricate architectural motifs on a miniature scale can be seen on the Beaton panels of the 1520s or 1530s.[3]

Even closer is some of the decoration on a wooden casket. Thought to have belonged to Margaret Tudor, queen of James IV, it also has plaited ornament not unlike the Eglinton and Fife caskets, alongside fleurs-de-lis, hearts, pansies and Tudor lettering.[4] These pieces show Scotland, like much of Europe in the early 16th century carrying Gothic motifs to their most extreme form, before embarking on the Renaissance style which was shortly to flower at Stirling Castle.

NOTES: [1] I am indebted to Henry Steuart Fothringham for this unpublished information. [2] Glenn 1998, pls XXVIII B and XXIX. [3] Caldwell 1994, pls XXVII C and D. [4] Edinburgh 1982, no E21, 72-5.

BIBLIOGRAPHY

ACHEN, Henrik von 1996, *Norwegian Medieval Altar Frontals in Bergen Museum*, Bergen.

ALEXANDER, Jonathan J G 1992, *Medieval Illuminators and their Methods of Work*, New Haven/London.

ANDERSEN, Håkon A 1997, *Kunsthåndverket i middelalderen fra Trondheims skattkammer*, Trondheim.

ANDERSON, Alan Orr and Marjorie 1990, *Early Sources of Scottish History AD 500 to 1286*, Stamford.

ANDERSON, Alan Orr and Marjorie 1991, *Scottish Annals from English Chroniclers AD 500 to 1286*, Stamford.

ANDERSON, Joseph 1878, 'Notices of a Mortar and Lion-Figure of Brass dug up in Bell Street, Glasgow and of six Lion-Shaped Ewers of Brass (the Manilia of the Middle Ages), exhibited to the Meeting', *PSAS*, vol XIII, 48-66.

ANDERSON, Joseph 1881, *Scotland in Early Christian Times*, Edinburgh.

ANDERSON, Joseph 1886, 'Notice of a Casket of Cetacean Bone, carved with Interlaced Patterns in Panels, exhibited by Miss Drysdale, Kilrie House, Kirkcaldy', *PSAS*, vol XX, 390-96.

ANDERSON, Joseph 1889, 'Notice of the Quigrich or crosier, and other relics of St Fillan, in the possession of their hereditary keepers or Dewars in Glendochart in 1549-50', *PSAS*, vol XXIII, 110-18.

ANDERSON, Joseph 1910, 'The Architecturally shaped Shrines and other Reliquaries of the early Celtic Church in Scotland and Ireland', *PSAS*, vol XLIV, 259-81.

ANDERSSON, Britt-Marie 1976, 'Les trésors d'émaux limousins en Suède médiévale', *Bulletin de la Société Archéologique et Historique du Limousin*, tome CIII, 107-36.

ANDERSSON, Britt-Marie 1980, 'Emaux Limousins en Suède – les châsses, les croix', *Antikvariskt arkiv, 69*, Stockholm.

ARBROATH LIBER 1848, *Liber de S. Thome de Aberbrothoc*, [*Bannatyne Club*], Edinburgh.

ARNE, T J 1914, *La Suède et l'Orient*, Uppsala.

ASH, Marinell 1981, '"A fine, genial, hearty band": David Laing, Daniel Wilson and Scottish Archaeology', in Bell, A S (ed), *The Scottish Antiquarian Tradition*, 86-113, Edinburgh.

ASH, Marinell 1999, in Hulse, Elizabeth (ed), *Thinking with Both Hands – Sir Daniel Wilson in the Old World and the New*, Toronto.

AUGUSTSSON, Jan-Erik, BLENNOW, Anna-Maria, BONSDORFF, Jan von, ESTHAM, Inger, KARLSSON, Lennart, LINDGREN, Mereth, NOCKERT, Margareta, PILTZ, Anders, SVANBERG, Jan, TEGNÉR, Göran, TÅNGEBERG, Peter, and ULLÉN, Marian 1996, *Den Gotiska Konsten*, [*Signums svenska konsthistoria*], Lund.

AVRIL, François 1978, *Manuscript Painting at the Court of France – The Fourteenth Century (1310-1380)*, London.

BACKHOUSE, Janet 1985, *Books of Hours*, London.

BAIN, Joseph 1881-88, *Calendar of Documents relating to Scotland*, [CDS], Edinburgh.

BARROW, Geoffrey W S 1960, *The Acts of Malcolm IV 1153-1165*, [*Regesta Regum Scottorum I*], Edinburgh.

BARROW, Geoffrey W S 1971, *The Acts of William I King of Scots 1165-1214*, [*Regesta Regum Scottorum II*], Edinburgh.

BARROW, Geoffrey W S 1973, *The Kingdom of the Scots*, London.

BARROW, Geoffrey W S (ed) 1974, *The Scottish Tradition: Essays in honour of Ronald Gordon Cant*, Edinburgh.

BARROW, Geoffrey W S 1988, *Robert Bruce and the Community of the Realm of Scotland* (3rd edition), Edinburgh.

BARROW, Geoffrey W S 1992, *Scotland and its Neighbours in the Middle Ages*, London.

BARROW, Geoffrey W S 1998, 'The Social Background of the Bute Mazer', in Fawcett, Richard (ed), *Medieval Art and Architecture in the Diocese of Glasgow*, [*The British Archaeological Association Conference Transactions XXIII*], 122-32.

BARROW, Geoffrey W S 1999, *The Charters of David I*, Woodbridge.

BARTLETT, Robert (ed and trans) 2003, *The Miracles of St Æbbe of Coldingham and St Margaret of Scotland*, Oxford.

BECKWITH, John 1972, *Ivory Carvings in Early Medieval England*, London.

BEDOS, Brigitte 1980, *Corpus des sceaux français du Moyen Age. Tome I:Les sceaux des villes*, Paris.

BEDOS-REZAK, Brigitte 1993, *Form and Order in Medieval France*, Aldershot.

BELL, A S (ed) 1981, *The Scottish Antiquarian Tradition*, Edinburgh.

BERESFORD, G 1987, 'Goltho: the development of an early medieval manor c850-1150', *English Heritage Archaeological Reports*, no 4.

BERGEN 1978, *Handbook to the cultural history of the Middle Ages, supplementary to the displays and exhibits in Bryggens Museum*, Bergen.

BERGENDAHL HOHLER, Erla 1999, *Norwegian Stave Church Sculpture*, 2 vols, Oslo.

BIRCH, Walter de Gray 1895, *Catalogue of Seals in the Department of Manuscripts in the British Museum – Seals of Scotland and Ireland*, vol IV, London.

BIRCH, Walter de Gray 1907, *History of Scottish Seals – Ecclesiastical and Monastic Seals of Scotland*, vol II, Stirling.

BLAIR, Claude 1958, *European Armour circa 1066 to circa 1700*, London.

BLAIR, Claude (ed) 1998, *The Crown Jewels*, 2 vols.

BLAIR, John and RAMSEY, Nigel (eds) 1991, *English Medieval Industries*, London

BLINDHEIM, Martin 1965, *Norwegian Romanesque Decorative Sculpture 1190-1210*, London.

BLINDHEIM, Martin 1988, 'St Magnus in Scandinavian Art', in Crawford, Barbara (ed), *St Magnus Cathedral and Orkney's Twelfth Century Renaissance*, Aberdeen, 165-182.

BLOCH, Peter 1992, *Romanische Bronzekruzifixe*, [*Bronzegeräte des Mittelalters*, 5], Berlin.

BOARDMAN, Stephen 1996, *The Early Stewart Kings – Robert II and Robert III 1371-1406*, East Linton.

BOCCIA, L G 1991, *L'Armeria del Museo Civico Medievale de Bologna*, Busto Arsizio.

BORENIUS, Tancred 1929, 'The Iconography of St Thomas of Canterbury', *Archaeologia*, vol LXXIX, 29-54.

BOURKE, Cormac 1980, 'Early Irish hand-bells', *Journal of the Royal Society of Antiquaries of Ireland*, vol CX, 52-66.

BOURKE, Cormac 1983, 'The hand-bells of the early Scottish church', *PSAS*, vol CXIII, 464-8.

BOURKE, Cormac (ed) 1997, *Studies in the Cult of Saint Columba*, Dublin.

BRANNER, Robert 1977, *Manuscript Painting in the Reign of Saint Louis*, Berkeley/London.

BREVIARIUM ABERDONENSE 1854, [*Bannatyne Club*], London, 2 vols.

BRITISH MUSEUM 1925, *Catalogue of Additions to the Manuscripts in the British Museum in the years 1911-1915*, London.

BROOKE, Daphne 1994, *Wild Men and Holy Places – St Ninian, Whithorn and the Medieval Realm of Galloway*, Edinburgh.

BROWN, Iain Gordon 1989, '"This Old Magazine of Antiquities" – The Advocates' Library as National Museum', in Cadell, Patrick and Matheson, Ann (eds), *For the Encouragement of Learning – Scotland's National Library 1689-1989*, 149-85, Edinburgh.

BRUNA, Denis 1996, *Enseignes de Pèlerinages et Enseignes Profanes*, Paris.

BRYDALL, R 1895, 'The monumental effigies of Scotland', *PSAS*, vol XXIX, 329-410.

BUCHON, J A C (ed) 1840, *Jean Froissart – Les Chroniques*, 3 vols, Paris.

BURGESS, C and CHURCH, M 1995, 'Uig Landscape Survey: Uig Sands to Aird Uig, Isle of Lewis, Uig Parish', *University of Edinburgh, Department of Archaeology, Annual Report*, 41, 35-6.

BURNS, James H 1962, *Scottish Churchmen and the Council of Basle*, Glasgow.

CADELL, Patrick and MATHESON, Ann (eds) 1989, *For the Encouragement of Learning*, Edinburgh.

CADELL, Patrick, 'Charles Kirkpatrick Sharpe', *DNB*, forthcoming.

CALDWELL, David H 1976, 'A medieval crescent-shaped dagger-pommel from Fortingall, Perthshire', *PSAS*, vol CVII, 322-3.

CALDWELL, David H 1978, 'An enamelled plaque from Borve, Benbecula', *PSAS*, vol CIX, 378-80.

CALDWELL, David H 1981, 'Metalwork', in Good, George L and Tabraham, Christopher J, 'Excavations at Threave Castle, Galloway, 1974-78', *Medieval Archaeology*, XXV, 106-16.

CALDWELL, David H 1991, 'Tantallon Castle, East Lothian: a catalogue of the finds', *PSAS*, vol CXXI, 335-57.

CALDWELL, David H 1994, 'The Beaton Panels – Scottish Carvings of the 1520s or 1530s', in Higgitt, John (ed), *Medieval Art and Architecture in the Diocese of St Andrews*, [The British Archaeological Association Conference Transactions, XIV], 174-84.

CALDWELL, David H 1995, in Lewis and Ewart 1995, 82-3, 84-93.

CALDWELL, David H and LEWIS, John 1996, 'Linlithgow Palace: an excavation in the west range and a note on finds from the palace', *PSAS*, vol CXXVI (2), 823-69.

CAMPBELL, M and SANDEMAN, M L S 1962, 'Mid Argyll: an Archaeological Survey', *PSAS*, vol XCV, 1-125.

CAMPBELL, Marian 1979, '"Scribe faber lima": a crozier in Florence reconsidered', *The Burlington Magazine*, vol CXXI, 364-70.

CAMPBELL, Marian 1991, 'Gold, Silver and Precious Stones', in Blair, John and Ramsay, Nigel (eds), *English Medieval Industries*, London, 107-66.

CANT, Ronald G 1972, 'The church in Orkney and Shetland and its relations with Norway and Scotland in the middle ages', *Northern Scotland*, vol I, 1-18.

CARFRAE, Robert 1890, 'Donations to the Museum', *PSAS*, vol XXIV, 411-12.

CDS *Calendar of Documents relating to Scotland preserved in H.M. Public Record Office*, Bain, J (ed) 1881-83, 4 vols, Edinburgh.

CHERRY, John 1981, 'Medieval Rings', in Ward, Anne, Cherry, John, Gere, Charlotte and Cartlidge, Barbara, *The Ring from Antiquity to the Twentieth Century*, 53-86, London.

CHERRY, John 1989, 'Seal Matrix', in Stones, J A (ed), *Three Scottish Carmelite Friaries – Excavations at Aberdeen, Linlithgow and Perth 1980-1986*, 154.

CLANCHY, M T 1993, *From Memory to Written Record*, Oxford.

CLANCY, Thomas O 1998, *The Triumph Tree – Scotland's Earliest Poetry*, Edinburgh.

CLARKE, David 2003. The foremost figure in all matters relating to Scottish archaeology: aspects of the work of Joseph Anderson, *PSAS*, vol CXXXII, forthcoming.

COCHRAN, Patrick, R W 1872, 'Notice of some Antiquities recently discovered in North Ayrshire', *PSAS*, vol IX, 385-7.

COCKERELL, Sydney C and PLUMMER, John c 1970, *Old Testament Miniatures*, London.

CONSTABLE, Thomas and Archibald 1890, *The Kennet Ciborium*, Edinburgh.

COWAN, Ian B and EASSON, D E 1976, *Medieval Religious Houses: Scotland*, London.

CRAWFORD Barbara E (ed) 1988, *St Magnus Catherdral and Orkney's Twelfth-Century Renaissance*, Aberdeen.

CROSS, Morag 1994, *Bibliography of Monuments in the Care of the Secretary of State for Scotland*, Glasgow.

CURLE, Alexander O 1924, 'A note on four silver spoons and a fillet of gold found in the Nunnery at Iona: and on a finger-ring, part of a fillet and a fragment of wire, all of gold, found in St Ronan's Chapel, the Nunnery, Iona', *PSAS*, vol LVIII, 102-111.

CURSITER, Stanley 1949, *Scottish Art to the close of the Nineteenth Century*, London.

DALRYMPLE, Hew 1894, 'The Seal of the Priory of Whithorn', *Archaeological and Historical Collections relating to Ayrshire and Galloway*, vol VII.

DALTON, O M 1909, *Catalogue of the Ivory Carvings of the Christian Era in the British Museum*, London.

DEAN, B 1926, 'Early Gothic Spurs', *Bulletin of the Metropolitan Museum of Art New York*, vol XXI, 129-30.

DEEVY, Mary B 1998, *Medieval Ring Brooches in Ireland*, Bray.

DILLEY, James W 1948, 'German Merchants in Scotland 1297-1327', *Scottish Historical Review*, vol XXVII, 142-55.

DILWORTH, Mark 1994, *Whithorn Priory in the Late Middle Ages*, Whithorn.

DNB *Dictionary of National Biography,* Stephen, Leslie (ed), London, 1885-1900, 63 vols.

DONALDSON, Gordon 1950, 'The Bishops and Priors of Whithorn', *Transactions of the Dumfriesshire and Galloway Natural History and Antiquarian Society*, 3 Ser, vol XXVII, 127-54.

DONALDSON, Gordon and MORPETH, Robert 1988, *A Dictionary of Scottish History*, Edinburgh.

DOWDEN, John 1899, 'The Inventory of Ornaments, Jewels, Relicks, Vestments, Service-Books, etc., belonging to the Cathedral Church of Glasgow in 1432, illustrated from various sources and more particularly from the Inventories of the Cathedral of Aberdeen', *PSAS*, vol XXXIII, 280-329.

DOWDEN, John 1912, *Bishops of Scotland*, Glasgow.

DOYLE, A 1957, 'A Scottish Augustinian Psalter', *Innes Review*, vol VIII, no 2.

DRYSDALE, William 1857, 'Notice of an Ancient Gold Seal, in the possession of J. W. Williamson, Esq. Kinross', *Archaeologia Scotica*, vol IV, 420-21.

DUFFY, Seán 1992, 'Irishmen and Islesmen in the Kingdoms of Dublin and Man, 1052-1171', *Ériu*, vol XLIII.

DUFFY, Seán 1997, *Ireland in the Middle Ages*, London.

DUNCAN, A A M 1988, *Acts of Robert I 1306-1329*, [*Regesta Regum Scottorum V*], Edinburgh.

DUNCAN, A A M 1992, *Scotland – The Making of the Kingdom*, Edinburgh.

DUNCAN, A A M and BROWN, A L 1956, 'Argyll and the Isles in the earlier Middle Ages', *PSAS*, vol XC, 192-220.

DUNS, Prof 1883, 'On a silver brooch from Mull', *PSAS*, vol XVII 76-8.

EAMES, Penelope 1977, *Medieval Furniture*, London.

EASSON, David E 1947, *Charters of the Abbey of Coupar Angus*, 2 vols, Edinburgh.

EELES, Francis 1926, 'The Guthrie Bell and its Shrine', *PSAS*, vol LX, 409-20.

EGAN, Geoff and PRITCHARD, Frances 1991, *Medieval Finds from Excavations in London: 3 – Dress Accessories c1150-c1450*, [Museum of London], London.

EGGEN, Erik 1968, *The Sequences of the Archbishopric of Nidaros*, Copenhagen, Munksgaard.

ELLIS, Blanche 1995, in Clark, John, *The Medieval Horse and its Equipment,* [Museum of London], London, 128.

EVANS, Joan 1953, *A History of Jewellery 1100-1870*, London.

EWAN, Elizabeth 1990, *Townlife in Fourteenth-Century Scotland*, Edinburgh.

FAIRHOLT, Frederick William and WRIGHT, Thomas 1857, *Miscellanea Graphica – Representations of Ancient, Medieval and Renaissance Remains in the possession of Lord Londesborough*, London.

FALKE, Otto von and MEYER, Erich 1935, *Romanische Leuchter und Gefässe der Gotik*, [*Bronzegeräte des Mittelalters*, 1], Berlin.

FARMER, David Hugh 1992, *The Oxford Dictionary of Saints*, Oxford.

FARRER, William 1923-25, *Honors and Knights' Fees*, vols I-III, Manchester and London.

FAWCETT, Richard 1990, 'Ecclesiastical Architecture in the Second Half of the Thirteenth Century', in Reid, Norman H (ed), *Scotland in the Reign of Alexander III 1249-1286*, 148-80.

FAWCETT, Richard 1995, 'The architectural development of the abbey church', in Lewis and Ewart 1995, 159-74.

FAWCETT, Richard 2001, *Elgin Cathedral*, (Historic Scotland), Edinburgh.

FERGUSON, William 1994, *Scotland's Relations with England*, Edinburgh.

FINLAY, Ian 1991, *Scottish Gold and Silverwork*, revised and edited by Henry Fothringham, Stevenage.

FISKE, Willard 1905, *Chess in Iceland and in Icelandic Literature*, Florence.

FLEMING, David Hay 1899, 'Articles Exhibited to the Society', *PSAS*, vol XXXIII, 76-8, fig 6.

FLETCHER, William Younger 1902, *English Book Collectors*, London.

FOOTE, Peter 1988, 'Observations on *Orkneyinga Saga*', in Crawford 1988, 192-207.

FRANCOVICH, G de 1938, 'L'Origine e la Diffusione di Crocofisso Gotico Doloroso', *Kunstgeschichtliche Jahrbuch der Biblioteca Hertziana*, 145-261.

FRASER, William 1859, *Memorials of the Montgomeries, earls of Eglinton*, Edinburgh.

FRASER, William 1868, *The Red Book of Grandtully*, 2 vols, Edinburgh.

GABORIT-CHOPIN, Danielle 1978, *Ivoires du Moyen Age*, Fribourg.

GABORIT-CHOPIN, Danielle 1992, 'Walrus ivory in Western Europe', in Roesdahl, Else and Wilson, David M (eds), *From Viking to Crusader*, Paris, Berlin, Copenhagen, 204-205.

GAMER, Helena M 1954, 'The earliest evidence of chess in western literature: the Eidsiedeln verses', *Speculum*, vol XXIX, 734-50.

GAMMACK, James 1887, 'Notice of a bronze censer found under the floor of the old church of Garvock, Kincardineshire', *PSAS*, vol XXI, 180-2.

GAUTHIER, Marie-Madeleine 1972, *Émaux du moyen âge occidental*, Fribourg.

GIBSON, Margaret 1994, *The Liverpool Ivories*, London.

GILLIES, William A 1938, *In Famed Breadalbane*, Perth.

GILRUTH, J D 1937, 'The Abbey of Aberbrothock: Two early Thirteenth-century Seals', *PSAS*, vol LXXII, 56-67.

GIMSON, G S 1995, 'Lion hunt: a royal tomb-effigy at Arbroath Abbey', *PSAS*, vol CXXV, 901-16.

GLENN, Virginia 1998, 'Court patronage in Scotland 1240-1340', in Fawcett, Richard (ed) *Medieval Art and Architecture in the Diocese of Glasgow*, [*The British Archaeological Association Conference Transactions XXIII*], 111-21.

GLENN, Virginia 1999, 'Thirteenth-century seals – Tayside Fife and the wider world', *Tayside and Fife Archaeological Journal*, vol 5, 146-162.

GLENN, Virginia 2001, 'Survival and Revival of the Insular style in later medieval Scottish Art', in Rednap, Mark (ed), *Pattern and Purpose in Insular Art*, [*Proceedings of the 4th International Conference on Insular Art*], Cardiff, 275-84, pl XXII.

GLENN, Virginia 2003, 'The late 13th century chapter seals of Dunkeld and Oslo cathedrals', *PSAS*, vol CXXXII, forthcoming.

GOLDSCHMIDT, Adolph 1918, *Die Elfenbeinskulpturen aus der Romanischen Zeit. XI-XIII Jahrhundert*, vol III, Berlin (reprint Berlin 1975).

GOLDSCHMIDT, Adolph 1926, *Die Elfenbeinskulpturen aus der Romanischen Zeit. XI-XIII Jahrhundert*, vol IV, Berlin (reprint Berlin 1975).

GORDON, James Frederick Skinner 1868, *Monasticon – an account (based on Spottiswoode's) of the Abbeys, Priories, Collegiate Churches and Hospitals in Scotland, at the Reformation*, Glasgow.

GORET, Jean-François and POPLIN, François 1998, 'Autour d'un fou d'échecs en ivoire trouvé à Château-Thierry (Aisne): matières dures d'origine animale et pièces de jeu médiévaux', in *A quoi joue-t-on ?*, papers of the Festival d'Histoire de Montbrison, 497-508, pls XXIX-XXXII.

GRAHAM, B J 1975, 'Anglo-Norman Settlement in County Meath', *Proceedings of the Royal Irish Academy*, vol 75C, 223-48.

GRAHAM, B J and PROUDFOOT, L J (eds) 1993, *An Historical Geography of Ireland*, London.

GRAHAM CALLANDER, J 1924, 'Fourteenth-century Brooches and other ornaments in the National Museum of Antiquities of Scotland', *PSAS*, vol LVIII, 160-84.

GRAHAM CALLANDER, J 1926, 'Notes on (1) casket of cetacean bone, and (2) a Highland brooch of silver', *PSAS*, LX, 105-22.

GRANCSAY, S V 1955, *Equestrian Equipment*, loan exhibition catalogue, J B Speed Art Museum, Kentucky.

GRANT, Alexander 1884, *The Story of the University of Edinburgh*, London, 2 vols.

GRANT, Alexander 1984, *Independence and Nationhood – Scotland 1306-1469*, Edinburgh.

GRAY, H St George 1930, 'A Medieval Spoon found at Taunton Castle', *The Antiquaries Journal*, X, 156-8.

GRIMME, Ernst Günther 1972, *Der Aachener Domschatz*, [*Aachener Kunstblätter*, Band 42], Düsseldorf.

GRINDER-HANSEN, Keld and POSSELT, Gert (eds) 1992, *Danmarks middelalderlige skattefund c 1050-c 1550*, [*Nordiske Fortisminder, Serie B, Bind 12,1 and 12,2*], Copenhagen.

GUTHRIE, John 1855, 'The Guthrie Bell', *PSAS*, vol I, 54-7.

HARBISON, Peter 1992, *Guide to National and Historic Monuments of Ireland*, Dublin.

HARTHAN, John 1977, *Books of Hours*, London.

HARVEY, Paul D A and McGUINNESS, Andrew 1996, *A Guide to British Medieval Seals*, London.

HENDERSON, George 1983, 'The seal of Brechin cathedral', in O'Connor, Anne and Clarke, D V (eds), *From the Stone Age to the 'Forty-Five'*, Edinburgh, 385-415.

HESLOP, T Alexander 1980, 'The Lewis Chessmen', *Journal of the British Archaeological Association*, vol CXXXIII, 108-109 (review of Taylor 1978).

HESLOP, T Alexander 1986, 'Seals as Evidence for metalworking in England in the later twelfth century', in Macready, Sarah and Thompson, F H (eds), *Art and Patronage in the English Romanesque*, London, 50-60.

HIGGITT, John 1987, 'The Jedburgh Comb', in Stratford, Neil (ed), *Romanesque and Gothic – Essays for George Zarnecki*, Woodbridge, 119-28.

HIGGITT, John 1995, 'The comb, pendant and buckle', in Lewis, John H and Ewart, Gordon J 1995, *Jedburgh Abbey – the archaeology and architecture of a border abbey*, Edinburgh, [*Society of Antiquaries of Scotland Monograph Series*, 10], 83-4.

HIGGITT, John 2000, *The Murthly Hours – Devotion, Literacy and Luxury in Paris, England and the Gaelic West*, London.

HILL, Peter 1997, *Whithorn and St Ninian – The Excavation of a Monastic Town 1984-91*, Stroud.

HOHLER, Christopher 1957, 'The Badge of St James', in Cox, Ian (ed), *The Scallop*, London, 49-70.

HOPE, W H St John 1887, 'The Seals of English Bishops', *Proceedings of the Society of Antiquaries of London*, 2nd series, vol XI, 271-306.

HOPE, W H St John 1895, 'Municipal Seals of England and Wales', *Proceedings of the Society of Antiquaries of London*, 2nd series, vol XV, 434-55.

HORGEN, Randi (ed) 2000, *Middelaldersalen i Historisk Museum*, Oslo.

HORSTMANN, C 1881, *Altenglische Legenden, Neue Folge*, Heilbronn.

HOW, George Evelyn Paget 1935, 'Early Scottish Spoons', *PSAS*, vol LXIX, 138-57.

HOW, George Evelyn Paget 1952, *English and Scottish Silver Spoons – Mediaeval to Late Stuart*, London.

HUME BROWN, P 1891, *Early Travellers in Scotland* (facsimile ed), Edinburgh (reprint 1978).

HUNTER BLAIR, R 1915, 'Scottish Private Seals', *Archaeologia Aeliana*, vol XII, 287-332.

HUNTER BLAIR, R 1919, 'Scottish Ecclesiastical Seals', *Archaeologia Aeliana*, vol XVI, 156-83.

HUTCHESON, Alexander 1885, 'Notice of the discovery, near Broughty Ferry, of an antique ecclesiastical gold finger-ring', *PSAS*, vol XIX, 156-9.

HUTCHINSON, Gillian 1997, *Medieval Ships and Shipping*, Leicester.

HUTTON, George Henry *c*1795, *Sigilla*, National Archives of Scotland, ms GD.103/2/15.

HUTTON, George Henry 1800, *Seals*, National Archives of Scotland, ms GD.103/2/16.

HUYSHE, Wentworth 1913, *Devorgilla, Lady of Galloway and her Abbey of the Sweetheart*, Edinburgh.

JAMES, Henry 1855, 'Notice of the discovery of a beautiful enamelled gold ring, believed to have belonged to King James V, found in the ruins of Tantallon Castle', *PSAS*, vol I, 168-9.

JAMES, Montagu Rhodes 1926, 'The drawings of Matthew Paris', *Walpole Society*, vol XIV, 1-26.

JANSSON, Ingmar (ed) 1996, *The Viking Heritage – a Dialogue between Cultures*, Stockholm.

JARDINE, Fergus 1843, 'Parish of Kinghorn', in *The New Statistical Account of Scotland*, vol IX, 1845, 800-821.

JARDINE, Henry 1822, 'Report relative to the Tomb of King Robert Bruce, and the Church of Dunfermline', *Archaeologia Scotica*, vol II, 312-455.

JERVISE, Andrew 1861, *Memorials of Angus and the Mearns*, Edinburgh.

KARLSSON, Lennart, LINDGREN, Mereth, NOCKERT, Margareta, PILTZ, Anders, SVANBERG, Jan, TÅNGEBERG, Peter, ULLÉN, Marian 1995, *Den Romanska Konsten*, [*Signums svenska konsthistoria*], Lund.

KEITH, R 1824, *An Historical Catalogue of the Scottish Bishops to the year 1688*, Russell, M (ed), Edinburgh.

KELSO LIBER 1846, *Liber S. Marie de Calchou*, [*Bannatyne Club*], Edinburgh, 2 vols.

KINGSFORD, H S 1940, 'Some English Medieval Seal-Engravers', *Archaeological Journal*, vol XCVII, 155-77.

KLNM *Kulturhistorisk leksikon for nordisk middelalder*, vol I-XXII, 1956-78 (reprint 1980-82, København, Oslo, Stockholm).

KLUGE-PINSKER, Antje 1991, *Schach und Trictrac*, Sigmaringen.

LAING, David 1857, 'A Brief Notice of the small Figure cut in Ivory, supposed by Pennant to represent the King of Scotland in his Coronation Chair, and which was discovered in Dunstaffnage Castle', *Archaeologia Scotica*, vol IV, 366-71.

LAING, Henry 1850, *Descriptive Catalogue of Impressions from Ancient Scottish Seals*, Edinburgh.

LAING, Henry 1866, *Supplemental Descriptive Catalogue of Impressions from Ancient Scottish Seals*, Edinburgh.

LANGBERG, Harald 1979, *Gyldne Billeder fra Middelalderen*, Copenhagen.

LANGBERG, Harald 1992, *The Lundø Crucifix*, Copenhagen.

LAPERRIERE, Charles Baile de (ed) 1991, *The Royal Scottish Academy Exhibitors 1826-1990*, Hilmarton Manor.

LASKO, Peter 1972, *Ars Sacra 800-1200*, Harmondsworth.

LEWIS, John H and EWART, Gordon J 1995, *Jedburgh Abbey – the archaeology and architecture of a border abbey*, Edinburgh (Society of Antiquaries of Scotland Monograph Series Number 10).

LIDDELL, Donald M 1938, *Chessmen*, London.

LIEBGOTT, Niels-Knud 1985, *Elfenben – fra Danmarks Middelalder*, Copenhagen (Nationalmuseet).

LIGHTBOWN, Ronald 1978, *Secular Goldsmiths' Work in France*, London

LIGHTBOWN, Ronald 1992, *Medieval European Jewellery*, London.

LOCKWOOD, Glenn L 1989, *Beckwith – Irish and Scottish Identities in a Canadian Community, 1816-1988*, Ottawa.

LONGHURST, Margaret H 1927, *Catalogue of Carvings in Ivory. Part I. Up to the Thirteenth Century*, Victoria and Albert Museum, London.

LONGHURST, Margaret H 1929, *Catalogue of Carvings in Ivory. Part II*, Victoria and Albert Museum, London.

MACDONALD, George 1919, 'The Mint of Crossraguel Abbey', *PSAS*, vol LIV, 20-26.

McDONALD, R Andrew 1997, *The Kingdom of the Isles – Scotland's Western Seaboard, c.1100-c.1336*, East Linton.

MACGREGOR, Arthur 1985, *Bone, Antler, Ivory and Horn*, London.

MACKENZIE, W C 1903, *History of the Outer Hebrides*, Paisley.

McLEES, Christopher and EKROLL, Øystein 1990, 'A drawing of a medieval ivory chess piece from the 12th-century church of St Olav, Trondheim, Norway', *Medieval Archaeology*, vol XXXIV, 151-4.

MACLEOD, Alexander 1833, 'Island of Lewis. Parish of Uig', in *The New Statistical Account of Scotland – Ross and Cromarty*, vol XIV, Edinburgh, 1845, 150-6.

MACMILLAN, James E 1986, *Know Your Perth*, vol II, Perth.

McNEILL, Peter G B and MACQUEEN, Hector L (eds) 1996, *Atlas of Scottish History*, Edinburgh.

MACQUARRIE, Alan 1983, 'Notes on some charters of the Bruces of Annandale', *Transactions of the Dumfriesshire and Galloway Natural History and Antiquarian Society*, vol LVIII, 72-9.

MACQUARRIE, Alan 1997, *Scotland and the Crusades*, Edinburgh.

McROBERTS, David 1959, 'Material destruction caused by the Scottish Reformation', *Innes Review*, vol X, 126-72.

McWILLIAM, Colin 1978, *The Buildings of Scotland – Lothian except Edinburgh*, Harmondsworth.

MADDEN, Frederic 1832, 'Historical Remarks on the introduction of the game of Chess into Europe, and on the ancient Chessmen discovered in the Isle of Lewis', *Archaeologia*, vol XXIV, 203-291.

MAHR, Adolf and RAFTERY, Joseph 1976, *Christian Art in Ancient Ireland*, New York (reprint from 1932, 1941).

MÂLE, Émile 1961, *The Gothic Image* (reprint from the 1913 translation by Dora Nussey), London.

MAXWELL, Stuart 1958, 'A medieval gold ring from Shetland', *PSAS*, vol XCI, 193-4.

MAYO, Janet 1984, *A History of Ecclesiastical Dress*, London.

MELROSE LIBER 1837, *Liber S. Marie de Melros*, [*Bannatyne Club*], Edinburgh, 2 vols.

METCALFE, W M 1889, *Pinkerton's Lives of the Scottish Saints*, Paisley.

MICHEL, Francisque- 1862, *Les Écossais en France, les Français en Écosse*, London.

MICHELLI, Perette E 1986, 'Four Scottish crosiers and their relation to the Irish tradition', *PSAS*, vol CXVI, 375-92.

MIDDELDORF, Ulrich (ed) 1980, *Il tesoro della basilica di San Francesco ad Assisi*, Florence.

MIKET, Roger and ROBERTS, David L 1990, *The Mediaeval Castles of Skye and Lochalsh*, Portree.

MILLAR, Oliver (ed) 1972, 'Inventories and Valuations of the King's Goods 1649-1651', *Walpole Society*, XLIII, 1970-72, Glasgow.

MOIR BRYCE, W 1911, *The Black Friars of Edinburgh*, Edinburgh.

MOONEY, John 1935, *St Magnus, earl of Orkney*, Kirkwall.

MORGAN, Nigel J 1982, *Early Gothic Manuscripts [I] 1190-1250*, Oxford.

MORGAN, Nigel J 1988, *Early Gothic Manuscripts [II] 1250-1285*, London.

MORGAN, Nigel J 1995, 'Western Norwegian panel painting 1250-1350: problems of dating, styles and workshops', *Acta ad Archaeologiam et Artivm Historiam Pertinentia*, [*Institvtvm Romanvm Norvegiae*, XI], Rome, 9-56.

MUNRO, Jean and R W 1986, *Acts of the Lords of the Isles, 1336-1493*, [*Scottish Historical Society*], Edinburgh.

MURRAY, H J R 1913, *A History of Chess*, Oxford.

MURRAY, H J R 1941, 'The Mediæval Games of Tables', *Medium Ævum*, vol X, no 2, 57-69.

MYLN, Alexander 1823, *Vitae Dunkeldensis Ecclesiae Episcoporum*, [*Bannatyne Club*], Edinburgh.

NELSON, P 1936, 'Some British medieval seal-matrices', *Archaeological Journal*, vol XCIII, 13-44.

NILSÉN, Anna 1998, 'Kring ett Limogeskrucifix i Vårvik på Dal', *Fornvännen*, 93, Stockholm.

NMAS 1892, *Catalogue of the National Museum of Antiquities of Scotland*, Edinburgh.

OAKESHOTT, Walter 1981, *The Two Winchester Bibles*, Oxford.

O'DONOVAN, John 1847, *Leabhar na g-Ceart*, Dublin.

Ó FLOINN, Raghnall 1983, 'A Gold band found near Rathkeale, Co. Limerick', *North Munster Antiquarian Journal. Irisleabhar Seandáluíochta Tuadh-Mhumhan*, vol XXV, 3-8.

Ó FLOINN, Raghnall 1987, 'Schools of metalworking in eleventh- and twelfth-century Ireland', in Ryan, Michael (ed), *Ireland and Insular Art AD 500-1200*, Dublin, 179-87.

Ó FLOINN, Raghnall 1994, *Irish Shrines and Reliquaries of the Middle Ages*, Dublin.

OMAN, Charles 1957, *English Church Plate 597-1830*, London.

OMAN, Charles 1959, *English Domestic Silver* (4th edition), London.

OMAN, Charles 1967, 'The Whithorn crozier, a newly discovered English enamel', *Burlington Magazine*, vol CIX, 299-300.

OMAN, Charles 1974, *British Rings 800-1914*, London.

PÁLSSON, H and EDWARDS, P 1978, *Orkneyinga Saga – The History of the Earls of Orkney*, London.

PASTOUREAU, Michel 1995, 'Le roi aux fleur de lis', *L'Histoire*, no 184, 66-70.

PEDDIE, John M Dick 1883, 'Notice of a Crucifix of Bronze found in the Churchyard of Ceres, Fife', *PSAS*, vol XVII, 146-51.

PEDRICK, Gale 1904, *Borough Seals of the Gothic Period*, London.

PINKERTON, John Macpherson (ed) 1976, *Minute Book of the Faculty of Advocates 1661-1712*, Edinburgh.

POLLEXFEN, John H 1864, 'Notice of the coins of David I of Scotland, Henry I and Stephen of England, found with gold ornaments, &c, at Plan, in the Island of Bute, in June 1863', *PSAS*, vol V, 372-84.

PSAS *Proceedings of the Society of Antiquaries of Scotland*.

RAINE, J (ed) 1835, *Reginaldi Monachi Dunelmensis Libellus de Admirandis Beati Cuthberti*, [*Publications of the Surtees Society*], London.

RCAHMS Scot 1928, *Inventory of Monuments and Constructions in the Outer Hebrides, Skye and the Small Isles*, Edinburgh.

RCAHMS 1951, *An Inventory of the Ancient and Historical Monuments of the City of Edinburgh*, Edinburgh.

RCAHMS 1982, 'Iona', *The Royal Commission on the Ancient and Historical Monuments of Scotland, Argyll – an Inventory of the Monuments*, vol 4, Edinburgh.

RCAHMS 1996, *Tolbooths and Town-Houses – Civic Architecture in Scotland to 1833*, Edinburgh.

RICCI, Seymour de 1930, *English Collectors of Books and Manuscripts 1530-1930*, Cambridge.

RICKERT, Margaret 1965, *Painting in Britain – The Middle Ages* (2nd edition) Harmondsworth.

RIGOLD, S E 1977, 'Two common species of medieval seal-matrix', *The Antiquaries Journal*, vol LVII, 324-9.

ROESDAHL, Else and WILSON, David (eds) 1992, *From Viking to Crusader*, Copenhagen and New York.

ROGERS, Charles 1879, *Rental Book of the Cistercian Abbey of Coupar Angus*, [*Grampian Club*], 2 vols, London.

SANDLER, Lucy F 1986, *Gothic Manuscripts 1285-1385*, 2 vols, London.

SAWYER, Birgit and Peter 1993, *Medieval Scandinavia*, Minneapolis and London.

SCONE LIBER 1843, *Liber Ecclesie de Scon*, [*Bannatyne and Maitland Clubs*].

SCOTT, W H 1853, 'Unpublished Counter-Seal of Kilwinning', *PSAS*, vol I, 70-71.

SHARPE, Richard 1995, *Adomnan of Iona – Life of St Columba*, Harmondsworth.

SIMMS, R S 1932, 'Medieval Spoon from Pevensey Castle', *Antiquaries Journal*, vol XII.

SIMPSON, Grant G (ed) 1996, *Scotland and the Low Countries 1124-1994*, [*The Mackie Monographs*, III], East Linton.

SIMPSON, W Douglas 1965, *Bishop's Palace and Earl's Palace, Kirkwall Orkney. Official Guide*, Edinburgh (HMSO).

SKAARE, Kolbjørn 1976, *Coins and Coinage in Viking-Age Norway*, Oslo.

SMELLIE, William 1782, *Account of the Institution and Progress of the Society of the Antiquaries of Scotland*, Edinburgh.

SMITH, David J 1991, 'Conventual Seal of the Dominican Friary at Edinburgh', *PSAS*, vol CXXI, 331-3.

SMITH, John Alexander 1862, 'Notice of Bronze relics &c found in the Isle of Skye', *PSAS*, vol III, 101-6.

STALLEY, Roger 1977, 'Irish Art in the Romanesque and Gothic Periods', in *Treasures of Early Irish Art 1500 BC to 1500 AD* Dublin, 187-220.

STARKIE GARDNER, J 1902, in *Old Silverwork from the XVth to the XVIIIth Centuries*, London, *passim*.

STEER, K A and BANNERMAN, J W M 1977, *Late Medieval Monumental Sculpture in the West Highlands*, Edinburgh.

STEVENSON, J H 1931, 'The Bannatyne or Bute Mazer and its carved bone cover', *PSAS*, vol LXV, 217-55.

STEVENSON, J H and WOOD, M 1940, *Scottish Heraldic Seals – Royal, Official, Ecclesiastical, Collegiate, Burghal, Personal*, vols I-III, Glasgow.

STEVENSON, Robert B K 1962, 'The Kames Brooch', *PSAS*, vol XCV, 308-9.

STEVENSON, Robert B K 1981, 'The Museum, its Beginnings and its Development', in Bell, A S (ed), *The Scottish Antiquarian Tradition*, 31-85, 142-211, Edinburgh.

STEWART, I J and WATKINS, M J 1984, 'An 11th century Bone Tabula Set from Gloucester', *Medieval Archaeology*, vol XXVIII, 185-90.

STONE, Lawrence 1972, *Sculpture in Britain – the Middle Ages*, Harmondsworth.

STRATFORD, Neil 1997, *The Lewis Chessmen and the enigma of the hoard*, London (British Museum).

STRUTHERS, J 1870, 'Note of a gold brooch of the 13th or 14th century, found in the Water of Ardoch, near Doune Castle', *PSAS*, vol VIII, 330-3.

STUART, John 1877, 'Historical Notices of St Fillan's Crozier and the devotion of King Robert Bruce to St Fillan', *PSAS*, vol XII, 134-82.

SWARZENSKI, Hanns 1954, *Monuments of Romanesque Art*, London.

SWARZENSKI, Hanns and NETZER, Nancy 1986, *Catalogue of Medieval Objects in the Museum of Fine Arts, Boston – Enamels and Glass*, Boston.

SZABO, Vicki Ellen 1997, 'The Use of Whales in Early Medieval Britain', in Lewis, C P (ed), *The Haskins Society Journal – Studies in Medieval History*, vol IX, Woodbridge, 137-57.

TABRAHAM, Christopher 1986, *Scottish Castles and Fortifications*, Edinburgh.

TAIT, C B and NISBET, T (auctioneers) 1851, *Catalogue of the Collection of Charles Kirkpatrick Sharpe*, Edinburgh.

TAYLOR, Michael 1978, *The Lewis Chessmen*, London (British Museum).

THOBY, Paul 1953, *Les croix Limousins de la fin du XIIe siècle au début du XIVe siècle*, Paris.

THOMPSON, J D A 1956, *Inventory of British Coin Hoards AD 600-1500*, London.

THOMSON, Thomas 1827, 'A Letter giving some Account of an Ancient Ecclesiastical Bell and Chain, discovered in the parish of Kilmichael-Glassrie, in the County of Argyll, and presented to the Society of Antiquaries of Scotland by John Macneill of Oakfield, Esq.', *Archaeologia Scotica*, vol IV, 116-8.

THORP, Nigel 1987, *The Glory of the Page – Medieval and Renaissance Illuminated Manuscripts from Glasgow University Library*, London/Glasgow.

TODD, John M 1997, *The Lanercost Cartulary*, [Surtees Society], Durham.

TRÆTTEBERG, Hallvard 1953, 'Geistlige segl i Nidaros' in Marstrander, Sverre (ed), *Katalog over den Historiske Utstilling*, 41-55, Trondheim.

TRÆTTEBERG, Hallvard 1977, *Geistlige segl i Oslo bispedømme ca. 1200-1537*, Oslo-Bergen-Tromsø.

TRAILL, William 1883, *A Genealogical Account of the Traills of Orkney*, Kirkwall.

TRENHOLME, E C 1909, *The Story of Iona*, Edinburgh.

VAUGHAN, Richard 1958, *Matthew Paris*, Cambridge.

WAGNER, Anthony Richard 1956, *Heralds and Heraldry in the Middle Ages*, Oxford.

WAGNER, Anthony Richard (ed) 1967, *Rolls of Arms: Henry III (Aspilogia; Being Materials of Heraldry II)*, Oxford.

WARDEN, Alexander J 1872, *Burgh Laws of Dundee*, London.

WATKINS, Aelred 1947 *Inventory of Church Goods, temp. Edward III*, [*Norfolk Record Society*, vol XIX], parts 1 and 2.

WATSON, William J 1926, *The History of the Celtic Place-names of Scotland*, Edinburgh (reprinted 1993).

WATT, Donald E R 1969, *Fasti Ecclesiae Scoticanae Medii Aevi ad annum 1638*, [Scottish Record Society], St Andrews (revised edition 2003).

WEITZMANN-FIEDLER, Josepha 1981, *Romanische Gravierte Bronzeschalen*, Berlin.

WESTWOOD, J O 1876, *A Descriptive Catalogue of the Fictile Ivories in the South Kensington Museum*, London.

WHEELER, R E Mortimer 1943, *Maiden Castle, Dorset*, Oxford.

WHITFIELD, Niamh 1997, 'The Waterford kite-brooch and its place in Irish metalwork', in Barry, Terry, Cleary, Rose M and Hurley, Maurice F (eds), *Late Viking Age and Medieval Waterford – Excavations 1986-1992*, Waterford, 490-517.

WHITFIELD, Niamh 1998, 'The Manufacture of Ancient Beaded Wire: Experiments and Observations', *Jewellery Studies*, vol VIII, 57-86.

WILLIAMSON, Paul 1982, *An Introduction to Medieval Ivory Carvings*, London.

WILSON, Christopher 1984, 'Medieval Buildings' in Gifford, John, McWilliam, Colin and Walker, David, *Edinburgh – the Buildings of Scotland*, Harmondsworth, *passim*.

WILSON, Daniel 1849, *Synopsis of the Museum of the Society of Antiquaries of Scotland*, Edinburgh.

WILSON, Daniel 1863, *Prehistoric Annals of Scotland*, London.

WILSON, Daniel 1877, 'Notices of the Quigrich or crozier of St Fillan and of its Hereditary Keepers', *PSAS*, vol XII, 122-31.

WILSON, Daniel 1884, 'The Kilmichael-Glassrie Bell-shrine', *PSAS*, vol XVIII, 79-93.

WORMALD, Jenny 1991, *Mary Queen of Scots – a study in failure*, London.

YOUNG, Alan 1997, *Robert the Bruce's Rivals: The Comyns, 1212-1314*, East Linton.

EXHIBITION CATALOGUES

BRUGES 1998, *Bruges and the Renaissance – Memling to Pourbus*, Memlingmuseum – Oud-Sint-Janshospitaal, Martens, Maximiliaan, P J (ed).

COLOGNE 1972, *Rhein und Maas – Kunst und Kultur 800-1400*, Kunsthalle Köln, Musées royaux d'Art et d'Histoire, Bruxelles.

COPENHAGEN 1996, *Margrete I – Regent of the North*, Nationalmuseet.

DUBLIN 1983, *Treasures of Ireland 3000BC – 1500AD*, Royal Irish Academy – National Museum of Ireland, Ryan, Michael (ed).

EDINBURGH 1982, *Angels, Nobles and Unicorns – Art and Patronage in Medieval Scotland*, National Museum of Antiquities of Scotland, Caldwell, David H (ed).

FLORENCE 1989, *Arti del Medio Evo e del Rinascimento – Omaggio ai Carrand 1889-1989*, Museo Nazionale del Bargello.

LONDON 1902, *Old Silverwork from the XVth to the XVIIIth Centuries*, Royal Academy.

LONDON 1978, *British Heraldry from its Origins to c1800*, British Museum and British Library, Marks, Richard and Payne, Ann (eds).

LONDON 1984, *English Romanesque Art 1066-1200*, Hayward Gallery, Zarnecki, George, Holt, Janet and Holland, Tristram (eds).

LONDON 1987, *Age of Chivalry – Art in Plantagenet England 1200-1400*, Royal Academy of Arts, Alexander, Johnathan and Binski, Paul (eds).

LONDON, EDINBURGH, DUBLIN 1989, *The Work of Angels*, British Museum, National Museums of Scotland, National Museum of Ireland, Youngs, Susan (ed).

MADRID, BRUSSELS, SILOS 2001, *De Limoges a Silos*, Bibloteca Nacional, Espace Cultural BBL, Monasterio de Santo Domingo de Silos.

NEW YORK 1977, *Treasures of Early Irish Art 1500 B.C. to 1500 A.D.*, Metropolitan Museum of Art, Cone, Polly (ed).

OSLO 1972, *Middelalderkunst fra Norge i Andre Land – Norwegian Art Abroad*, Universitetets Oldsaksamling, Blindheim, Martin (ed).

OTTAWA 1972, *Art and the Courts – l'art et la cour*, The National Gallery of Canada, Brieger, Peter and Verdier, Philippe (eds).

PARIS 1956, *France – Écosse*, Les Archives Nationales – Hotel de Rohan, by Mahieu, Bernard and Gand de Vernon, Noëlle.

PARIS 1968, *L'Europe Gothique XIIe XIVe siècles*, Musée du Louvre, 12th Council of Europe Exhibition.

PARIS 1981, *Les fastes du Gothique – le siècle Charles V*, Galeries Nationales du Grand Palais.

PARIS, BERLIN, COPENHAGEN 1992-1993, *From Viking to Crusader – The Scandinavians and Europe 800-1200*, Grand Palais, Paris; Altes Museum, Berlin; Danmarks Nationalmuseet, Copenhagen; Roesdahl, Else and Wilson, David (eds), 22nd Council of Europe Exhibition.

PARIS 1995, *L'Œuvre de Limoges – Emaux limousins du Moyen Age*, Musée du Louvre, Taburet-Delahaye, Elisabeth and Drake Boehm, Barbara (eds).

PARIS 1996, *Un trésor gothique – La châsse de Nivelles*, Musée National du Moyen Âge – Thermes de Cluny.

PARIS 1997, *Enseignes de pèlerinage et enseignes profanes*, Musée National du Moyen Âge – Thermes de Cluny, by Bruna, Denis.

PARIS 1998, *L'Art au temps des rois maudits – Philippe le bel et ses fils 1285-1328*, Galeries Nationales du Grand Palais.

REYKJAVÍK 1997, *Church and Art – the Medieval Church in Norway and Iceland*, Norwegian Institute for Cultural Heritage Research, National Museum of Iceland, Árnadóttir, Lilja and Ketil, Kiran (eds).

ROME 1994, *I Normanni – popolo d'Europa 1030-1200*, Palazzo Venezia, D'Onofrio, Mario (ed).

INDEX